D0714007

PRAGMATIC LIBERALISM
AND THE CRITIQUE OF MODERNITY

In this book Gary Gutting offers a powerful account of the nature of human reason in modern times. The fundamental question addressed by the book is what authority human reason can still claim once it is acknowledged that our fundamental metaphysical and religious pictures of the world no longer command allegiance. If ethics and science remain sources of authority, what is the basis of that authority?

Gutting develops answers to these questions through critical analysis of the work of three major philosophical voices in our time: Richard Rorty, Alasdair MacIntyre, and Charles Taylor. His own position is defined as "pragmatic liberalism". Epistemologically, pragmatic liberalism shows that an understanding of rationality as the social practice of reason-giving is consistent with a realism about both the commonsense and scientific worlds. Ethically, it shows that we can make sense of our ethical commitments without asserting the objectivity of values. In contrast to other versions of liberalism, pragmatic liberalism accepts the value of traditions without privileging one absolutely, and is also open to religion as an ineliminable possibility of our mysterious existence.

This robust defense of the modern ideal of Enlightenment reason will appeal to a broad swathe of readers across the humanities and social sciences, especially in such fields as philosophy, literature, and political theory. The interpretations of Rorty, MacIntyre, and Taylor will make the book suitable as a coursebook for those teaching the history of modern philosophy.

Gary Gutting is Professor of Philosophy at the University of Notre Dame. His previous Cambridge books are *Michel Foucault's Archaeology of Scientific Reason* (1989) and *The Cambridge Companion to Foucault* (1994).

MODERN EUROPEAN PHILOSOPHY

General Editor
ROBERT B. PIPPIN, *University of Chicago*

Advisory Board
GARY GUTTING, *University of Notre Dame*
ROLF-PETER HORSTMANN, *Humboldt University, Berlin*
MARK SACKS, *University of Essex*

This series contains a range of high-quality books on philosophers, topics, and schools of thought prominent in the Kantian and post-Kantian European tradition. It is nonsectarian in approach and methodology, and includes both introductory and more specialized treatments of these thinkers and topics. Authors are encouraged to interpret the boundaries of the modern European tradition in a broad way and in primarily philosophical rather than historical terms.

Some Recent Titles:

Frederick A. Olafson, *What Is a Human Being?*
Stanley Rosen, *The Mask of Enlightenment: Nietzsche's Zarathustra*
Robert C. Scharff, *Comte after Positivism*
F. C. T. Moore, *Bergson: Thinking Backwards*
Charles Larmore, *The Morals of Modernity*
Robert B. Pippin, *Idealism as Modernism*
Daniel W. Conway, *Nietzsche's Dangerous Game*
John P. McCormick, *Carl Schmitt's Critique of Liberalism*
Frederick A. Olafson, *Heidegger and the Ground of Ethics*
Charles Griswold, *Adam Smith and the Virtues of Enlightenment*
Günter Zöller, *Fichte's Transcendental Philosophy*
Warren Breckman, *Marx, the Young Hegelians, and the Origins
of Radical Social Theory*
William Blattner, *Heidegger's Temporal Idealism*

PRAGMATIC LIBERALISM AND THE CRITIQUE OF MODERNITY

GARY GUTTING

CAMBRIDGE
UNIVERSITY PRESS

PUBLISHED BY THE PRESS SYNDICATE OF THE UNIVERSITY OF CAMBRIDGE
The Pitt Building, Trumpington Street, Cambridge CB2 1RP, United Kingdom

CAMBRIDGE UNIVERSITY PRESS
The Edinburgh Building, Cambridge CB2 2RU, UK   http://www.cup.cam.ac.uk
40 West 20th Street, New York, NY 10011-4211, USA   http://www.cup.org
10 Stamford Road, Oakleigh, Melbourne 3166 Australia

© Gary Gutting 1999

This book is in copyright. Subject to statutory exception
and to the provisions of relevant collective licensing agreements,
no reproduction of any part may take place without
the written permission of Cambridge University Press.

First published 1999

Printed in the United States of America

Typeface Baskerville 10/13 pt.   *System* Quark Xpress™ 4.0   [AG]

A catalog record for this book is available from the British Library.

Library of Congress Cataloging in Publication Data
Gutting, Gary.
Pragmatic liberalism and the critique of modernity / Gary Gutting.
p.   cm. – (Modern European philosophy)
Includes index.
ISBN 0-521-64013-X (hc.). – ISBN 0-521-64973-0 (pbk.)
1. Reason.   2. Rorty, Richard.   3. MacIntyre, Alasdair.
4. Taylor, Charles, 1931– .   5. Ethics, Modern – 20th century.
6. Philosophy, Modern – 20th century.   I. Title.   II. Series.
B833.G88   1999
148 – dc21   98-36501
                                                        CIP

ISBN 0 521 64013X hardback
ISBN 0 521 649730 paperback

TO ANASTASIA

δῖα γυναικῶν

CONTENTS

ACKNOWLEDGMENTS

I am very grateful to those who read and commented on earlier drafts of this book: Karl Ameriks, Gerald Bruns, David Burrell, Charles Guignon, Anastasia Friel Gutting, Thomas McCarthy, Philip Quinn, Richard Rorty, Joseph Rouse, Charles Taylor, Jerald Wallulis, and two anonymous readers for Cambridge University Press.

My thanks also to the participants in my graduate seminars in 1996 and 1997, which provided superb sounding boards for my ideas: Hayden Anderson, Philip Bartok, Noell Birondo, Timothy Bayne, Alissa Branham, Lori Clifford, Kevin Connor, Eric De Place, Rebecca DeYoung, Paul Gomez, Benjamin Huff, David Lewis, Benjamin Lipscomb, Robert Piercey, Andrew Roos, Michael Ryan, Michael Thrush, Christopher Toner, Manuel Vargas, and Angela Wenz. And special thanks to David Dudrick for many rewarding hours of searching conversation.

I am also grateful to Terry Moore at Cambridge University Press for his interest and encouragement, to Louise Calabro for production editing, and to Helen Greenberg for her copyediting.

As always, my primary gratitude goes to my family: to my children, Tasha, Edward, and Tom, who have grown so splendidly from remarkable children to admirable and likeable adults; and to my wife, Anastasia, who makes every day a special delight.

ABBREVIATIONS

The following abbreviations will be used for frequently cited titles:

AV: Alasdair MacIntyre, *After Virtue,* Notre Dame, IN: University of Notre Dame Press, 2nd edition, 1984.

CIS: Richard Rorty, *Contingency, Irony, and Solidarity,* Cambridge: Cambridge University Press, 1989.

EHO: Richard Rorty, *Essays on Heidegger and Others,* Cambridge: Cambridge University Press, 1991.

ELP: Bernard Williams, *Ethics and the Limits of Philosophy,* Cambridge, MA: Harvard University Press, 1985.

ORT: Richard Rorty, *Objectivity, Relativism, and Truth,* Cambridge: Cambridge University Press, 1991.

PMN: Richard Rorty, *Philosophy and the Mirror of Nature,* Princeton, NJ: Princeton University Press, 1979.

SS: Charles Taylor, *Sources of the Self,* Cambridge, MA: Harvard University Press, 1989.

TP: Richard Rorty, *Truth and Progress,* Cambridge: Cambridge University Press, 1998.

TRV: Alasdair MacIntyre, *Three Rival Versions of Moral Enquiry,* Notre Dame, IN: University of Notre Dame Press, 1990.

WJWR: Alasdair MacIntyre, *Whose Justice? Which Rationality?* Notre Dame, IN: University of Notre Dame Press, 1988.

INTRODUCTION
THE QUESTION OF MODERNITY

The question of modernity is the fundamental intellectual issue of our time. "Modernity" means at a minimum a way of thought and life that announces our independence of arbitrary, external authorities and urges that we put ourselves under the control of our own rational faculties. The modern age began with surges of optimism about what a liberated and enlightened humankind might achieve, particularly through science and politics. There were always questions about the project, and these have increased rapidly since the end of the nineteenth century. Surveying, from our fin-de-siècle peak, the debris of the twentieth century, we are tempted to renounce the enterprise. Certainly, outside the "hard sciences", almost every major intellectual and cultural domain has centrally engaged questions about the nature and value of the modern commitment to rational autonomy.

Analytic philosophy, which has defined the American and British mainstream for most of this century, is a prominent exception. Most analytic philosophers pursue clarity of explication and rigor of argument with no thought that there might be some fatal corruption at the heart of their projects of rational analysis. Analytic philosophy appears as an arch-modernism – a manifestation of the problems of modernity rather than a means to their solution. Among humanistic disciplines, there is no better example of wholehearted commitment to the original ideals of the Enlightenment. This explains the marginal position of mainstream analytic philosophy on the contemporary intellectual scene. Intellectuals centrally concerned with critiques of modernity see analytic philosophers as begging all the key questions. For their part, analytic philosophers typically cherish their separation from the confusions of intellectuals who do not share their standpoint. Thomas Nagel speaks for many when he says that "arid technicalities are preferable to the blend of oversimplification and fake profundity that is too often the form taken by popular philosophy."[1]

Whether analytic philosophy should be as marginal as it is depends on our understanding of the current debates over modernity. "Modern" means "happening now", a "now" that for us encompasses the roughly 500 years since people in the West began questioning long established political, religious, and intellectual authorities in the name of autonomous human reason.[2] The idea that there is something distinctive about this period is still best formulated in Kant's terms. The modern age is one of "enlightenment", where enlightenment means a rejection of the "self-incurred tutelage" of humankind.[3] Previously, Kant said, we accepted outside authorities as the guide to what we should think or do. Now (in the modern age) we should accept only what our own reason tells us.

As long as the dichotomy of authority versus reason is understood as a contrast between an arbitrary imposition of standards and an acceptance of what can be reasonably shown to constrain us, hardly any of us now will opt for arbitrary external authority; in this sense we are all moderns. (Nor should we forget that having gotten even this far is a major advance in human history.) But this minimal commitment to modernity leaves open the question of whether there might be some external authorities that are not arbitrary, authorities to which we reasonably should subordinate ourselves. A typical Enlightenment figure such as Voltaire, for example, thought that the authoritative claims of dogmatic theology and Aristotelian philosophy were merely arbitrary, but that we should accept the claims of natural science and of commonsense morality. The multiple and ever-shifting disputes about

---

1   Thomas Nagel, *Other Minds*, New York: Oxford University Press, 1995, 8–9.
2   Although I will often speak of "reason" in this generic way, the convenient locution should not be taken to imply that I think there is some ahistorical essence of rationality or even, à la Hegel, some privileged manifestation of reason in any given historical period. As my argument develops, it should be clear that generic talk of "reason" is just a marker for specific disputes about the role of experience and argument, as opposed to other alleged sources of cognitive authority (faith, feeling, divine commands), in various domains such as science, philosophy, religion, ethics, and politics. The "question of reason" is merely a series of – sometimes interestingly related – questions about what sorts of appeal should have ultimate weight in various domains of inquiry.
3   Immanuel Kant, "What Is Enlightenment?" translated by Lewis White Beck, in Lewis White Beck (ed.), *On History*, New York: Bobbs-Merrill, 1963, 3.

"modernity" over the last 400 years have mostly concerned just what authorities a reasonable person should accept. For us (i.e., educated citizens of the Western democracies), some of these disputes have been pretty much resolved. We have, for example, concluded that political claims of privileged nondemocratic authority are arbitrary and nonbinding. We have also concluded that, even though individuals may have a right to accept the claims of specific religious revelations, such claims are not generally compelling. We have accordingly gone a stage beyond the minimal modernity of mere preference in principle for reasoned constraints over arbitrary authority. We have decided that some of the main traditional external authorities do not meet our standards of rationality and so should be rejected.

Beyond this, most moderns have, over the last few centuries, agreed with Voltaire that the authorities of natural science and ethics are reasonable constraints on our thought and behavior. Moreover, a long tradition, from Descartes through Kant, holds that the rationality of science and ethics is grounded in a general philosophical account of the world. In this century, there has been a strong trend toward accepting science as the only rational authority but rejecting both the rational status of ethics and the need for a philosophical foundation for scientific rationality. But there remain those who insist on the rational authority of ethics and those who maintain that such authority (and perhaps that of science too) requires a philosophical grounding. Let us reserve the plain term "modernity" for the view that combines a rejection of religious and (nondemocratic) political authority with an acceptance of scientific results as deliverances of reason. To go further and maintain that science is the only rational authority is to embrace "scientistic modernity". This is opposed by "philosophical modernity", which maintains that there is a distinctive realm of philosophical rationality grounding either or both science and ethics. My project in this book is to defend a commitment to modern reason that avoids both scientistic and philosophical modernity.

Contemporary intellectual life is full of "critiques" of modernity and suggestions that we are now in, or quickly moving toward, a "postmodern" age. The unavoidability of this parasitic term suggests a continuing dominance of modernity; we need it even to characterize alleged alternatives. Most of what are taken as critiques of modernity are in fact internal disputes about the nature of the reason to which modernity commits us. This is obviously the crux of the disagreement between scientistic and philosophical modernity. But even for those who have opted for a given side in this disagreement, there remain quarrels about the proper understanding of the scientific or the philosophical reason that is taken to define our commitment to modernity.

The idea that a commitment to reason itself is at stake often arises from the tendency of proponents of specific conceptions of reason to denounce alternatives as renunciations of reason (as, in premodern times, proponents of conflicting conceptions of God called each other atheists). There are no doubt cases of genuine challenge to anything that might be plausibly regarded as a commitment to reason, particularly in literature and the arts and among certain religious believers. The phenomenon is not unknown among philosophers (I think, for example, of certain tendencies of the early Foucault and of the late Heidegger). But what look like philosophical challenges to reason (e.g., on the part of empiricists or of pragmatists) often turn out on examination to be merely critiques of some particular construal of reason and proposals of an alternative that critics find obviously inadequate. In other cases, there is a rejection of reason for certain key levels of human concern – for example, religion, ethics, art – but this rejection itself is rationally supported. This is a typically modern move, at least since Hume and Kant, whereby reason engages in a self-critique that reveals certain domains where it is not appropriate. Then our fundamental commitment to reason requires abandoning its claims in particular regions.

The widespread fascination with postmodernism notwithstanding, we have not been able to think ourselves beyond our commitment to modernity. The imputation of a fundamental rejection of the authority of reason remains an effective reductio ad absurdum. The question of modernity does dominate our thought, but the question is not whether to reject it but how to understand it. Those who see analytic philosophy as irrelevant because it does not question the very idea of a commitment to reason as the vehicle of human autonomy have misconstrued the question of modernity. On the other hand, much analytic philosophy has been justly marginalized because it ignores serious questions about its own particular conception of reason. As a result, analytic philosophy has not fully faced the question of whether it is trapped in a false conception of reason. The issue has typically arisen only when criteria of rationality appear to be internally inconsistent (e.g., the positivist verification principle); analytic philosophers are exceptionally good at dealing with this kind of concern. But they have been much less alert to the possibility that they are maintaining a consistent but false view of reason through unawareness of alternatives. Here analytic philosophers are often at a disadvantage because of their narrow cultural and historical perspectives. They often simply do not see as relevant to their philosophizing the historical and cultural perspectives that might offer alternatives to their conception of reason (often for the circular reason that these alternatives don't meet their assumed standards of rationality).

Herein lies the special importance of the philosophers with whom this book engages: Richard Rorty, Alasdair MacIntyre, and Charles Taylor.[4] They are analytic in their philosophical formation and style of thought. But at the same time, they have broad historical and cultural interests that have led them to critical examinations of the modern commitment to reason, and particularly of the commitment involved in analytic philosophy.[5] I suspect that I am not alone in experiencing a special intellectual exhilaration when reading Rorty, MacIntyre, and Taylor. They offer the conceptual clarity and respect for careful argument of good analytic philosophy, but without numbing technicalities, claustrophobic restriction of topics, and depressing isolation from nonphilosophical culture. At the same time, they provide the historical and cultural breadth of good continental philosophy without the pretension and obscurity. Why, I think, can't philosophy always be like this?

It is, nevertheless, not surprising that Rorty, MacIntyre, and Taylor are often regarded as marginal to "mainstream" philosophy of both the analytic and the continental variety. More sober analytic philosophers will remind me that, for all its interest and excitement, the work of Rorty, MacIntyre, and Taylor is generally marginal to the central projects of philosophical analysis. It is too historical, too metaphilosophical, too interdisciplinary for hardnosed epistemologists, metaphysicians, and philosophers of mind, science, and language. A steady diet of such philosophy would lead us away from our rigorous and fundamental tasks into a fuzzy world of history and even poetry. In a parallel vein, serious continentalists will tell me that, for all their superficial appeal, these writers lack the depth and originality of a Heidegger or a Derrida, that they are helpful as metalevel commentators but are not themselves major creative thinkers.

I quite agree that *Philosophy and the Mirror of Nature*, *After Virtue,* and *Sources of the Self* should not replace *Word and Object* and *Being and Time.* But I am also convinced that our standard division of analytic and continental philosophy does not exhaust the discipline's possibilities and that Rorty, MacIntyre, and Taylor offer a distinctive and essential approach to issues fundamental for

4   There are, of course, many other important philosophers with similar appoaches – for example, Bernard Williams, Ian Hacking, Thomas Kuhn, Stanley Cavell, and the later Hilary Putnam. I will pay particular attention in Part III to Williams's views on ethics.

5   In this regard, of course, they are returning to what had been a primary concern of modern philosophy, particularly in the days of Kant and his immediate successors, the German idealists. Analytic philosophy originated in a reaction against idealism, one less fortunate aspect of which was an unreflective acceptance of science and mathematics as the paradigms of rationality. (The case for the centrality of German idealism in the critique of modernity is well argued in Robert Pippin, *Modernism as a Philosophical Problem*, Oxford: Blackwell, 1991.)

contemporary philosophy. This approach provides the historical and meta-philosophical perspective we need to situate culturally and evaluate humanly analytic and continental projects. It also, as this book intends to show, offers a particularly fruitful perspective on the problem of modernity. My specific project is to show how this approach can lead us to a very attractive and plausible version of the modern ideal of Enlightenment.

I call my version of the Enlightenment ideal "pragmatic liberalism". Roughly, the "liberalism" expresses commitment to human freedom through the deployment of reason, and the "pragmatic" means that this commitment is not grounded on any deep (philosophical) theory of human nature.[6] The position, particularly as I initially develop it in Part I, owes much to Rorty, although it differs with him on such central issues as the status of scientific truth and the nature of ethical norms. In Part II, I consider MacIntyre's critique of modernity in the name of Aristotelian tradition, concluding that his criticisms are telling against only one version of modernity and, in any case, are in tension with his own implicit acceptance of modernist assumptions. Further, I argue, MacIntyre's implicit modernity allows pragmatic liberalism to correct and enrich its account of ethics by appropriating his notion of a tradition. In Part III, I refine pragmatic liberalism in the light of Taylor's penetrating analysis of modernity in *Sources of the Self*. Although I reject his effort to articulate in modern terms an Augustinian conception of the self, I appropriate some of his key ideas – particularly regarding the affirmation of everyday life and the nature of self-creation – to deepen my formulation of pragmatic liberalism. I also reflect on his critique of ethical naturalism to improve my account of the place of objectivity in ethics.

Since pragmatic liberalism raises serious questions about the pretensions of traditional philosophy, there will be a persistent metaphilosophical undercurrent to my discussions. In my conclusion, I bring these issues briefly to the surface and offer an account of philosophy that rejects its traditional role as arbiter of fundamental truths but still allows it a distinctive and important place in our cultural world.

---

6 Pragmatic liberalism is an ethical and metaphilosophical view that needs to be distinguished from liberalism as a position in political theory. The commitment to human freedom is, of course, shared with political liberalism, but pragmatic liberalism as such takes no position on the political issues of just how freedom is to be understood and what are the best means to achieve it. As I understand it, liberalism is no more characteristic of Rawls than it is of Nozick.

PART I

RICHARD RORTY

THE RUDIMENTS OF PRAGMATIC LIBERALISM

Richard Rorty has flirted with the label "postmodern";[1] and, in any case, critics typically see his views as a rejection of modernist rationality. There is no doubt that he rejects classical modern construals of rationality in terms of representationalism and foundationalism. The question is whether his critique of epistemology is an attack on reason itself. He may think he is merely exhibiting the deficiencies of modern explications of knowledge, but, his critics maintain, he excludes any coherent notion of knowledge and leaves us caught in a morass of relativism, subjectivism, or skepticism. Critics are even more disturbed by what they take to be the moral consequences of Rorty's pragmatism.[2] I think there are some important deficiencies in Rorty's position: in epistemology, it fails to come to terms with the fundamental truth of realism (both in science and in everyday life) and, in ethics, it tends toward a deeply misleading decisionism and overrates the value of moral pluralism. Nonetheless, I still regard Rorty's pragmatic appoach as one of the best starting points for contemporary philosophical reflection, and this chapter is intended to develop the rudiments of my pragmatic liberalism by

---

1   He characterized his position as "postmodernist bourgeois liberalism" in an essay with that title (ORT, 197–202) but has subsequently distanced himself from the postmodern label (cf. EHO, 1).

2   For vigorous statements of both the epistemic and the moral critique of Rorty, see Norman Geras, *Solidarity in the Conversation of Mankind*, London: Verso, 1995.

a critical appropriation of some of his key ideas. Rorty's pragmatism is certainly critical of classical formulations of the Enlightenment project. But, as I will show, properly clarified and modified, it renews rather than rejects the fundamental Enlightenment idea of human autonomy through reason.

I begin (Section 1) with a brief reconstruction of Rorty's *Geistesgeschichte* of modern epistemology. This is followed by a discussion (Section 2) of the epistemological behaviorism Rorty offers as an alternative to the representationalism of modern epistemology. Section 3 discusses his view of justification as a social practice in the light of standard criticisms. The next three sections take up the issue of truth. Section 4 presents what I see as the proper formulation of a pragmatic view of truth, and Section 5 shows how this view is supported by Davidson's approach to knowledge. Section 6 argues that we should take a more realistic view of science than Rorty allows. Sections 7 and 8 discuss Rorty's ethical views. They sketch his pragmatic approach to ethics, the view he calls "liberal ironism", reformulating and revising it in light of major criticisms of his position. At the end of this engagement with Rorty, we will have the fundamentals of the position I am calling pragmatic liberalism.

1. The Philosophy of Representations

Rorty's historical work does not fit neatly into either of the two standard categories of historical reconstruction or rational reconstruction.[3] It is not, like rational reconstruction, an effort to scan the philosophical past for contributions relevant to contemporary problematics. For such an enterprise, the starting point is our own understanding of the relevant issues; and the great thinkers of the past are admitted to our discussions only to the extent that they say something we can appropriate for our own purposes. Rorty, by contrast, employs history to question the fundamental presuppositions of contemporary problematics. At the same time, Rorty is not seeking the historical reconstructionist's faithful presentation of past philosophers' ideas in their own terms. His history tries to uncover just those aspects of the past (and our standard interpretations of it) that are relevant to understanding the nature and limits of current philosophizing. Its goal then is neither to understand what past philosophers thought in their own terms nor to discover timeless philosophical truths. The enterprise is rather a variety of what

---

3   Rorty distinguishes these two sorts of reconstruction in "The Historiography of Philosophy: Four Genres", in R. Rorty, J. B. Schneewind, and Quentin Skinner (eds.), *Philosophy in History*, Cambridge: Cambridge University Press, 1984, 49 (TP, 247).

Foucault has called "history of the present": the illumination and critique of current views and practices by tracing relevant historical lines back to their origins.[4]

Whatever the inadequacies of Rorty's account as a rigorous historical reconstruction of individual thinkers, it is very plausible as an understanding and critique of the way many readers of modern philosophy have interpreted its overall thrust. Rorty captures a very influential way of thinking about the role of philosophy in the Enlightenment project of human autonomy through reason. Once we assert this autonomy against traditional external authorities, we need to get clear about just what this newly liberated reason amounts to. One enduring temptation has been to identify it with the methods of modern empirical science. The only alternative to this radical and problematic move has seemed to be to recognize philosophy as a distinctive and central deployment of secular reason. Rorty's *Geistesgeschichte* of modernity, however unfaithful it may be to the true intentions of particular modern philosophers, is a fair expression of how they have been read by generations of moderns committed to the Enlightenment ideal of autonomy.

Rorty's account is based on a sharp contrast between the ancient and the modern status of philosophy. For the ancients, philosophy was the "queen of the sciences", first, crowning and synthesizing the efforts of the special sciences and, second, providing a basis for the good human life. These two functions were closely connected because knowledge of nature – particularly of human nature – was regarded as the ground for knowledge of the good; our vision of the world and of our place in it was the basis for our knowledge of how to live. (The Middle Ages, of course, brought a significant modification of the role of philosophy, which, having been trumped by divine revelation, fell to the place of "handmaid" to the new queen, theology.) The modern period was characterized by the replacement of the ancient sciences (Aristotelian physics, biology, etc.) of which philosophy had been the culmination and queen by the new modern sciences of Galileo, Newton, Dalton, and (eventually) Darwin.

The triumph of these new sciences was quickly seen by many intellectuals – Hobbes and Descartes, for example – as the destruction of the ancient

4 See Michel Foucault, *Discipline and Punish*, trans. A. Sheridan, New York: Pantheon, 1997, 30–1; and my "Introduction" to *The Cambridge Companion to Foucault*, Cambridge: Cambridge University Press, 1994, 10. I do not, of course, mean to suggest that Rorty's history of the present shares the ethical and political intentions introduced into Foucault's histories by their linking of knowledge and power.

system of philosophy, what had become the philosophy of the schools. This was fundamentally because the new science, taken realistically, undermined the metaphysical heart of scholastic philosophy. The new scientific world was one merely of inert matter and mechanistic forces; a world of, to use the old terminology, material and efficient but no formal or final causes. Then as now, this new view was most plausible for the external, material world, less so for the phenomena that we have come to call mental. Descartes initiated the modern period's efforts to come to terms with this disparity by drawing in a new way the distinction between mind and body.

Before Descartes, philosophers had typically seen the mind–body distinction as one between reason and nonreason, thus including sense perception, for example, on the side of the body rather than the mind. Descartes, in an effort to make the entire bodily realm the domain of the new mechanistic science, needed a sense of the distinction that eliminated from our understanding of "body" anything that could not be explained by this science. This led him to assign to the mind everything intentional and phenomenal (hence all "thoughts" in his maximally extended sense of all consciousness). Later modern philosophers might reject Descartes's dualism of two substances, mind and body; but they accepted his fundamental way of understanding the division between the mental and the physical as one between what was conscious and what was not. Even those who denied one or the other term of the distinction (materialists and idealists) accepted this understanding of the categories.

For Rorty, Descartes is the "father of modern philosophy" in the sense that his sharp division between mind and body provided the basis for the distinctively modern view of the mind as the object of philosophical inquiry. This was a particularly attractive approach, since, as noted earlier, the new mechanistic sciences seemed quite capable of an adequate account of matter but less capable of dealing with the mind. However, the full development of this new conception of philosophy was not achieved for over a century, with Kant's critical philosophy.

The development continued with Locke, who, like Descartes, took the mind as the proper domain of philosophical investigation. Locke, however, did not himself have a clear notion of philosophy as an independent discipline. He was inclined to see his work as the construction of a mechanistic account of the mind, a moral philosophy paralleling Newton's natural philosophy. (Similarly, Hume aspired to be "the Newton of the moral sciences".) But at the same time, Locke was interested in questions about the justification of knowledge, the very questions that later (with Kant) come to define the distinctively philosophical discipline of epistemology. According to Rorty, the central feature of Locke's work is his collapse (Rorty says confusion) of these two interests, in mechanistic explanation and in epistemological justification, into a single conception of knowledge. On this conception, to know something is simply for the mind to have been affected in an appropriate way by the object known. The normative state of being justified in making a given assertion is identified with the factual state of having been causally determined in a given way. To take an example from Wilfrid Sellars, Locke would identify *knowing* a red triangle with *having a sense impression of* a red triangle (i.e., having an image of a red triangle produced in one's mind).[5]

Locke is led to this identification because, like Aristotle and his medieval successors, he regards knowledge as fundamentally of an object rather than of a proposition (knowing *a* rather than knowing that *a* is *B*). Knowing a proposition requires being *justified* in making various assertions, and knowledge in this sense is not readily identified with being causally determined in a certain way. (Such an identification would seem to involve, as Sellars remarks, an epistemological version of the naturalistic fallacy.[6]) But to know an object presumably requires being somehow related to it, and it is natural to take this relation as one of causality. For Aristotle the causality was formal; the mind "became" (assumed the intentional form of) the object. But for Locke, who was trying to sustain a mechanistic picture of the mind, the causality could be only efficient, a matter of the object's somehow making an "impression" on the mind.

With Locke, then, the Cartesian mind emerges as the locus of the fledgling discipline of epistemology, the philosophical study of knowledge. The mental was the domain of certainty (indubitability), since we could, as Descartes said, be entirely sure about the contents of our mind. Accordingly, these contents were the obvious starting point for the effort to build an entirely reliable body of knowledge, a project enjoined by the desire to overcome the skepticism about established truths encouraged by Renaissance humanists such as Montaigne and by the modern revolutions in science and religion. The great problem was to move from the mind's certainty about itself to knowledge of things outside it. According to Rorty, then, epistemology is based, first, on Descartes's assumption that knowledge of the external world is a matter of having mental representations that accurately picture

---

5 Cf. Wilfrid Sellars, *Philosophical Perspectives,* Springfield, IL: Charles C. Thomas, 1967, 211; PMN, 143.

6 Cf. Wilfrid Sellars, "Empiricism and the Philosophy of Mind", in his *Science, Perception, and Reality,* London: Routledge and Kegan Paul, 1963, 131; PMN, 141.

that world and, second, on Locke's assumption that the accuracy of a representation depends on the manner of its causal production.

But these assumptions, at least as they were understood by the standard empiricist and rationalist accounts of knowledge that followed Locke, allowed no way of guaranteeing the accuracy of our mental representations of extramental reality and avoiding the skeptical conclusion that we are trapped behind a "veil of ideas". It was Kant's frustration with this failure that led to his Copernican revolution. The two assumptions of truth as representation and of origin as guarantee of accurate representation continue in Kant's account, but in an inverted and transformed manner. Our ideas (e.g., of space, time, substance, causality) accurately represent the world not because they are causally produced by the world but because they themselves are necessary conditions of the mind's noncausal production ("constitution") of the world as an object of knowledge. Knowledge of this constitution and its conditions is unproblematic in view of Descartes's assumption of the mind's privileged access to itself.

The key to Kant's approach is his distinction between two types of mental representations: concepts and intuitions. He saw his predecessors as either empiricists, who tried to reduce concepts (generalized ideas) to intuitions (immediate sense impressions), or rationalists, who tried to reduce intuitions to concepts. Both, he maintained, failed to realize that an experience of an object requires both conceptual and intuitive elements, the conceptual providing the framework of intelligibility without which the object could not be presented and the intuitive providing the content without which the framework would be merely an empty scheme. The answer to the defining question of epistemology – How can our representations accurately represent objects? – was that the very meaning of "object" (at least in the crucial context of empirical knowledge) requires that an object be properly correlated with the mind's rules for forming representations of it.

Kant restored philosophy to an autonomous and privileged position in the domain of knowledge. Every other type of knowledge presupposed the conceptual (analytic or synthetic a priori) truths to which philosophy alone had access. Moreover, only the conceptual truths of philosophy could be known with the maximal certainty of direct intellectual insight. Philosophy is no longer, as in ancient times, the *culmination* of human knowing. But it is the *foundation* of human knowing, providing the ultimate justification of all epistemic claims and adjudicating conflicts between rival bodies of alleged knowledge.

Kant's Copernican revolution did not provide a generally accepted solution to the problem of knowledge. But, according to Rorty, it did establish that problem as the defining issue of philosophy as a modern discipline in its own right. It did this by convincing subsequent thinkers that an adequate account of knowledge required an irreducible distinction between general conceptual structures and specific experiential content. Such a distinction provided the basis for philosophy as an autonomous discipline, that is, a discipline with the tasks of delineating the mind's general conceptual structures and of explaining how they combined with experiential content to produce knowledge. The privileged status of philosophy was guaranteed by a sharp distinction between the a priori knowledge proper to it and the a posteriori knowledge of empirical science. Philosophers after Kant frequently rejected his conception of philosophy as the domain of transcendental truths necessary for any possible experience. But, in one way or another, they all preserved a distinction of kinds of knowledge that provided philosophy with a privileged access to a domain of foundational truth. Thus, idealists distinguished the necessary from the contingent, positivists the analytic from the synthetic. All modern epistemologies are based on a division between knowledge in its formal, structural dimension and knowledge in its material, contentual dimension, with the former always the domain – at least in part – of the philosopher.

Modern epistemology has taken many forms, and by no means all of them are good fits to the simple account Rorty most often has in mind. Frequently, his target is a naive foundationalism for which there is, strictly speaking, no knowledge apart from an absolutely certain basis provided by philosophical intuition and argument. Without such a basis, all knowledge, both commonsense and scientific, is said to crumble, and skepticism triumphs. Historians of modern philosophy are rightly dubious of this simplistic interpretation of thinkers such as Descartes, Hume, and Kant. It is not at all clear, for example, that any of these three thought that scientific knowledge had no epistemic standing without a philosophical vindication. Insofar as Rorty's critique is aimed specifically at naive foundationalism, it affects primarily certain forms of empiricism, particularly (and most important for Rorty) logical positivism. But Rorty's history of modern philosophy is still important – and has much wider relevance – in its focus on the centrality of an epistemology of representations and the role such epistemology has played in defining a distinct and privileged place for philosophy as a cognitive authority.[7] An

---

7   Charles Taylor emphasizes, against Rorty, that representationalism is more central than foundationalism in modern thought. Cf. "Overcoming Epistemology", in *Philosophical Arguments*, Cambridge, MA: Harvard University Press, 1995, 2–3. Taylor ties representationalism to characteristic modern views not only in epistemology and philosophy of mind but also in ethics and politics.

independent and authoritative philosophy has seemed and to many still seems to be the only way, short of reducing all knowledge to empirical science, of maintaining the Enlightenment ideal of autonomous reason. Rorty maintains that conceptions of philosophy as an autonomous discipline depend on an indefensible distinction between formal and material knowledge. The essential function of his historical reflections on philosophy from Descartes to Kant is to show that this division is not inevitable, that it reflects just one historically contingent way of thinking about knowing, not an eternal truth about it.

Of course, as Rorty himself points out (PMN, 38ff.), the distinction of formal and material knowledge is hardly unique to modern philosophy. Even if he succeeds in undermining formulations of the distinction in terms of modern representationalism, this will not refute other, even more venerable, formulations of a distinction that has pervaded philosophical thought since Plato. Some such distinction is implicit in the separation between necessary and contingent truth, a division that has seemed inevitable ever since the discovery of mathematical truths distinct from what we could know from sense perception.

Rorty, however, maintains that the idea that there is a sharp distinction between necessary (e.g., mathematical) and contingent (e.g., sensory) truth is itself a product of the entirely optional metaphor of knowledge as vision. This metaphor goes back to Plato, and it is still at work in the modern assumption, noted in our discussion of Locke, that knowledge is primarily *of* an object, not *that* a proposition is true.[8] Given this picture, it has been natural to think that different degrees of certainty in knowledge are a matter of being constrained (in the limit, compelled) to belief by the object known. I cannot, for example, avoid believing that twice 2 is 4, because of the force exerted on my mind by the relevant mathematical concepts. (Note also how the metaphor lends itself to the further modern assumption that justification has to do with causes rather than reasons.) Without the visual metaphor, we could regard certainty as nothing more than our confidence that no one will be able to offer reasons sufficient to cast doubt on the propositions we assert. We could, in Rorty's terms, see knowledge as taking place entirely

---

8   Rorty would hardly deny that the metaphor was called into serious question at least as early as Kant, who, like many twentieth-century analytic philosophers, had a propositional rather than an objectual account of knowledge. Presumably, Rorty's view is that philosophers have had a hard time overcoming the ocular fascination and drawing the proper consequences of a propositional conception of knowledge.

within the space of reasons for asserting propositions rather than in the space of causes that compel belief; we could see knowledge as the outcome of conversation rather than confrontation. In the end, Rorty's critique of traditional philosophy – both ancient and modern – depends on the viability of this alternative view of knowledge. It is to this view that we now turn.

2. Knowledge without Representations

To know something, I must have a belief and that belief must be justified. These are necessary (though, of course, not sufficient) conditions implicit in our commonsense notion of knowledge. Let us for now focus on justification. Still keeping to the commonsense level, justification frequently means that I can say something on behalf of the belief that will pass muster among my peers. Thus: "It's raining in Chicago." "How do you know?" "I heard it on WBBM." "Okay, we'll take an umbrella." Here my belief is a proposition that I justify by citing another proposition that my interlocutors accept and see as properly supporting my belief. If they don't accept it, then I cite other propositions until we reach agreement. Rorty's view – which he calls "epistemological behaviorism" – is that we need nothing beyond this commonsense model as an account of epistemic justification. That is, justification, even in far more significant and complex cases, is just a matter of being able to give good reasons (put forward adequate supporting propositions) for the belief. Also, the norms specifying "good reasons" and "adequate support" are themselves based on the agreement of an epistemic community.

The alternative is to maintain that justification of a belief requires that it receive some further "inner authentication"; that there be some special *experience* (insight, awareness, perception) to justify my having the belief; that, in Rorty's term, I have certain "privileged representations". This, as we have just seen, is the view of classical modern epistemology, which has allowed for two kinds of experiential justification: via sensory awareness or via conceptual insight (understanding of meanings). Rorty's epistemological behaviorism denies any justificatory role to either sort of experience. This position does not, like logical or metaphysical behaviorism, deny the existence of "inner episodes" or try to reduce them to objective descriptions of behavior. It is perfectly happy to admit that there may be all manner of sensory and intellectual awarenesses (from raw feels, through ordinary sense perceptions, to mathematical "intuitions"). But it denies that any such episodes are involved in the justification of our beliefs. They may well have a great deal to do with the causal explanation of why we have these beliefs, but they are not reasons for having them.[9]

Epistemological behaviorism conflicts with the "empiricist" claim that beliefs such as "There is a tree outside the window" are justified by my sense experiences and with the "rationalist" claim that beliefs such as "All bachelors are unmarried" are justified by my awareness of meanings. Let us begin with the empiricist, who will say that, ultimately, the justification for "There is a tree outside the window" is my experience of seeing the tree. Can Rorty really deny so obvious a claim? He will, of course, admit that frequently the justification of this claim will involve appeal to a *proposition* such as "I see a tree outside the window". Surely, he must also agree that such an appeal is fruitless unless the proposition is true, that is, unless I have actually had the experience of seeing the tree? But, if so, doesn't the justification for "There is a tree outside the window" depend on the experience?

Here we need to recall that we are concerned only with justification, not with truth. For me to be justified in believing "I see a tree outside the window", it is not necessary that I actually have the experience of seeing a tree. I need only have good reason to believe that I see a tree, that is, I need only believe propositions that support the proposition "I see a tree". This illustrates Rorty's key claim: justification is a matter of giving reasons, and what is a good reason never depends on whether or not I have had a certain sort of experience. As far as justification (reason-giving) goes, what matters is whether I believe I have had the experience (or, if this belief is challenged, whether I have good reason to believe I have had the experience). The objection to Rorty assumes that the mere fact that a proposition is true can be a reason for believing it is true. He denies this, maintaining that just because something exists in reality doesn't mean it exists in the space of reasons.

But the empiricist will still not be satisfied. According to epistemological behaviorism, knowledge requires justification, which requires an ability to cite reasons, which requires linguistic ability. But, the empiricist will urge,

---

9   This point is particularly important in assessing recent work in the philosophy of mind (by, for example, Fodor), which gives representations a central role in explaining the mechanisms by which knowledge occurs, but without offering a representationalist account of justification as a normative, epistemological concept. As I understand it, epistemological behaviorism has no objections to this sort of appeal to representations. For the same reason, I think Rorty should have no difficulty accepting Michael Devitt's point that Rorty's critique of correspondence as an epistemological theory does not, in principle, exclude it as an element in a causal explanation of knowledge. See Devitt's *Realism and Truth,* 2nd edition, Oxford: Blackwell, 1991, chapter 11.

this ignores the knowledge of those – for example, infants, the severely retarded – who do not have linguistic ability. In other words, there are surely instances of pre- (or non-) linguistic awareness that are knowledge. Rorty's response to this objection is based on Sellars's distinction between "awareness-as-discriminative-behavior" and awareness as knowledge.[10] Many entities without linguistic ability – from photoelectric cells and computers to frogs and babies – are able to respond to stimuli in systematically differentiated ways. In the case of at least some organisms – certainly babies – we have reason to think that this ability depends causally on the primitive form of awareness that philosophers call "raw feels". Thus, a baby feels hunger and cries for its bottle. Should we say that the baby knows it is hungry (its stomach is empty) – that is, believes it is hungry and is justified in its belief in virtue of its raw feeling of hunger? Well, does a photoelectric eye know that someone is approaching the door? Not in any literal sense; it merely has the mechanical ability to respond to such an approach by opening the door. It could not, for example, justify the claim that someone is approaching the door. What is the difference between the baby and the electric eye? Merely that the baby responds in virtue of a "feeling" and the electric eye doesn't. (We could invent an electronic gadget that monitored a baby's stomach secretions and emitted a crying sound just whenever the baby itself cried. But we wouldn't say the gadget literally knew that the baby was hungry.) But why should the mere fact of the baby's feeling make a difference?

The only answer supporting the empiricist would be that having the feeling justifies the claim that the baby is hungry, whereas whatever is going on in the electric eye does not justify the claim that someone is approaching the door. But what does it mean to say that the feeling of hunger justifies the claim that the baby is hungry? Only that someone who knew that the feeling was occurring could put this fact forward in support of the claim. So then the question is, Does the baby know that it is feeling hungry? And the answer is no, since, by hypothesis, the baby is pre-linguistic and therefore lacks propositional knowledge. In fact, the situation is the same for the electric eye as for the baby. Someone who knew about the electromagnetic processes going on in the eye could appeal to them to justify the claim that someone is approaching the door. But the electric eye can't do this, since it lacks propositional knowledge. The only difference between the two cases is that the infant's response depends on its awareness. But to think that this matters epistemically is to make the same empiricist mistake we encountered

10 Cf. PMN, 182, and Wilfrid Sellars, "Empiricism and the Philosophy of Mind", in *Science, Perception, and Reality*, 169.

earlier. It is to think that the mere fact of an experience's occurring can constitute a reason for believing a proposition.[11]

Consider next the rationalist's claim that our knowledge of necessary truths (e.g., of "All bachelors are unmarried") is a matter of our awareness of meanings. Rorty cites Quine's famous discussion in "Two Dogmas of Empiricism" as undermining the effort to distinguish a class of truths-in-virtue-of-meaning from a class of truths-based-on-experience. Certainly, to the extent that Quine shows that no such distinction can be drawn, the rationalist (or logical empiricist) claim we are examining becomes indefensible. However, even without Quine's critique, epistemological behaviorists can handle claims about insights into necessary truths the same way they handle claims about sense experiences. In both cases, the key point is that the mere occurrence of an experience (whether sensory or conceptual) has no justificatory force. At best, justification is supplied by a belief that such an experience has occurred. Thus, the case against rationalist conceptual insights is the same as that against empiricist sense experience.

It is also worth noting that epistemological behaviorism need not follow Quine's predilection for austere ontology. Denying any justificatory role for mental entities, whether raw feels or meanings, says nothing about the actual existence of such entities. Assertions about existence depend on what we need (or find convenient) to describe and explain our world. Rorty is rightly unimpressed by the (essentially positivist) reasons Quine has for insisting that we accept the existence of nothing more than sets and elementary particles. He thinks that there is no ontological force in the criteria of unity and clarity to which Quine appeals, and he endorses Davidson's tolerance for cultivating any ontology that suits our local needs. But for our present purposes, the point is simply that refusing mental entities a role in epistemology does not of itself exclude them from our ontology (and, conversely, including them in our ontology does not give them epistemic status).

Even if we agree that justification is a process of giving reasons that has no role for experiences, there are two further aspects of Rorty's account that raise serious questions. The first is his claim that reason-giving is an essentially social practice, so that to justify a belief is to justify it to a community.

---

11   Rorty notes (PMN, 183–5; 188–90) two ways in which we can, without abandoning epistemological behaviorism, allow a sense in which the infant has knowledge of its hunger. First, it knows "what it is like to be hungry", where this simply means that it feels hungry and does not constitute knowledge in the sense of *justified* true belief. Second, we may ascribe propositional knowledge to the pre-linguistic infant in *anticipation* of the linguistic abilities it will someday develop (and we may even make such ascriptions to "the more attractive-looking sort of animals" in virtue of our ability to *imagine* them speaking).

The second is his effort to develop an antirepresentationalist view of truth to complement his social-practice view of justification.

3. Justification as a Social Practice

How can reason-giving be nothing more than a social practice? Couldn't I have perfectly good reasons for believing something that everyone else thought was false and unjustified? Why should enough recalcitrant Athenians be able to put Socrates in the wrong? Epistemological behaviorism seems to erase the boundary between objective knowledge and subjective opinion.

In treating justification as a social practice, Rorty generalizes Thomas Kuhn's account of the natural sciences.[12] This account fits Rorty's purposes in two ways. First, it rejects the idea that there is any necessarily shared epistemic ground (e.g., a neutral observation language or a priori methodological rules) that we can use to resolve scientific disagreements. This is Kuhn's doctrine of incommensurability, which corresponds to Rorty's rejection of privileged representations. Second, Kuhn locates the ultimate source of science's cognitive authority in the consensus of the scientific community, a view that corresponds to Rorty's insistence on the primacy of conversation (reason-giving as a social practice). Rorty's idea is to extend what Kuhn says about natural science to the entire domain of human knowledge.

Rorty begins by generalizing Kuhn's distinction between normal and revolutionary science. Normal discourse (his generalization of normal science) occurs when the participants are in sufficient agreement on fundamentals to allow the evaluation of contested claims by shared standards. Such discourse is the "behavioral" equivalent of the discourse that would be possible if the privileged representations of epistemology were available. Such representations (i.e., foundational sensory and/or conceptual certainties) would always provide, in principle, clear criteria for adjudicating any cognitive dispute. Normal discourse is not supported by any privileged representations, but the deep agreement of the interlocutors allows them to proceed as if it were. Abnormal discourse arises when someone, for whatever reason, speaks in a manner counter to the consensus of normal discourse (as when a Galileo says that the earth is not at rest). Unlike Kuhn, Rorty does not insist on a stage of "crisis" between those of normality and of revolution. He seems to think that new ways of speaking need not be motivated by acute strains in

---

12   Cf. PMN, 322–42, and Thomas Kuhn, *The Structure of Scientific Revolutions,* 2nd edition, Chicago: University of Chicago Press, 1970.

the old ways. In any case, most of the time such abnormal remarks simply fall by the wayside as mere foolishness or eccentricity. But sometimes the remarks are gradually picked up by the rest of the community and effect a radical change in the nature of its discourse. Then the innovators are hailed as revolutionary geniuses. But, of course, this means only that the community has accepted their new discursive standards.[13]

The charge that Rorty's view destroys the distinction between objectivity and subjectivity can take a number of forms. One version is that it entails a metaphysical idealism (indeed, a subjectivist form of idealism, which relativizes reality to different mental configurations). Kuhn opened himself to such a charge by saying that the adherents of different paradigms (systems of normal discourse) "live in different worlds".[14] Kuhn said this because he thought there was no way of giving a description of the world that would be shared by (and neutral between the conflicting claims of) rival paradigms. If this were so, then the paradigm, which is surely in the ideal realm, would determine the world. Rorty, however, maintains that Kuhn can readily admit that for any two paradigms we can find a description of the world that is neutral between them. Incommensurability requires only that no such description be a basis for deciding the issues in dispute between the paradigms. We can, for example, always find some way of describing a sunset that will be acceptable to both Ptolemeians and Copernicans (thus: "the perceived distance between the horizon and the sun gradually decreases"). The sunset is an objective reality for adherents of each paradigm; their disagreement is only about how this reality is to be further interpreted and explained.

This modification of Kuhn's view may avoid metaphysical idealism, but critics will still wonder how Kuhn (and Rorty) can preserve any meaningful epistemological distinction between objective knowledge and subjective belief. Scientists know that the earth moves relative to the sun; but for Kuhn, doesn't this mean merely that all members of the relevant scientific community agree that the earth moves? It seems that group consensus – which in fact is no different from what Lakatos called "mob psychology" – has become the only standard of knowledge.

As both Rorty and Kuhn note, coming to terms with this objection requires getting clear about the distinction between "objective" and "subjective". Building on Kuhn's comments, Rorty in effect distinguishes three

---

13   Rorty also develops his views on "conceptual change" via a Davidsonian account of metaphor. See "Unfamiliar Noises: Hesse and Davidson on Metaphor", ORT, 162–72; and "Philosophy as Science, Metaphor, Politics", EHO, 12–17.

14   Kuhn, *Structure of Scientific Revolutions*, 120–1.

cases. Sometimes "subjective" refers to what is a matter of individual preference and "objective" to what is generally accepted. In this sense, "Chateau Lafite is Bordeaux" is objective, whereas "Chateau Lafite 1959 is the best Bordeaux" is subjective. Rorty and Kuhn obviously do not make all knowledge subjective in this sense. The consensus of a scientific, literary, or political community is not a matter of personal opinion. It is objective at least in the sense of being *inter*subjective. Sometimes "subjective" refers to what is a matter of judgment as opposed to what can be unequivocally demonstrated (e.g., proven algorithmically). Kuhnian consensus is subjective in this sense, but then so is virtually every form of knowledge available to us outside of the most rigorous mathematical demonstrations. (Indeed, even mathematical demonstrations involve ineliminable acts of judgment regarding, for example, the applicability of a general principle to a particular case.) So for these first two cases, Kuhn and Rorty can respond to the charge of subjectivism with, respectively, "Not guilty" and "So what?".

The third sense of the distinction takes "subjective" to mean "how things appear to us" as opposed to "how things really are". This is surely the sense of "subjective" Rorty's critics have in mind. If knowledge is nothing more than group consensus, then it expresses only how things seem to us, which may well not be how they really are. Rorty's response to this charge is that this formulation of the distinction is ambiguous. One meaning is quite acceptable but innocuous to his position. The other meaning, which would undermine his position, is incoherent.

The innocent version of the distinction understands "things as they appear to us" as "how things appear in first impressions, before serious inquiry", and contrasts this to "how things appear after the fullest possible scrutiny". Rorty's understanding of knowledge is obviously objective if the objection is understood in this way. But the critic may rather take the distinction as between "things as they are described by our most careful and thorough inquiries" and "things as they are just in themselves, entirely apart from how they are described by our inquiries". But, Rorty maintains, to accept this distinction is to endorse the classical modern view that we directly know only mental representations ("things as we describe them"), which may or may not "match up" with reality outside the mind ("things as they are in themselves"). Once, with Rorty, we reject this distinction, there is no sense to the third meaning of objectivity.

We may still suspect that Rorty is improperly reducing objectivity to intersubjectivity, ignoring the fact that an individual can be in the right in opposition to his entire society. But such Socrates-versus-the-Athenians objections miss the point by confusing a social practice with group consensus.

Justification is social because it is linguistic and because we learn a language only in becoming part of a community. Belonging to a community means coming under the norms that constitute that community, but not every opinion shared by all or most members of a community expresses a communal norm. It is, in fact, quite possible for a single individual to be in accord with a community's norms when the rest of the community is not. For example, I could be the only person who pronounces my name correctly or the only person who knows that the twenty-first century does not begin until 2001. It may also happen that the norms of a community are not all mutually consistent, and an individual may be entitled to assert the claim of one norm against another that everyone else accepts. Of course, enough changes in the views and practices of the members of a community will eventually lead to changes in its norms, since norms have no basis outside of the community itself. But this does not mean that norms are changeable at the whim of a group, even if the group includes everyone. Even if we all say something different, we may not all be able to believe it or be able to reflect it in our practices.

Rorty himself does not always avoid confusion on this point. Consensus is closely tied to reason-giving in both origin and outcome. Like any social practice, reason-giving proceeds from an intersubjective acceptance of a set of norms; and it tends toward agreement on claims that have been justified by the practice. Rorty tends to collapse these two points into the misleading claim that consensus is what justifies a proposition. But on his own account this is true only in a very indirect sense. At some ultimate point, further demands for justification of the norms governing our reasoning-giving no longer make sense; and we can do no more than point out that these *are* the norms that we accept. But this acceptance is by no means an optional choice by individuals. It is the outcome of the deep-rooted and complex process whereby they have become reason-givers. At the other end, consensus is (at least in ideal cases) the outcome of successful reason-giving: the process of discussing the evidence, presenting arguments, and answering objections leads, when things go right, to widespread agreement on what to believe. So consensus about norms is the ultimate source of the practice of reason-giving, and consensus in specific beliefs is often the outcome of the practice.

None of this, however, implies that our beliefs are justified only to the extent that we agree on them. Rorty sometimes seems to think otherwise, as in the following passage from a response to Putnam:

> Suppose everybody in the community . . . thinks S must be a bit crazy [to assert p]. They think this even after patiently listening to S's defense of p, and

after making sustained attempts to talk him out of it. Might S still be *warranted* in asserting p? Only if there were some way of determining warrant *sub specie aeternitatis,* some natural order of reasons that determines, quite apart from S's ability to justify p to those around him, whether he is *really* justified in holding p.[15]

Here Rorty ignores the fact that S might have good reasons to believe that everyone else in the community is ignorant of, misinterpreting, or simply incapable of understanding the revelant community norms appropriate for evaluating p. Perhaps, for example, the rest of the community has lost the ability to understand the millennial significance of the fact that there is no year zero. In such a case, S will be justified against everyone else – not necessarily *sub specie aeternitatis* but in light of his superior understanding of norms implicit in his community. In this same discussion, Rorty suggests that S has warrant for asserting p simply if "S was in a good position, given the interests and values of himself and his peers, to assert p".[16] This is correct, but it is consistent with the possibility that, on a particular issue at a particular time, S may be warranted in believing that he does not have any epistemic peers. In such a case, S is justified in asserting p against everyone else.

Justification by consensus occurs only in special cases. When astrophysicists accept the existence of black holes, their justification is a complicated body of evidence and arguments based on it, not the fact that they agree that black holes exist. Nonexperts who accept the results of astrophysics on authority may justify their belief in black holes by the consensus of astrophysicists. But this is a derivative sort of justification that does not define the nature of the practice.

Because of his confusion about consensus, Rorty often wrongly portrays it as a casual, readily alterable agreement, as when he says that everything we know is known only under "optional descriptions" (PMN, 379) or that "man is always free to choose new descriptions" (PMN, 362, n. 7). In fact, to take an obvious case, the main elements of our scientific picture of the world (atomic structure, evolutionary development) are deeply rooted and extremely unlikely to change. Any such change would require either profound alterations in our norms of reason-giving or entirely improbable changes in the evidence available. Even our firmest beliefs may well be contingent in the sense that they might turn out to be wrong. But Rorty tends to confuse this modest fallibilism with a wildly implausible decisionist (or voluntarist) view of knowledge. For many of our beliefs, learning that they are wrong and

15 "Putnam and the Relativist Menace", *The Journal of Philosophy* 90 (1993), 451 (TP, 50).
16 Ibid.

coming to give them up would be an extended, arduous, excruciating process.[17]

Epistemic decisionism is abetted by our tendency to think that "accepting norms" is a matter of acquiescing to explicitly formulated criteria that govern our practice of reason-giving. But, as Charles Taylor, among many others, has emphasized, a practice such as reason-giving will always derive from an implicit understanding that is only partially and imperfectly caught by explicit formulations. Appreciating this point is perhaps the best way to counter the tendency to decisionism.

Rorty's confusions in this area show up in his discussion of the (eventual) emergence of the sharp modern distinction between science and religion from the Galileo–Bellarmine dispute. Denying that there are "rational" or "objective" standards behind our acceptance of this distinction (PMN, 331), he attributes it to such things as "the Enlightenment's decision that Christianity was mostly just priestcraft" (PMN, 329) and, more generally, to "three hundred years of rhetoric" in favor of the distinction (PMN, 330). But in fact the distinction was – to use another, more felicitous phrase of Rorty's – "hammered out" through long years of lively and subtle argument, argument that eventually convinced almost everyone that there were good reasons for, say, excluding Scriptural citations from science. Of course, after a certain point, what was won by careful argumentation becomes part of our unquestioned intellectual heritage. The heirs are easy with their legacy only because of their ancestors' hard work.

Rorty is rightly criticized for his insouciant tendency to assimilate justification to voluntary consensus, as though norms of belief depended on the majority vote at the next epistemic town meeting. But there is no need to formulate the view of reason-giving as a social practice in this decisionistic way. Admitting that justification is ultimately a matter of sharing a practice rather than, say, attaining self-evident insights does not make the routine results of ordinary epistemic deliberations a matter of arbitrary choice.[18] In his critique of Rorty, Thomas McCarthy has rightly maintained that "'our' culture is shot through with transcultural notions of validity". As he says, our

---

17   For a similar critique in the context of Rorty's effort to appropriate the work of Heidegger and Gadamer, see John Caputo, "The Thought of Being and the Conversation of Mankind", *Review of Metaphysics* 36 (1983), 661–85.

18   For an excellent discussion of this point (and with particular reference to Rorty's treatment of the Galileo–Bellarmine case), see Richard Bernstein's classic review of PMN, "Philosophy and the Conversation of Mankind", *Review of Metaphysics* 33 (1980), reprinted in his *Philosophical Profiles*, Philadelphia: University of Pennsylvania Press, 1986, especially 50–7.

actual practices of justification "involve constructing arguments that claim to be universally valid", not appealing to our agreement on a given claim. "In general, it is not *because* we agree that we hold a claim to be valid; rather, we agree because we have grounds for granting its validity."[19] But a properly formulated epistemological behaviorism will have no quarrel with McCarthy here. Epistemological behaviorism is not a view about the content of the norms involved in our practice of justification, but only about the ultimate basis of these norms. Its claim is that, in the final analysis, there is nothing underlying these norms other than the practice that they define. This is not a contradiction of our practice but merely a rejection of an indefensible philosophical interpretation of that practice. Properly understood, Rorty's pragmatic approach to justification is a coherent and plausible alternative to what representationalism has to offer.

4. The Problem of Truth

There still remains the question of truth. Rorty has somewhat altered his views on this topic over the years. But there is one key point on which he has always insisted. No matter what else we say about truth (e.g., whether we define it as warranted assertibility within a language or as correspondence with reality, or eschew any substantive definition and take it as a primitive), there is no way for us to know the truth other than the social practice of giving reasons. We have no reliable source of truth other than our ongoing conversation with one another. Perhaps we may or must understand truth as something beyond the best or ultimate outcome of that conversation. Even so, we have no trustworthy means of deciding what to accept as the truth other than what goes on in that conversation. For, as we have seen, "nothing counts as justification unless by reference to what we already accept, and . . . there is no way to get outside our beliefs and our language so as to find some test other than coherence" (PMN, 178). Given this, saying that a belief is true in any sense other than its being "justified to the hilt" (saying, for example, that it corresponds to the way reality is in itself) is to pay it an empty compliment. The most we can know is that it is justified.

The line of thought just described sketches one major motivation for Rorty's eventual conclusion that we should abandon the effort to produce

---

19   Thomas McCarthy, "Philosophy and Social Practice: Richard Rorty's 'New Pragmatism'", in *Ideals and Illusions,* Cambridge, MA: The MIT Press, 1991, 17, 19. This is a revised version of "Private Irony and Public Decency", *Critical Inquiry* 16 (1990) 355–70. (See also Rorty's response, "Truth and Freedom", 633–43, in the same volume.)

a serious philosophical theory of truth. Another motive is the failure of 2,500 years of philosophizing to produce anything like a satisfactory theory. But is such an abandonment really possible, and just how should we understand it? To answer these questions, we need to reflect a bit on the modern debate about metaphysical realism (or, equivalently, the correspondence theory of truth).[20]

In this debate, the weapon of choice has often been a caricature of the opposing view. The case against metaphysical realism, for example, is unanswerable if the theory's proponent can be saddled with a simplistic commitment to the thing-in-itself. Such a commitment is senseless if, for example, the thing-in-itself is regarded as cognitively inaccessible to our consciousness (which is only of things-as-they-appear-to-us). Then, the realist would be saying that what we are aware of (e.g., our "ideas") are representations of something that we cannot in principle know about. Certainly, it makes no sense to say that we can *know* that this is the case.

But, as Charles Taylor maintains, this kind of absurdity does not show that there is no sense in which our knowledge "corresponds" to reality. Talk of knowledge of reality does not require the picture of representations that mirror an inaccessible thing-in-itself. We might, for example, claim that we are simply aware of things that are independent of us – not of ideas (or whatever) that represent what we are not aware of. We simply find ourselves "at grips with a world of independent things".[21]

---

20 Strictly speaking, metaphysical realism and the correspondence theory of truth are independent claims. (Michael Devitt has particularly emphasized this point in "What Has Truth to Do with Realism?", chapter 4 of his *Realism and Truth*. Marian David, to whom I am indebted for very helpful discussion on this topic, also makes the point in his *Correspondence and Disquotation*, Oxford: Oxford University Press, 1994, 18, n. 2.) I could think everything is mind-dependent (and so deny metaphysical realism in favor of metaphysical idealism) and still understand truth as correspondence (i.e., the adequate representation of objects by beliefs). Conversely, I could accept mind-independent realities but deny that knowing the truth about these realities is a matter of having beliefs that correctly represent them. The way to do this would be to say, with Frege, that the content of my belief *is* – not merely *represents* – an abstract state of affairs and that its truth consists in the instantiation of that state of affairs. If, however, we reject both metaphysical idealism and Fregean Platonism, realism and correspondence become inextricably linked. For then the truth of a belief can consist neither in its idealistic coherence with other beliefs nor in its nonrepresentational correspondence to a fact that instantiates its abstract content. This leaves the non-Platonic metaphysical realist with no option but to understand the truth of a belief as its adequate representation of its object. Because contemporary debates about metaphysical realism typically assume a rejection of both idealism and Platonism, they do not distinguish realism from the correspondence theory of truth.

21 Charles Taylor, "Rorty in the Epistemological Tradition", in Alan Malachowski (ed.), *Reading Rorty*, Oxford: Blackwell, 1990, 270.

Similarly, the opponents of metaphysical realism are readily defeated if we can saddle them with the claim that objects of knowledge cannot be causally independent of us; that, for example, the Big Bang could not exist except as an object of human thought. But, as Rorty rightly insists, the opponents of realism need not claim that there is nothing *causally* independent of us.[22] The issue is not, Did the Big Bang occur before there were any human beings to experience it? It obviously did. The issue is rather whether the Big Bang, as we know it, has any features that are *representationally* independent of us. That is, do the categories we use to characterize it somehow mirror features it has entirely apart from our characterizations? It is this claim that the opponent of metaphysical realism questions.

So both proponents and opponents of metaphysical realism will, if they are sensible, begin by agreeing that the notion of an inaccessible thing-in-itself is senseless and that there are things causally independent of us. As a result, they will agree that the object of knowledge lies between the two extremes of total independence of and total dependence on the knower. Given this, however, we may wonder what they have left to disagree about. It would seem that, in rejecting the extreme versions of each position, we have converged on what we can call the "scheme-content" view of knowledge. The "scheme" is the set of categories in terms of which the mind understands objects of knowledge; this constitutes the idealist moment in our view of knowledge. The "content" is the object as a determinate something entirely independent of the mind's categorial system; this constitutes the realist moment in our view of knowledge. If both sides of the realism debate accept the role of conceptual schemes (which seems entailed by the rejection of the thing-in-itself) and also accept an irreducible content organized by the schemes (which seems entailed by the acceptance of the causal independence of the object), what could remain in dispute?

As Rorty has eventually realized, the answer to this question is: the very distinction between scheme and content. Particularly through the influence of Davidson, he has come to see that his critique of epistemology must include a firm rejection of this distinction, which Davidson has labeled "the third dogma of empiricism".[23] Unfortunately, Rorty's earlier discussions, particularly in PMN, do not always reflect this realization. In such discussions, he agreed that, to avoid metaphysical idealism, he needed to accept

---

22 Rorty, "Taylor on Truth", in James Tully (ed.), *Philosophy in an Age of Pluralism: the Philosophy of Charles Taylor in Question*, Cambridge: Cambridge University Press, 1994, 22 (TP, 86).

23 Donald Davidson, "The Very Idea of a Conceptual Scheme", *Inquiries into Truth and Interpretation*, Oxford: Oxford University Press, 1984, 189.

a world entirely independent of us that is the object of our knowledge. But, to avoid metaphysical realism, he insisted that the content of that knowledge comes from categories of the mind that do not correspond to any features of that world. From this standpoint, the "world" is epistemic prime matter, providing nothing but the brute resistance of things to our minds. Any structure, any properties we attribute to it reflect nothing more than the consequences of the consensus of our epistemic community.

As a result, Rorty balked at speaking of truth and objectivity as characteristics of even our most favorable epistemic situations. He denounced, for example, "the absurdity of thinking that the vocabulary used by present science, morality, or whatever has some privileged attachment to reality which makes it *more* than just a further set of descriptions" (PMN, 361). But such thinking is absurd only if the "privileged attachment to reality" is understood in terms of representationalist epistemology (e.g., by saying that the privilege derives from the fact that we can show that our scientific or moral representations match up with a reality of which we have no direct knowledge). Why, we want to respond, can't the best results of our science, for example, be said to be privileged just because they are, in all likelihood, true?

Rorty has disavowed his earlier position as merely a linguistic version of transcendental idealism. It gave in to the temptation "to use Kantian form–matter metaphors", which presuppose a scheme–content distinction. In particular, "we are tempted to say that there were no objects before language shaped the raw material (a lot of *ding-an-sichy*, all-content-no-scheme stuff)". But such talk left Rorty open to the charge "of making the false causal claim that the invention of the term 'dinosaur' caused dinosaurs to come into existence".[24] Similarly, his effort to understand truth in terms of our agreement about a given vocabulary left him the unpleasant alternative of either finding an adequate response to the powerful standard objections against *defining* truth in terms of consensus or else simply trying to do without the concept of truth.

In later essays, Rorty sometimes endorses what seem like decisively realistic assertions, such as "common-sense physical entities objectively exist independently of the mental" ("Pragmatism, Davidson, and Truth", ORT, 149)[25] and "if one follows Davidson [as Rorty says he does], . . . one will feel in touch with reality *all the time*" (ibid., 145). But such assertions lose much of their force when we put them in the context of other passages in which

---

24   Rorty, "Taylor on Truth", in James Tully (ed.), *Philosophy in an Age of Pluralism:* 26 (TP, 90).
25   Rorty is quoting (with approval) from Michael Devitt, "Dummett's Antirealism", *The Journal of Philosophy* 80 (1983), 76.

Rorty seems to say that the specific characteristics of (the facts about) the "independent" world are entirely dependent on our cognitive attitudes. Speaking, for example, of such apparently "hard facts" as a piece of litmus paper's turning blue or a column of mercury's reaching a certain level in a tube, he says: "The hardness of fact in all these cases is simply the hardness of previous agreements within a community about the consequences of a certain event" ("Texts and Lumps", ORT, 80). Rorty's language about the reality of the world has continued to be ambivalent.

To further our understanding of Rorty's views on truth and realism, it will be useful to focus on his debate with Charles Taylor on these issues.[26] Taylor focuses on Rorty's reluctance to admit that worldviews (including his own philosophical views) could be regarded as true or false, and argues effectively that Rorty's position shows a residual adherence to the modern epistemology he claims to reject. As Taylor puts it, although Rorty explicitly rejects the representationalist picture, "his conception of the alternatives still seems to be commanded by that view",[27] since he assumes that the only possible meanings for truth and objectivity are those specified by that picture. This point is nicely illustrated by Rorty's otherwise puzzling endorsement of Sartre's view that "the notion of 'one right way of describing and explaining reality' . . . is just the notion of having a way of describing and explaining *imposed* on us in that brute way in which stones impinge on our feet" (PMN, 375). As Taylor puts it, Rorty seems to think that "a representation which is not made true by some independent reality might just as well not be considered a candidate for truth at all".[28]

In his response to Taylor, Rorty admits the accuracy of Taylor's account of his earlier views, and acknowledges that he should not have eschewed truth but only the construal of truth in terms of the adequacy of a scheme to its content. But, given this correction, he thinks he has an entirely persuasive case against the metaphysical realism involved in a correspondence theory of truth. His opening point, with which Taylor will agree, is that realism makes no sense if it requires positing a cognitively inaccessible thing-in-itself. But he maintains that for metaphysical realism the only alternative to positing the thing-in-itself is to maintain that things with which we *are* in cognitive contact possess intrinsic features – that is, properties that they have

---

26   The debate was initiated by Taylor's "Rorty in the Epistemological Tradition", in A. Malachowski (ed.), *Reading Rorty*, 256–75. It continued with Rorty's reply, "Taylor on Truth", in James Tully (ed.), *Philosophy in an Age of Pluralism*, 20–33 (TP, 84–97), and Taylor's response, "Reply to Rorty", 219–22, in the same volume.

27   "Rorty in the Epistemological Tradition", in Alan Malachowski (ed.)., *Reading Rorty*, 271.

28   Ibid., 272.

quite apart from any ways in which we describe them. Talk of intrinsic features, however, assumes that we can draw a meaningful distinction between the independent content our descriptions are about and the conceptual schemata imposed by those descriptions. It assumes, that is, a distinction between scheme and content. But Davidson has shown that no such distinction can be drawn. Hence, there is no sense to the notion of an intrinsic property, and we are back with the incoherent thing-in-itself as the only way of making sense of the metaphysical realism.

Taylor's response is that we simply "cannot do without" the scheme–content distinction. He agrees with Rorty's point that we cannot "distinguish the role of our describing activity . . . and the role of the rest of the universe, in accounting for the truth of our beliefs".[29] But, Taylor says, this would require dropping the scheme–content distinction only if making the distinction means that we have "to disaggregate and isolate somehow a component of pure precategorised reality, which could then somehow be compared or related to language".[30] This, he says, is no more plausible than the claim that there is no distinction between form and color because we can't isolate the one element from the other. Taylor cites what he regards as clear cases of the distinction. If yesterday there were twelve chairs in a room and today there are ten, then reality has changed, not our language for classifying it. But when Aristotle says the sun is a planet and we say it is a star, the reality has remained the same, and we have employed a new classification scheme. Not only is there a distinction between scheme and content; it is also clear that some schemes are better than others for dealing with the content they organize. This does not mean that any scheme can be "compared to reality unframed by any scheme" or that all schemes can be ranked regarding adequacy against one another ("because some raise quite different questions"). "But when all this is said, some schemes can be ranked; and ranked because they permit us to grasp, or prevent us from grasping features of reality, including causal features, which we recognise as being independent of us". "This", Taylor says, "is the nub of what I want to call realism".[31]

Taylor is right in the sense that, once we have a certain description of reality as an unproblematic given (e.g., agree that there are twelve chairs in this room), then we can readily distinguish a change in reality from a mere change in descriptive scheme. But the issue between the realist and Rorty is whether the scheme–content distinction applies "all the way down" – that is,

29   "Taylor on Truth", in James Tully (ed.), *Philosophy in an Age of Pluralism*, 23 (TP, 87).
30   "Reply to Rorty", ibid., 219.
31   Ibid., 220.

whether all our descriptions of the world must involve a distinguishable scheme and content. Taylor's examples say nothing to this issue. His debate with Rorty identifies the issue as a crux of their disagreement but fails to resolve it. Further progress requires discussion of the resources Davidson provides Rorty for an alternative to the scheme–content distinction.

On the other hand, Taylor is right that we simply begin from a realist stance. We are, from the beginning, in cognitive contact with objects independent of us, not only knowing that there is such a world, but also knowing many specific things about it. However, this baseline knowledge of the world is simply a matter of knowing certain commonplaces, not of having any theoretical account of this knowledge – in terms, for example, of representations. Rorty may still be right that there is no prospect for our arriving at a substantive theoretical account of our knowledge.

In fact, I think he is right. Although we always start inquiry and reflection from baseline, humdrum truths, these are, of course, only privileged de facto. There is no reason in principle why they could not be criticized – analyzed, questioned, justified, or even eventually rejected. Such criticism is the business of philosophy. Philosophers have successfully criticized baseline truths about science, morality, religion, and politics. However, a couple of millennia of frustration should have taught us that there is no fruitful (or even coherent) way of criticizing baseline truths about truth itself. We can and must subscribe to all the commonplaces: we know truths, many truths are about the world, such truths tell us the way the world is, and so on. But whenever we try to get a critical perspective on these truths about truth, we wind up with dubious assumptions, misleading pictures, incoherent formulations. This view is not itself the conclusion of a philosophical perspective on truth, but merely a prudential judgment based on the historical record.

Accepting this sort of humdrum, philosophically unloaded sense of truth allows us to avoid the pitfalls of many of Rorty's formulations, which run aground by trying to avoid talk of our knowing truths about the world.[32] Without a forthright acceptance of humdrum realism, Rorty is tempted to replace truth with group consensus and hesitates to say that philosophical

---

32   The humdrum view of truth shares the spirit of a number of other recent views, including Arthur Fine's "natural ontological attitude" (cf. "The Natural Ontological Attitude" in J. Leplin (ed.), *Scientific Realism*, Berkeley: University of California Press, 1984) and Paul Horwich's "minimal truth" (*Truth*, Oxford: Blackwell, 1990). Rorty often seems to endorse the humdrum view, for example, in the "Introduction" to CP and in "Realism and Anti-realism", in L. Nagl and R. Heinrich (eds.), *Wo Steht die Analytische Philosophie Heute?*, Vienna: Oldenbourg, 1986, 103–15. In the latter discussion, he emphasizes the similarity of his view to that of Fine.

views opposed to his are wrong, maintaining only that he offers preferable "alternative descriptions". Such equivocations leave him open to charges of incoherent relativism and skepticism. But these difficulties dissolve once we accept humdrum realism.[33]

The remaining question is whether we can accept just humdrum realism and not also be committed to a representationalist theory of knowledge based on the scheme–content distinction. Donald Davidson shows how we can do this, thereby walking the narrow line between transcendental idealism and metaphysical realism.

5. Davidsonian Therapy

Davidson's view can be developed from the standard preliminary characterization of knowledge as (at least) justified true belief.[34] Given this, understanding knowledge requires understanding justification, truth, and belief. The classical modern view develops this understanding in terms of representation. A belief is taken to be a mental representation. Its truth is a matter of its accurately corresponding to an external (nonrepresentational) object. Since, on the representationalist view, we are directly aware of only our representations, the great problem becomes justification: showing that our beliefs do in fact correspond to external objects. This project requires showing that some representations (a subset of our beliefs or perhaps some other, more basic representations – e.g., sensations) have a privileged status that makes the connection to the world.

Davidson (like Rorty) thinks that the representationalist approach to knowledge fails, primarily because it poses but cannot solve the problem of

---

33   In a similar manner, Kai Nielsen defends Rorty against Jaegwon Kim's criticism by distinguishing the "common-sense" realism Rorty holds from the metaphysical realism that he rejects. See J. Kim, "Rorty on the Possibility of Philosophy", *The Journal of Philosophy* 78 (1980), 588–97; K. Nielsen, *After the Demise of Tradition: Rorty, Critical Theory, and the Fate of Philosophy*, Boulder, CO: Westview Press, 1991, 43–7.

34   Rorty's major discussion of Davidson is in the four essays that compose Part II of ORT. For Davidson's (almost entirely positive) response to Rorty's appropriation of his ideas, see "Afterthoughts, 1987", appended to the reprint of his "A Coherence Theory of Truth and Knowledge" in Alan Malachowski (ed.), *Reading Rorty*. See also Davidson's endorsement of Rorty's interpretation in his comments to Thomas Kent in "Language Philosophy, Writing, and Reading: A Conversation with Donald Davidson", Gary A. Olson (ed.), *Philosophy, Rhetoric, Literary Criticism: (Inter)view*, Carbondale: Southern Illinois University Press, 1994: "I would say nobody seems to me to have done as well in seeing what my overall picture is than [sic] Rorty. Even though Rorty and I think of things in quite a different way, he has made an effort to follow what I was up to, and it seems to me he gets the main thing right" (26).

skepticism. It cannot, that is, show that our representations accurately correspond to the world. He thinks, moreover, that the problem is with the very notion of representation as an epistemological category. There may be such things, but they have nothing to do with knowledge. His project, accordingly, is to show how we can understand belief, justification, and truth without appeal to representations.

Begin with belief. If it is not a mental representation, it must be simply an assertion (or a disposition to assert). To say that I believe a proposition p is simply to say that, given appropriate circumstances, I would assert p. As for justification, since it cannot be a matter of finding privileged representations, it must be a matter of giving reasons, that is, supporting one assertion with other assertions.

But what about truth? Without representations, it cannot be the correspondence of the mental to the world. On the other hand, we do not seem to be able to give an account of it, as we did for belief and justification, simply in terms of whether or how we assert a given proposition. The skeptic will always rightly point out that any assertion – no matter how emphatic, how widely accepted, how thoroughly justified – might not be true.

Davidson's solution is simply to reject the idea that we need an epistemological account of truth. Why make this apparently extreme move? Well, our humdrum knowledge about truth tells us that an account of its role in knowledge (an epistemological account) would have to present it as some sort of relation between our beliefs and the world. After all, humdrumly, a true belief is one that somehow "gets the world right". However, if we exclude representationalism, we exclude any intentional relations between beliefs and the world. We can countenance only causal relations.[35] We should, accordingly, have to say either that beliefs causally affect the world in virtue of their truth or that beliefs are true in virtue of the way that the world causally affects them. The first approach uses truth to explain certain features of the world – its existence and/or nature in the idealistic case, our ability to deal successfully with it (e.g., predict and control it) in the "pragmatic"[36] case. The second approach holds that beliefs are made true by the causal action of the world.

Rorty rejects both of these approaches.[37] Regarding the first approach,

---

35 This is Rorty's thesis (2) in "Pragmatism, Davidson, and Truth", ORT, 128.

36 Here, of course, "pragmatic" refers to an epistemological theory, not to Rorty's anti-epistemological pragmatism.

37 These rejections are expressed in theses (1) and (3) of "Pragmatism, Davidson, and Truth", ORT, 128.

the idealistic version is a nonstarter, since it violates the obvious truth that the world is causally independent of our minds. Idealism makes sense only if it is formulated in terms of a representational account of the relation of mind and world. The "pragmatic" version of the first approach is the "best-explanation" argument for realism that, as we shall see, Rorty dismisses on grounds of excessive generality. Other versions of this approach – for example, Dummett's – slip back into representationalism (in Dummett's case by giving an essential role to "senses").

The second approach is that of metaphysical realism. Rorty has no problem agreeing that beliefs (true or false) are caused by the world. The question is whether their truth itself is produced by the world. Does the world "make them true"? Once again, the thesis at least makes sense from a representationalist viewpoint. If true beliefs are accurate "pictures" of reality, we can at least imagine the pressures of reality forcing them into the appropriate shape. But if a belief is not a representation, what can the world do to it to make it true? At best, a belief might be caused to exist by whatever (thing, fact, state of affairs – take your ontological pick) it is about. Suppose, for example, that my belief that there is a tree outside is in fact caused by a tree outside. Even so, the belief is not true in virtue of its being so caused. The belief might have been caused in many different ways – for example, by a friend telling me there is a tree outside – and it would still be true. All that the truth of the belief requires is that the tree be outside. Given this, it doesn't matter what caused the belief.

Without representationalism, then, there is no possibility of an epistemological account of truth. We can only follow Davidson in taking truth as a primitive. That is, we must be content with our humdrum knowledge of truth, along with purely logical explications of this knowledge in terms of Tarksi's T-sentences.[38] The commitment to humdrum realism is, however, crucial, as we can see by reflecting on John McDowell's perceptive criticism of Rorty's appropriation of Davidson.

McDowell maintains that Rorty posits an unacceptable division between an external view of beliefs as merely the effects of causal processes and an internal view of beliefs, implicit in Rorty's account of justification as reason-

---

38 As Davidson puts it, summing up the "minimalist attitude towards truth" that he and Rorty share: "Truth is as clear and basic a concept as we have. Tarski has given us an idea of how to apply the general concept (or try to apply it) to particular languages on the assumption that we already understand it; but of course he didn't show how to define it in general (he proved, rather, that this couldn't be done). Any further attempt to explain, define, analyse or explicate the concept will be empty or wrong" ("Afterthoughts, 1987", in Alan Malachowski [ed.], *Reading Rorty*, 135).

giving, as the outcome of rational inquiry. McDowell points out that knowledge makes no sense if we simply set up these two views in total independence of one another. Without some connection between the two, there is, in particular, no basis for identifying a belief as the result of a given causal process with a belief as the conclusion of an argument. Rorty's hesitation (at least in his earlier writings) to admit that knowledge is of truths about the world makes it impossible for him to make this connection.[39] McDowell is, for example, rightly shocked at Rorty's claim that, when our perceptual or scientific language-game leads us to assert "There are rocks", "there seems no obvious reason why the progress of the language-game we are playing should have anything in particular to do with the way the rest of the world is" (ORT, 129). As McDowell says, "It is the whole point of the idea of norms of inquiry that following them ought to improve our chances of being right about 'the way the rest of the world is'. If following what pass for norms of inquiry turns out not to improve our chances of being right about the world, that just shows we need to modify our conception of the norms of inquiry."[40]

McDowell's point should not, however, be taken to mean that Rorty must provide a philosophical theory to bridge the mysterious gap between the external domain of causality and the internal domain of epistemic norms. The point is rather that separating the two domains, instead of admitting from the beginning that we know truths about the world, is precisely to fall back into the traditional epistemology Rorty wants to avoid. Admitting this prevents the problem epistemology purports to solve from arising. Nor is admitting the "world" in this sense a lapse into metaphysical realism. "The world as I invoke it here . . . is not the world that is well lost. . . . It is the perfectly ordinary world in which there are rocks, snow is white, and so forth".[41] It is, in other words, the humdrum world, the object of the humdrum realistic truths I have insisted Rorty needs to accept.

---

39 Susan Haack makes essentially the same point in terms of belief, beginning from the truism that *to believe that p is to accept p as true*. Because of this, she says, denying "any connection between a belief's being justified according to our practices, and its being true" makes it "impossible to see why a belief's being justified [in the sense of] conforming to [our] practices should be thought to have any bearing on whether one should hold it" ("Vulgar Pragmatism", in Herman J. Saatkamp, Jr. [ed.], *Rorty and Pragmatism: the Philosopher Responds to His Critics.* Nashville, TN: Vanderbilt University Press, 1995, 137). In other words, "justified" means "justified in believing", and "justified in believing" means "justified in believing to be true". So, if Rorty's concept of justification excludes any relation to truth, he does not really have a concept of justification; he must "think of justification always in covert scare quotes" (136). See also Rorty's response to Haack in the same volume.

40 John McDowell, *Mind and World,* Cambridge, MA: Harvard University Press, 1994, 151.

41 Ibid. McDowell is referring to Rorty's essay, "The World Well Lost", in *Consequences of Pragmatism,* Minneapolis: University of Minnesota Press, 1982.

Rorty's own response to this criticism is to distrust McDowell's claim that his talk of "being right about the way the world is" is harmless. He says he thinks McDowell's view "will lead one back to the distinction between scheme and world" and so to representationalism ("The Very Idea of Human Answerability to the World: John McDowell's Version of Empiricism", TP, 151). Rorty may have a point, given McDowell's insistence that, before we are entitled to walk away from the problems of representationalist epistemology, we need a precise formulation of just why these problems cannot be coherently formulated. It is easy to get caught up in the argument while trying to explain that there is nothing to argue about. But the fact remains that it is possible simply to rest with humdrum realism, staying clear of representationalist readings into it; and failing to endorse humdrum realism is incoherent.

The notion of humdrum truth similarly provides a response to Putnam's otherwise devastating critique of Rorty. Putnam points out that, for all his criticism of philosophical conceptions, Rorty cannot avoid using difficult and controversial notions such as that of a disposition, which he takes for granted in speaking of consensus among members of a group:

> To reject talk of "meanings" as mythology – as both Quine and Rorty do – while rejoicing . . . in talk of dispositions of one's fellow "postmodern bourgeois liberals" to agree . . . is irresponsible. If we should now let the project of saying what the noumena are, and whether there are noumena, and whether or not the whole question was a mistake, have a long respite, well and good! . . . But that is quite different from saying that we have achieved a coherent standpoint from which we can see what is and what is not mythological. . . . If we are allowed to go on using dispositional idioms without a metaphysical account of how dispositionality "emerges" in the world (without a "foundation"), then why should we be forbidden to talk of true and false, right and wrong, rational and irrational, in exactly the same way?[42]

As I see it, Rorty should respond by simply agreeing with Putnam. He can and must allow himself the use of truth in the humdrum sense, with no commitment to substantive philosophical theory.

Humdrum truth is also what Rorty needs to make his peace with John Searle. Searle cogently defends "realism" and "the correspondence theory of truth", but only by in effect reducing these views to the humdrum conception. He begins by characterizing his position as a set of utterly obvious "platitudes" and, toward the end of his discussion, remarks that "the hard-

---

42   Hilary Putnam, "A Comparison of Something with Something Else", *New Literary History* 17 (1985), 75–6.

est thing to keep in mind in this whole discussion is that we are dealing with a small bunch of tautologies and their entailments".[43] This is consistent with Rorty's view as long as Searle does not (as he seems not to) think that the entailments of his tautologies amount to a nontrivial theory of truth.[44]

The key point is that our "discourse on truth" should be limited to an assertion, without philosophical commentary or elaboration, of the baseline commonplaces about truth and a review of the arbitrariness and/or incoherence of efforts to criticize (i.e., analyze, modify, or justify) the baseline truths. As Rorty's work and its reception show, this is not an easy line to walk. Assertions of the baseline truths are readily taken in the sense imposed on them by standard philosophical theories of truth. Thus, "There is a world outside of us" is taken as a rejection of metaphysical idealism in favor of metaphysical realism; or "we have to judge for ourselves whether or not a reason is a good reason" is taken as endorsing linguistic idealism. In the same way, criticism of the flaws of a philosophical theory of truth is too readily seen as an endorsement of an opposing theory. Often it is Rorty's critics who are misunderstanding what he is trying to do. But sometimes he himself has forgotten his policy of disengagement and has started saying things (e.g., "Truth is what our peers let us get away with") he shouldn't want to say. This occurs when he makes positive claims about truth that venture beyond the commonplace. On the subject of truth, whenever Rorty is provocative and unsettling, he is, by his own best lights, wrong.[45]

Rorty's ambivalence regarding truth shows up in his tendency, even after Davidsonian therapy, to make claims that implicitly reject the humdrum view of truth. A good recent example is his rejection of the concept of ideology as formulated by Terry Eagleton. Eagleton, in a broadly Marxist mode, has defined ideology as "ideas and beliefs which help to legitimate the interests of a ruling group or class specifically by distortion and dissimulation". Rorty maintains that such a definition conflicts with the pragmatic view of truth, since "'distortion' presupposes a medium of representation which, intruding between us and the object under investigation, produces an appearance that does not correspond to the reality of the object. This representationalism

43 John Searle, *The Construction of Social Reality*, New York: The Free Press, 1996, 152, 214.

44 For Searle's explicit critique of Rorty, see his "Rationality and Realism: What Is at Stake?", *Daedalus* 122 (1992), 55–84. Rorty's reply, in "Does Academic Freedom Have Philosophical Presuppositions?", *Academe*, November–December 1994, 52–63, strikes me as vacillating confusingly between assertions and denials of humdrum realism. (This reply is reprinted as "John Searle on Realism and Relativism" in TP, 63–83.)

45 Michael Devitt has a good treatment of the fundamental realism of Rorty's position in his *Realism and Truth*, chapter 11.

cannot be squared with the pragmatist insistence that truth is not a matter of correspondence to the intrinsic nature of reality." He goes on to maintain that "pragmatists . . . agree that everything is a social construct and that there is no point in trying to distinguish between the 'natural' and the 'merely' cultural".[46] Here Rorty acts as though his rejection of representationalism forbids all talk of accuracy or distortion, even in a political context far removed from philosophical theory. This is the sort of rejection of humdrum realism for which his critics rightly reproach him. There is a commonsense distinction between the way things are and the way the interests of an exploitative regime represent them. The fact that his distinction does not translate into a substantive philosophical theory of truth does not, as Rorty here implies, eliminate the practical political force of the distinction.

Rorty's ambivalence toward humdrum truth derives from what he sees as elements of representationalism in our commonsense views on truth. So, at the end of his discussion of Crispin Wright's "minimalist conception of truth", he says, "If contemporary intuitions are to decide the matter, 'realism' and representationalism will always win. . . . [Pragmatists] should see themselves as involved in a long-term attempt to change the rhetoric, the common sense, and the self-image of their community".[47] But it is one thing to be alert to metaphysical excesses wearing the mask of common sense and another to reject the humdrum realism at the core of our commonsense view of truth. Rorty unfortunately sometimes lets the former lead to the latter.

If, however, we stick to the distinction between humdrum and philosophical realism, Davidson's perspective allows us to develop Rorty's pragmatic approach to knowledge in a coherent and convincing manner. Davidson shows how we can, contrary to Taylor, reject the scheme–content distinction and eliminate representationalism while maintaining a humdrum realism that slips into neither transcendental idealism nor metaphysical realism.

Our discussion so far has, however, ignored a major difficulty for any antirepresentationalist. We have dealt with knowledge (justification, truth, and belief) but not meaning. The topic can hardly be avoided. We cannot believe or know what we don't understand, and what we understand (e.g., a belief) surely has meaning. Meanings, however, are paradigms of represen-

---

46 "Feminism, Ideology, and Deconstruction: A Pragmatist View", *Hypatia* 8 (1993), 98. The quotation from Eagleton is from his *Ideology: An Introduction*, London: Verso, 30.

47 Rorty, "Is Truth a Goal of Enquiry? Davidson vs. Wright", *The Philosophical Quarterly* (1995), 299–300 (TP, 41). This is a response to Crispin Wright, *Truth and Objectivity*, Cambridge, MA: Harvard University Press, 2nd edition, 1992. Rorty rejects Wright's "minimalist" account as a vehicle for fruitless "metaphysical activism" about truth.

tationalist entities. Somehow, Rorty needs to be able to talk of meaning without introducing meanings, to show that a belief can be meaningful without being related to a meaning that it represents.

Here too Davidson offers Rorty crucial assistance. Davidson begins from a point we mentioned earlier in passing: that although there is no place for an epistemological theory of truth, it is possible to develop a logical theory of truth. Such a theory (Tarski *fecit*) is not concerned with defining truth or giving it a role in explaining knowledge. It is, rather, interested simply in providing, for any given language, an axiomatic system capable of deriving as theorems the truth conditions for every sentence in the language. The truth conditions for a sentence s of a language L are given by a statement in a metalanguage that specifies the state of the world that must obtain if (and only if) the sentence is to be true. If we take German as our L and English as the metalanguage, then a typical simple statement of truth conditions (T-sentence) is

"Schnee ist weiss" is true iff snow is white.

The job of constructing an axiomatic system capable of deriving all such T-sentences would be trivial if, for each sentence of L we could take as an axiom,

"s" is true iff T(s),

where T(s) is the translation of s into the metalanguage. But a meaningful axiomatization requires deduction of the theorems (in this case an infinite set) from a *finite* set of axioms. So the job cannot be done by brute force.

The fact that the right-hand side of a T-sentence is a translation (into the metalanguage) of the sentence named on the left-hand side suggests a connection with the problem of meaning. Why not simply say that the right-hand side of the T-sentence (derivable from our axioms) for a given sentence s is the meaning of the sentence?

To this it will be objected that our ability to construct the axiom system capable of deriving the T-sentences presupposes that we already know the meaning of the sentences of L. We knew, for example, that "Schnee ist weiss" meant "Snow is white"; otherwise, we would not have designed our axioms to yield the T-sentence they did. So we can hardly say that the T-sentence provides us with the meaning of s.

Suppose, however, that we could derive all the T-sentences for L from observation of the linguistic and other behavior of the users of L. With no background knowledge at all of the meaning of German terms, we probably could not start from anything as complicated as "Schnee ist weiss". But through slow stages of development (beginning with the fact that Germans say "Schnee" when pointing to snow), we might be able to construct *the empirical hypothesis* that "Schnee ist weiss" is true iff snow is white. Doing this for every T-sentence of L would provide, without circularity, the meaning of every sentence s of L. Trying to establish this possibility is the point of Davidson's discussion, following Quine, of the field linguist and radical translation (or interpretation). Of course, the philosopher's interest in this situation is not at all the same as that of the field linguist. The linguist merely wants to develop a usable translation manual for a previously unknown tongue. The philosopher is interested in showing that the linguist's (necessarily) behaviorist methodology is in principle able to define meaning without recourse to meanings.

But the critic will now object that, even if this method can yield the meaning of German sentences without our previously knowing their meanings, it still presupposes that we know the meanings of our (English) sentences. So what has been the gain for an understanding of meaning?

This objection misses the point of Davidson's exercise. He is not trying to show how we come to know the meanings of English sentences. This is done merely by learning to speak English, an achievement that needs no philosophical explanation and that obviously involves a complex implicit understanding of language that could never be exhaustively reproduced by the field linguist's explicit formulations. Davidson's task is rather to begin with our ability to speak English and then show how we can develop the capacity to speak *explicitly* about the meanings of sentences (in German, English, or any other language). The possibility of empirically deriving T-sentences from the situation of radical interpretation does just this. The point is simply to show how we can understand talk of meanings solely in terms of a logical characterization of truth à la Tarski. Once this is achieved, there is no need for a substantive philosophical theory of meaning.

6. Truth and Science

We have seen how Rorty can avoid incoherence by staking his right to minimal senses of truth and objectivity. He has acknowledged that his ambivalence toward truth was a mistake and that, for example, "Whatever dumb things I may have said in the past, I am now . . . happy to say that when I put forward large philosophical views I am making 'claims to truth' . . . rather than simply a recommendation to speak differently".[48] However, Rorty has still not been able to get beyond his (ultimately representationalist) reluctance to accept a realistic construal of the true sentences of natural science. I will argue that he can and should take this further step. In this regard, it is helpful to reflect on a thought experiment Rorty proposes. "Imagine," he says, "that a few years from now you open your copy of the *New York Times* and read that philosophers, in convention assembled, have unanimously agreed that values are objective, science rational, truth a matter of correspondence to reality, and so on" ("Science as Solidarity", ORT, 43). He notes that the public reaction to such an event "would not be 'Saved!' but rather 'Who do these philosophers think they *are*?'" And rightly so, he says, since what we should expect of philosophers (and all intellectuals) is not "getting it right" but "making it new", not truth but originality.

Perhaps the most interesting thing about Rorty's thought experiment is that, if we substitute "natural scientists" for "philosophers", it is no longer a fantasy but an everyday fact. Nuclear physicists, industrial chemists, molecular biologists, et al. do routinely announce agreement on previously controversial issues. The public reaction, however, is the opposite of what Rorty imagines it being to a similar philosophical development. And, I would add, rightly so.

Why? The obvious answer, which Rorty rejects, is that science has access to the truth about the natural world in a way that philosophy – along with all other humanistic and most social scientific disciplines – does not. He acknowledges that there is something strikingly distinctive about the natural sciences: their remarkable success in predicting and therefore controlling events in the world. But, he asks, "What is so special about prediction and control?" By which he means, Why should we think that success at prediction and control is an indication of some special access to the truth about reality? "Why," for example, "should we think that the tools which make possible the attainment of these particular human purposes are less 'merely' human than those which make possible the attainment of beauty or justice?" ("Is Natural Science a Natural Kind?", ORT, 58).

On Rorty's view, the only epistemological difference between the natural sciences and their less vaunted counterparts in the *Geisteswissenschaften* is that the former are able to achieve a high degree of consensus. "If we say

---

48 "Taylor on Truth", 28, n.14 (TP, 92, n.16); Rorty maintains that he has not voiced these "dumb views" since 1986. He also acknowledges an "only half-erased decisionism in PMN – an unhappy tendency to make existentialist noises". But, as we have seen, Rorty still sometimes slips back into his rejection of truth.

that sociology or literary criticism 'is not a science,' we shall mean merely that the amount of agreement among sociologists or literary critics on what counts as significant work . . . is less than among, say, microbiologists" ("Science as Solidarity", ORT, 40). But doesn't it seem likely that the agreement among microbiologists is connected with their ability to make successful predictions? If you think antibiotics are an effective treatment for ulcers and I don't, the best way for you to convince me will be to show a high rate of recovery for ulcer patients who took antibiotics. Predictive success is one of the best sorts of evidence for the truth of a scientific hypothesis; and, since scientists want the truth about the world, they tend to accept hypotheses with a high degree of predictive success.

Rorty sometimes gives the impression that any scientific interest in truth is an unfortunate misdirection, that we should "replace the desire for objectivity – the desire to be in touch with a reality which is more than some community with which we identify ourselves – with the desire for solidarity with that community" ("Science as Solidarity", ORT, 39). But, in accord with our previous discussions of realism, such remarks misleadingly suggest that scientific knowledge is entirely constituted by our agreement to think and talk in a certain way. This obscures the fact that the "human community" is, to adapt the Heideggerian phrase, a "community-in-the-world", from the start interacting with things that exist in causal independence of it. Our rejection of metaphysical realism must not lead us to deny (or, like Berkeley, to reinterpret philosophically) the existence of anything ordinary people believe in. In the same vein, there is no reason to agree with fictionalists and instrumentalists, who, on the basis of philosophical theories, deny the existence of the theoretical entities postulated by science.

We can, however, share Rorty's concern that we not interpret the predictive success of science as a sign of its ability to reach some special sort of truth – a truth beyond that of ordinary experience and thought. He rejects the idea that "some of our true beliefs are related to the world in a way in which others are not" ("Is Natural Science a Natural Kind?", ORT, 51). Any true belief is, humdrumly, true of the world with which we find ourselves engaged from the beginning. But no belief – not even those of the most successful science – is true in some deeper sense.

Those who think there is some deeper truth in science appeal to the idea that science has a special method (e.g., abductive inference) that reveals to us special objects of knowledge (e.g., the "really real"). Such ideas are typically formulated in terms of the classical modern picture of a mind that knows directly only representations and needs the special scientific method to ground an inference to the existence of, for example, the microentities that are the realities to which true representations correspond. This is often the thinking behind efforts to argue that the truth of scientific theories (and hence the existence of the entities they postulate) is the best explanation of their predictive success. Here, an argument for scientific realism (the existence of theoretical entities) is equated with an argument for metaphysical realism (the existence of a noumenal world beyond that of the world that appears to us).

Rorty is right to reject such arguments. There is no basis for asserting the existence of a noumenal world or of a special scientific method for knowing about it. If the cognitive privilege of natural science can be based only on the privileged representations of classical modern epistemology, then this privilege is an illusion. But this is not the only way. There is no need to take the predictive success of science as evidence, via an argument to the best explanation, for a special sort of scientific truth. Predictive success (of the right sort and sustained over time) itself makes natural science cognitively privileged. This privilege does not consist in knowing a world beyond that in which we all live by methods no one else uses. It consists rather in knowing the world in which we all live much better by making particularly effective use of one of the common ways of knowing this world.

More fully: from time immemorial, one of the ways of finding out more about the world has been to perform tests: guess on the basis of past experience what might happen in the future, see if our guess is correct, revise it if not, and so on. Over the centuries, and with increasing momentum since the 1600s, this "empirical" approach – this effort to know about things by trying to predict their behavior – has been made more refined, precise, and rigorous. And, particularly in the last 300 years, the resulting knowledge about the world has been spectacular. However, far and away the largest and most precise body of such knowledge has been about the nonhuman domain of the world, from stars and planets to the microstructures of animals and chemicals. The natural sciences, in short, are cognitively privileged simply because they have yielded so much more and so much more precise knowledge of the world than any other inquiries.

This privileged status has nothing to do with knowing a metaphysical world-beyond-the-world or with having gained access to some privileged set of representations. It does have something to do with the now evident superiority of studying the natural world through systematic empirical methods (as opposed to relying on traditional authorities, commonsense intuitions, or a priori philosophical analyses). But this is just to say that these methods have, as a matter of fact, been the most successful in telling us about the way the natural world behaves. Rorty is right to insist that the success of these methods in this context does not prove that they should be the model for inquiring about other things we are interested in (art, ethics, politics), or that inquiries not using these methods are senseless or unimportant. But he is wrong to say that, apart from a contingent consensus of opinion, natural science has no cognitively privileged status.

I acknowledge the entirely mundane character of the points I have been making about natural science. I have insisted on them only because Rorty has, in opposing a misunderstanding, gone past the truth in the other direction. In rightly arguing that science does not have the sort of privilege representationalism accords it, he ignores the substantial sort of privilege that it does have.

This obscuring of the true status of science is particularly evident in Rorty's discussion of the "ontological significance" of science's predictive success. He begins by rightly noting the vacuity of a general argument for the truth of scientific theories from their predictive success (e.g., in technological applications). A general argument of this sort is no more convincing than one from the success of Moslem armies to the truth of Islam. Rorty also rightly notes that the problem with such an argument is precisely the abstract, overly general level at which it operates. We would need to have detailed explanations of just how specific scientific procedures have led to specific successes. (This, for example, is the problem with the proof of Islam from military success. No one can explain just how and why the will of Allah has brought about just these victories in just this sort of way.) Rorty sets out what is required as follows: "They [proponents of a special cognitive status for science] are going to have to isolate some reliability-inducing methods which are not shared with all the rest of culture and then isolate some features of the world which gear in with these methods. They need, so to speak, two independently describable sets of cogwheels, exhibited in sufficiently fine detail so that we can see just how they mesh" ("Is Science a Natural Kind?" ORT, 55).

This requirement is acceptable, with two qualifications. First, as we saw earlier, what matters is that the results, not the methods, of science are distinctive. Science is superior to other cognitive efforts because of its distinctively successful developments of the standard methods we use to learn about the world. Second, it is misleading to portray the move from predictive success to cognitive significance as made by philosophers (or others) who reflect on scientific practice and somehow correlate it with "an independently describable" account of the world. Scientists themselves are after knowledge, and their practices involve constructing descriptions of the world, the truth of which they infer from their predictive success. Given these two qualifications, however, there is no problem pointing out in detail the case, from predictive success, for the truth of scientific results (and hence for the cognitive significance of the enterprise). We need only review the complex series of theoretical developments, mathematical calculations, and empirical tests whereby the scientific community has convinced itself of the correctness of a given hypothesis. We could, for example, trace the career of the atomic hypothesis from its initial modern employment by Dalton, through the decisive nineteenth-century triumphs that convinced even such skeptics as Mach, to our current ease with speaking of manipulating and even "taking pictures" of atoms. Such an account would show how specific scientific developments (e.g., certain of Lavoisier's experiments, specific solutions of the Schrödinger equation) convinced scientists that atoms had specific characteristics.[49]

I have said that the preceding sort of account provides what Rorty asks for as an explanation of just how predictive success leads to ontological significance. Rorty apparently would not agree, since his own discussion looks for (and fails to find) the explanation in a quite different direction. This is the direction of causal production rather than rational justification. His idea is that the realist would need to show just how the independently existing world brings it about that we have beliefs that accurately represent it. The sort of thing he is looking for is, for example, an explanation of "how gravity caused Newton to acquire the concept of itself". He says further that "the closest I can come to imagining what such an explanation would be like would be to describe what happens in the brain of a genius who suddenly uses new vocables. . . . " ("Is Natural Science a Natural Kind?" ORT, 57). We are hardly surprised that such a bizarre explanatory search comes up empty. But we should be surprised that Rorty thinks this is the sort of account required to explain the success of science in describing the world. It is, perhaps, the kind of account required to ground a representationalist move from the world as it appears to us to the world as it really is in itself. But, as I have been insisting, a realistic view of natural science need not endorse this sort of metaphysical realism.

On the view I'm supporting, realism is just the claim that natural science has been able to achieve a remarkable amount of knowledge about the

49 For an example of such an account, see Ernan McMullin, "What Do Physical Models Tell Us?" in B. van Rootselaar (ed), *Logic, Methodology, and Philosophy of Science*, Amsterdam: North Holland, 1968.

world (the one we all live in and know about); such a claim is justified by natural science's high level of success in predicting events in that world.[50] The explanatory accounts that show this connection between truth and predictive success are not given in the space of causes but, as fits Rorty's own account of justification, in the space of reason-giving. Such accounts – which merely rehearse the rational path natural science itself has followed in justifying its claims – show just how it is that natural science has achieved more cognitively than other modes of inquiry. They thus provide, in a way that entirely accords with his view of justification, the answer to Rorty's question, "What is so special about prediction and control?" This answer shows why, with no compromise in our critique of modern epistemology, we can and should accept a privileged role for natural science as a description of reality.[51]

Critics may suggest that my talk of science's ontological significance and cognitive superiority is merely fancy language for its obvious advantage in prediction and control. To make anything more of it will, they may urge, return us to a discredited representationalism. For such critics, I go wrong by arguing from predictive success to ontological significance in the sense of "conveying the truth about nature as it is in itself, independent of our beliefs and desires". But this sort of objection confuses the problematic sense of "ontological significance" that underlies representationalist theories of knowledge with the entirely unproblematic sense required by the humdrum realism of our everyday presence in the world. Quite apart from any philosophical theories, we have a good deal of knowledge about things that exist independent of the web of our beliefs and desires. Much of this is simply the result of ordinary sense experience (what we have seen, heard, or run up against); but much of it is also an extension of such knowledge by the focused and controlled efforts of experimental science. Some of the latter is just a matter of closer direct observation, perhaps aided by simple instruments such as calipers or magnifying glasses. But just as ordinary knowledge involves inferences from observed facts to unobserved explanations of these facts (e.g., from noises in the wall to a mouse making the noises), so scientific knowledge involves inferences to unobserved (though in principle ob-

---

50   This is the sort of realism Rorty defines as "the idea that inquiry is a matter of finding out the nature of something which lies outside the web of beliefs and desires" ("Inquiry as Recontextualization", ORT, 96). I remain puzzled as to why Rorty thinks he needs to reject this view.

51   I discuss Rorty's views on science more thoroughly in my "Paradigms and Hermeneutics: a Dialogue on Kuhn, Rorty, and the Social Sciences", *American Philosophical Quarterly* 21 (1984), 1–15.

servable) entities such as the earth's core, dinosaurs, and gases in the interior of stars. To say that natural science has achieved a body of objective knowledge beyond that of common sense is to say that such entities exist in the same sense that the ordinary objects of direct sense experience do, and are not merely convenient fictions facilitating prediction and control. To say that the natural sciences are cognitively superior to the social sciences is to say that, on the whole, sociology, anthropology, and even psychology and economics have not developed comparably rich and detailed extensions of commonsense knowledge.

My claims here about the ontological significance of natural science are, accordingly, independent of most of the issues currently debated by philosophers of science under the heading of scientific realism. My position is, for example, consistent with Hacking's combination of an acceptance of the existence of theoretical entities with a rejection of the detailed truth of specific theories about them.[52] It is even consistent with van Fraassen's thoroughgoing antirealism about theoretical entities.[53] The realism I am defending can be maintained simply in terms of the new *observable* entities and truths about them discovered by natural science; it does not require any particular view about the ontological status of unobservable entities.[54]

My realism about science is even consistent with many contemporary claims about the fundamentally social nature of the scientific enterprise – including claims about the socially negotiated nature of scientific concepts and justifications. It contradicts social constructivist accounts only when these are pushed to a skeptical limit; that is, when, in challenging claims of scientific truth, they also, incoherently, challenge the humdrum realism about the world of everyday experience that, as Hume urged, none of us can reject in a sustained way. This point can be generalized to express the core of my realism about science: a realistic view of science is necessary precisely to the extent that denying it will, in virtue of science's status as an extension of everyday knowledge, also require a denial of humdrum realism.

52 Ian Hacking, *Representing and Intervening*, Cambridge: Cambridge University Press, 1983.
53 Bas van Fraassen, *The Scientific Image*, Oxford: Oxford University Press, 1980.
54 In fact, however, I would argue that natural science has provided decisive evidence for the existence of at least some unobservable entities. For my criticism of van Fraassen on this issue, see "Scientific Realism vs. Constructive Empiricism", *The Monist*, 65 (1982), 336–49 (reprinted in P. Churchland and C. Hooker [eds.], *Images of Science*, Chicago: University of Chicago Press, 1985), and "How to Be a Scientific Realist", *The Modern Schoolman* 74 (1999).

7. Ethics without Foundations

Critics of modernity typically tie its epistemological defects to its moral deficiencies. As we shall see in our discussions of MacIntyre and Taylor, the connection is often made through the notion of the self. The modern view of knowledge, it is said, requires a self that is entirely disengaged from the world, an autonomous "point", with no externally imposed essence or structure. According to the critics, the consequences of such a conception are as disastrous in ethics as they are in epistemology. Just as there is no way for such a self to escape from the veil of its own ideas to the world of objective knowledge, so there is no way for it to climb out of the trough of its own desires to enter a world of objective moral obligation.

Although Rorty does not accept the hyper-individualism of a punctual self, in no way constituted by relations to others, he does see the self as simply a congeries of beliefs and desires, with no underlying nature that might ground a morality contrary to the total system of our beliefs and desires. He proposes to "think of the moral self . . . as a network of beliefs, desires, and emotions with nothing behind it – no substrate behind the attributes". Further, this network is not fixed once and for all, but is constantly "reweaving" itself, "not by reference to general criteria (e.g., 'rules of meaning' or 'moral principles') but in the hit-or-miss way in which cells readjust themselves to meet the pressure of environment" ("Postmodernist Bourgeois Liberalism", ORT, 199). He denies, of course, the cognitive isolation of this self from the material world, since he rejects representationalism and sees knowledge as a natural product of our causal interaction with the world. Similarly, he has no problem with locating this self in the social world, that is, seeing at least some of its beliefs and desires as constituted by its relations to a community. But he maintains that morality requires nothing more than the self so understood. There is no need for a "deeper self" in the manner of a Platonic soul or an Aristotelian nature to support or make intelligible our moral commitments. (It is likewise important to emphasize that Rorty's talk of beliefs and desires does not presuppose a representationalist construal of them as private mental entities, with a problematic connection to an external world.[55])

Rorty's approach reflects his commitment to what is often called "natu-

---

55   There are, in any case, viable nonrepresentationalist accounts of beliefs and desires, for example, Robert Brandom's Sellarsian account in *Making It Explicit*, Cambridge, MA: Harvard University Press, 1994. For excellent general discussions of Brandom's view, see Richard Rorty, "Robert Brandom on Social Practices and Representations", TP, 122–37, and Joseph Rouse, "Perception, Action, and Discursive Practices", forthcoming.

ralism". But we need to be careful in our use of this term in the present context. Rorty at one point defines naturalism as "the claim that there is no occupant of space-time that is not linked in a single web of causal relations to all other occupants; and that any explanation of the behaviour of any such spatio-temporal object must consist in placing the object within that single web" ("Taylor on Truth", 30; TP, 94). Given this definition, it might seem that the project of a naturalistic ethics is a nonstarter. If human beings are nothing but physical systems, presumably merely complexes of elementary particles, and can be related only to other such systems, in what sense can they be the bearers of moral properties? One might as well try to attribute moral qualities to rocks.

Rorty avoids this difficulty by distinguishing naturalism, which he holds, from reductionism, which he does not. Reductionism, he says, is "the insistence that there is not only a single web but a single privileged description of all entities caught in that web. . . . The reductionist thinks that we need explanatory unity as well as causal unity – a way of commensurating all explanatory vocabularies". We avoid reductionism (while maintaining naturalism) by, with Davidson, being "satisfied with token-token identities between entities differently described".[56] Accordingly, Rorty does not face the impossible task of developing an ethics out of elementary particle theory.

There are, however, still difficulties in bringing the metaphysical naturalism of Rorty's definition to bear on ethical issues. On the one hand, given its nonreductivism, such a naturalism does not in fact exclude all of the traditional ontological props of morality. Aristotelian natures, for example, would surely exist in the spatiotemporal nexus of Rorty's naturalism. On the other hand, there is no need to deny the existence of nonnatural entities to assert their irrelevance to ethics. I suggest, accordingly, that we distinguish metaphysical naturalism from ethical naturalism, where the latter is understood as the claim that our ethical values require grounding in nothing more than our beliefs and desires. So understood, ethical naturalism does not imply metaphysical naturalism, since it is consistent with the existence of "supernatural" entities. It is even consistent with the claim that such entities provide a foundation (e.g., justification or coherent explanation) for ethical principles. Ethical naturalism claims just that any such entities are not *needed* to justify or make sense of ethical principles. At the same time, ethical naturalism is inconsistent with any version of metaphysical naturalism that thinks, à la Aristotle, that understanding or justifying morality requires natural entities (e.g., a substantive human nature) beyond beliefs and desires.

56 "Taylor on Truth", in James Tully (ed.), *Philosophy in an Age of Pluralism*, 30; TP, 94.

Ethical naturalism can also be characterized as a subjectivism (or, in its more plausible forms, an intersubjectivism), in opposition to the objectivism for which ethical values must be grounded in something independent of our beliefs and desires. Ethical naturalists do, of course, acknowledge that, very early on, we perceive ourselves as moral agents guided by values and obligations that may conflict with what an individual wants. The trouble is that we also realize very early that these values and obligations are closely tied to the opinions and desires of other people. Consider the little boy who disobeys his mother and runs into a busy street. If he's hit by a car, he has undoubtedly "put himself in the wrong" with respect to a world whose dictates he cannot ignore. On the objectivist view of morality, the same thing is true even if his disobedience results in no physical injury. He has "put himself in the wrong" simply by disobeying. But, as the child may eventually begin to wonder, is there really anything he has "run up against" other than his mother's (or, more generally, society's) desire? Ethical naturalism maintains that there need be nothing to the moral world other than the social complex of human beliefs and desires. In the terminology I am employing, ethical objectivism is the denial of ethical naturalism.

The issues raised by ethical naturalism will be with us for the rest of this book. We will, in particular, discuss MacIntyre's defense of an Aristotelian objectivism and Taylor's claim that ethical naturalism is not adequate to our moral experience. I will argue for the incorporation of a version of ethical naturalism into my pragmatic liberalism. But the issues are complex, and I will, particularly in discussing Taylor, try to develop a more sophisticated naturalism that can come to terms with at least some of the intuitions driving objectivism. For the rest of this chapter, I will consider some standard objections to ethical naturalism in general, along with some specific problems raised by Rorty's formulation of an ethics of "liberal ironism".

Most of the objections to the naturalist grounding of ethics in our desires come from critics intent on reminding us that morality is serious business. When a belief or action is dubbed "moral", the implication is that it reflects a distinctive depth of commitment or obligation that separates it from run-of-the-mill matters. Critics of Rorty and other ethical naturalists frequently claim that their position lacks this moral seriousness.

The strongest form of this criticism is the charge that Rorty's view cannot be taken seriously because it is a self-refuting relativism, undermining its own claim by asserting that contrary claims are equally true (or, at least, equally justified). Such charges are cogent only if we insist that Rorty employ traditional senses of truth or justification that he has rejected as impossibly strong. If, in particular, we insist that truth involve correspondence to a transcendent reality and that justification have no dependence on specific social practices of reason-giving, then Rorty will not be able to mark out any moral position as epistemically superior to any other. But this simply reflects the critics' imposition of epistemic standards that Rorty finds incoherent. In terms of Rorty's own views of truth and justification, there is no reason he cannot claim that his ethical position is true and justified.

Other criticisms suggest that ethical naturalism, even if consistent, lacks a distinctively moral seriousness, particularly as this has been elucidated by Kant. According to Kant, the moral reflects what we unconditionally must do, as opposed to what we want (desire, are inclined) to do. In these terms, the problem with ethical naturalism is that it eliminates the duty–desire distinction, making the moral itself a matter of our desires. Rorty, in particular, is unequivocal about this elimination, emphasizing, for example, that he rejects the distinction of moral and prudential considerations. But if morality is merely what we want, not the will of God or the dictates of our nature or of reason, why should we take it seriously?

The presupposition of such a question is that we have certain attitudes and are searching for reasons to take them seriously, to accord them moral status. But this misdescribes the situation. The moral status of a desire derives precisely from the fact that we do take it seriously. To say that moral norms are rooted in nothing more than our desires is not to say that all desires are on a par and have the same moral status. The desires that ground morality, like the ultimate norms of epistemic justification, derive from the biological and cultural forces that have constituted us as epistemic and moral agents. Nor should we take talk of "desires" to imply commitment to a morality of self-centered pleasure rather than duty to others.[57] It may well be that my deepest desire is to subordinate my own selfish inclinations to the common good (perhaps even as defined by the dictates of universalizing reason).

Critics, following the Socrates of the *Euthyphro*, object that, in general, we think of ourselves as desiring things because they are valuable, not as finding them valuable because we desire them.[58] This is undeniable for ordinary

---

57 To the extent that "desire" has inappropriate connotations, we can substitute a more neutral term such as "attitude" or "orientation". Ethical naturalism need not be formulated in terms of desire, understood in some specific psychological sense. The naturalist might, for example, endorse something like Allan Gibbard's powerful expressivist account, developed in *Wise Choices, Apt Feelings*, Cambridge, MA: Harvard University Press, 1990. I use "desires" as simply a convenient shorthand for the variety of ways that naturalists can account for values without positing anything beyond our attitudes toward them.

58 David Brink offers a good formulation of this objection in his critique of what he calls the "desire-satisfaction" view of values (*Moral Realism and the Foundations of Ethics*, Cambridge: Cambridge University Press, 1989, 224–6). Brink quotes the passage from Spinoza cited at the end of this paragraph as an example of the position he is criticizing.

cases, when we are acting within a preestablished moral framework. I want to think about philosophical questions because I judge that activity to be worthwhile; the activity is not worthwhile because I want to engage in it. But such examples show merely that most of our desires are formed in the context of pregiven values. There still remains the question of the nature and source of the fundamental values that guide the formation of our ordinary desires. The naturalist's suggestion is that we should think of these values as themselves derived from desires that are deeper than our ordinary desires and that constitute our fundamental values. The many mundane cases in which judgments of value determine desires are not counterexamples to this suggestion. (Note the parallel between this view of value and the account of justification offered in Section 3.) It may still be that, at the deepest level, the truth is, as Spinoza said, "that we do not endeavor, will, seek after or desire because we judge a thing good. On the contrary, we judge a thing good because we endeavor, will, seek after, and desire it."[59]

The ethical naturalist's position is poorly served when it is formulated, as Rorty often does, in decisionistic language. He says, for example, that "personhood" is "a matter of decision rather than knowledge, an acceptance of another being into fellowship rather than recognition of a common essence" (PMN, 38). But we do not *decide* to accept newborn children into our community. Their acceptance as persons has much deeper roots. More generally, we do not typically simply decide at a given moment, à la the early Sartre, what we are going to believe about fundamental questions of morality, as we might decide to listen to a symphony rather than a quartet. In other passages Rorty offers a more plausible account: that our moral orientation is a matter of developing habits of thought and action ("The Contingency of Language", CIS, 6), something likely to be a complex and extended process over which we have at best very indirect control.[60] At times he explicitly notes that decisionism makes no sense on his view of the mind as merely a web of contingent beliefs and desires. For "there is no such thing as getting outside the web which constitutes oneself, looking down upon it, and deciding on one portion of it rather than another".[61]

Decisionist views of morality ignore this fact by discussing moral commitment in terms of contingent choices, as in Sartre's famous example of a young man torn between remaining with his mother and joining the Free

---

59   *Ethics*, III, 9, scholium, translated by S. Shirley, Indianapolis: Hackettt, 1982.
60   As I will suggest in the following chapter, cultural transmitters such as MacIntyre's traditions are plausible vehicles of such a process.
61   "A Reply to Six Critics", *Analyse & Kritik* 6 (1984), 95.

French. In fact such examples take for granted an entire framework of morality. Duty to family, hatred of fascism, and concern about the tension between personal and national loyalties themselves express the nexus of moral commitments that raise the young man's question of whether to stay at home. Sartre is correct in holding that these commitments do not determine a specific moral choice. But this is a point about the judgmental (as opposed to algorithmic) nature of the translation of moral commitments into action. It does not establish that these commitments themselves are the results of choices.

The sorts of attitudes we regard as moral have a status in the web of our desires and beliefs far different from that of transient whims or minor predilections. Far from being the objects of our choices, moral attitudes define the context of values in which choices themselves are made. They represent, so to speak, the biological and cultural hard-wiring that makes us moral agents.

A critic may respond that no amount of subtlety about the nature of the desires that constitute naturalist morality can evade the fact that there is no moral force in an attitude that is merely *ours*. A moral, as opposed to a prudential, reason for acting grips us precisely because it expresses our obligation to something or someone outside ourselves. Morality says: no matter *what you think, feel, or want,* this is *what you must do.* For Rorty, however, there is no more sense to moral compulsion by an external law than there is to epistemic compulsion by an external world. In both cases, justification can be only a social practice of reason-giving, not a confrontation with an outside reality. The only reasons we can have are our reasons.

The critic's point, however, may be about truth rather than justification. The latter is always a matter of internal reasons. But just as any science we can take seriously must be true of a physical world independent of beliefs about it, so, it will be urged, a morality we can take seriously must be true of a moral world independent of our desires. Proponents of this view have traditionally gone on to offer a vindication of morality from independent knowledge of nonnatural entities such as God, the soul, or human nature. Unfortunately, our present epistemic situation provides no compelling case for such knowledge. Moreover, we do not find ourselves, as with the physical world, from the beginning in uncontroversial contact with a moral world clearly independent of human desires. Nor is there any sign of a gradual extension of moral knowledge from a humdrum beginning. The critic who insists that we have no right to our morality until we can provide an objective grounding for it is simply making the case for moral skepticism. For those who insist on such a foundation for morality, the choice is not between an unserious morality based on desires and a serious morality based on objective, nonnatural fact, but rather between a morality based on desires and no morality at all.[62] But defenders of ethical objectivity have other alternatives. They may, in particular, argue, as Charles Taylor does, that, given the validity of moral norms, we must posit an objective basis as the account of their validity. Here the claim is not that morality remains questionable until a foundation is provided but rather that accepting morality requires also accepting its objectivity. We will discuss this approach in Part III.

In any case, worries about the moral adequacy of desire are not the only possible reason for thinking that naturalist morality is not serious. An even stronger concern may be its contingency. There might be desires that are expressions of the necessity of our nature as humans, and so properly have normative force. But ethical naturalism bases morality on desires that we merely happen to have. Another upbringing, different neural organization, would have given us – and perhaps has given others – quite different moral attitudes. Thus, Rorty himself admits that one of the strongest objections to his position is that it has the following disconcerting consequence:

> When the secret police come, when the torturers violate the innocent, there is nothing to be said to them of the form "There is something within you which you are betraying. Though you embody the practices of a totalitarian society which will endure forever, there is something beyond those practices which condemns you." ("Introduction", CP, xlii)

Strictly speaking, there *may* be "something within" the secret police or the torturers that condemns them; there may be some liberal values they share with us through which we could get them to see that what they are doing is wrong (though they might still do it). But Rorty's point is that there will be something we can appeal to only if our interlocutors' deepest desires *happen* to overlap ours in the right sort of way. If their fundamental moral formation has been sufficiently different from ours (if, for example, they are rational space aliens who are incapable of seeing us as anything but prey for their recreational hunting), there will be nothing we can say to them.

Why is this obvious consequence of our morality's contingency so disturbing? Some of the worry may be merely a hangover from our intoxication with foundationalist epistemology, a lingering conviction that a claim

---

62   This is not to say that a nonnaturalistic foundation of ethics is impossible in principle. The point is rather that, given a de facto lack of such a foundation, insisting that one is needed in effect supports moral skepticism. I engage the issue of ethical naturalism and the alleged objectivity of values in much more detail in Part III, where I discuss Charles Taylor's views on these issues.

is not justified if we cannot prove it to any rational agent. If this is our problem, Rorty can only suggest going back to Wittgenstein or Davidson for another round of epistemic therapy. An apparently deeper worry is that our fundamental desires themselves might be bad.[63] We can at least conceive of people who have fundamental desires for random murder or other ethical horrors. Isn't it possible that our deepest desires are as awful as those seem to be? But this worry makes sense only if we beg the question against the ethical naturalist by assuming that the moral is what conforms to some external standard of rectitude. Moreover, how could we even recognize such a standard if it did not itself conform to our deepest desires? The truth is that we have no conception of moral goodness other than that provided by the desires that constitute us as moral agents.

On the other hand, perhaps the worry is an empirical psychological one: that we are simply incapable of remaining seriously committed to views that we do not regard as objectively justified. If so, naturalist morality would turn out to be de facto unlivable, no matter how defensible in theoretical discussion. This problem will, of course, not arise if the view we hold is, to use William James's famous terminology, the only one that is a live option for us. On this assumption, every moral viewpoint other than our own would be a dead option; we might acknowledge it as a logical possibility, but we could not (psychologically) take it seriously as something we might actually accept. Alternative views would then resonate to nothing at all in us, and it is difficult to see how our inability to refute them could pose a psychological obstacle to seriously asserting our own. Why should we care about refuting views that we are not even capable of taking seriously?

The preceding possibility may obtain for people in what are called "traditional societies", in which the moral identity of individuals is essentially defined by their membership in the group. But for members of modern societies, there are live alternatives. I can easily imagine that I, without ceasing to be the person I am, might have had (or might come to have) a different fundamental morality. In this case, won't full commitment require objective justification?

Not at all. Full commitment to a given option when we know that there are alternatives we might easily (and with equal reason) have preferred is a psychological commonplace of human life. We cheer for our local baseball team, are partial to our mother's cherry pie, support our alma mater, knowing full well that they enjoy no objective superiority and that we prefer them

---

63 Rorty himself sometimes seems to slip into this worry, as we shall see later when considering his discussion of the ironist's "worry that she might be wrong".

only because of the contingent circumstances of our lives. Much more seriously, we are loyal to the death to our nation, religion, and spouse, knowing full well that, had things gone a bit differently, we would have had a different commitment. It is overwhelmingly clear that we can be content with who we are for no other reason than that this *is* who we are. We can comfortably assert the superiority of our commitments without believing that our assertion has an objective basis.

Even if we agree that ethical naturalism does not involve ethical incoherence, we may, moving to the other extreme, wonder whether anything at all ethically interesting follows from its rejection of foundations for morality. The point, after all, is that my morality does not need foundations, not that it should be other than it is. Suppose, for example, that I have from my earliest years accepted a rigorous Christian version of a natural law morality, grounded, so I have long thought, in Aristotelian and Thomistic metaphysics. Persuaded, perhaps by Rorty, I now agree that all the talk of God, natures, and essences, which I thought established the objective truth of my morality, was so much empty verbiage. Does this mean that I should give up my morality? Surely not, since Rorty himself insists that morality does not need the grounding of which he has deprived me. So I presumably should have no qualms about continuing on my moral course.

From this point of view, we might, odd as it may seem, compare what Rorty does for morality to what Plantinga does for religious belief. In both cases, a critique of foundationalism undermines the very idea of the need to provide a certain class of beliefs with justification, thereby allowing us to hold, in good epistemic conscience, beliefs that we cannot justify.[64]

I don't think that ethical naturalists need deny this. They might, however, suggest that we reflect on whether, knowing that the foundations we previously thought were present are not, we are still so keen to hold our previous beliefs. For the loss of foundations for a body of beliefs does at least make this difference: with the foundations, it was irrational not to believe (i.e., we had no epistemic right not to believe); without them we at most have a right, but surely not an obligation, to believe.[65]

64   See Alvin Plantinga, "Reason and Belief in God", in Plantinga and N. Wolterstorff (eds.), *Faith and Rationality*, Notre Dame, IN: University of Notre Dame Press, 1983. In this connection, it is interesting to note a comment of Rorty's connecting "right to believe" approaches to knowledge and his conversational alternative to epistemology: "If we see knowing not as having an essence, to be described by scientists or philosophers, but rather as a right, by current standards, to believe, then we are well on the way to seeing conversation as the ultimate context in which knowledge is to be understood" (PMN, 389).

65   For more on this line of thought, see my "Plantinga and the Rationality of Religious Belief", in T. Tessin and M. von der Ruhr (eds.), *Philosophy and the Grammar of Religious Belief*, London: Routledge, 1995, 332–47.

We may, however, think that the possibility of our changing our ethical stance in response to the undermining of our old foundations is a philosophically empty one. For, it may be argued, ethical naturalism makes rational deliberation and discussion irrelevant to ethical beliefs. Rorty encourages such an objection by sometimes suggesting that our views on basic moral issues cannot be formed by argument, that whether we are talking about cultural ontogeny or philogeny, the adaptation of a new "final vocabulary" cannot be a matter of rational persuasion.[66] But it is important not to be misled by this disavowal of argument. It amounts to nothing more than a recognition that we are in no position to derive, by deductive or inductive inference, our ethical conclusions from premises accepted by just about anyone who could understand our discussion. Rorty acts as though the only alternative to such a derivation is a "redescription" of the situation according to our own lights; that is, a statement, without supporting reasons, of what we think, presented in the hope of causing others to think the same; that is, to take on a new "habit" of thought.

But there are modes of effective argument that are not a matter of decisively proving a point from shared premises. This, as Kuhn has emphasized, is the difference between logic and rationality. Another way to put the point is to note that what Rorty calls "redescription" involves much more than just bare assertion in a new vocabulary. It is rather a matter of showing how this vocabulary can hold its own in discussion (conversation) with those we are trying to persuade. Rorty himself, for example, frequently begins by making his audience acutely aware of the difficulties, from its own standpoint, of some traditional position. This, for example, is the point of his constant references to critiques of foundationalism. He then shows how his position readily avoids these difficulties. Of course, this position faces difficulties of its own, and responding to these is generally the crux of Rorty's case. He needs, for example, to show that his deabsolutized morality and politics do not involve relativistic incoherence and are consistent with our most deeply entrenched views about what is good and what is evil.

If Rorty is successful, his audience will be, at a minimum, convinced that he has a right to his position, that is, that he can hold his own indefinitely while defending it in our conversation. Beyond this, they may be sufficiently impressed by the merits of Rorty's approach in comparison to the standard view that they try thinking and talking his way themselves. This may lead them to discover even more rational power in the position (ability to pose

---

66   See, for example, "The Contingency of the Liberal Community", CIS, 44, and especially "Beyond Realism and Anti-realism", in L. Nagl and R. Heinrich (eds.), *Wo Steht die Analytische Philosophie Heute?*, Vienna: Oldenbourg, 1986, 103–15.

and answer objections, to suggest fruitful new lines of discussion) and perhaps eventually to endorse it themselves. This sort of justification is far more than mere "redescription"; and Rorty sells himself short by suggesting that he is not persuading us by argument.

Our discussion so far supports ethical naturalism against some of the major reasons for claiming that it cannot sustain a serious moral stance. We will, however, return to this issue in our discussion, in Part III, of Charle's Taylor's critique.

8. Liberal Ironism

We turn next to Rorty's substantive ethical position, the view he calls "liberal ironism". The supreme value for liberalism is the freedom of all individuals: first, their freedom from suffering, but then also freedom to form their lives with whatever values they find most compelling. Usually, Rorty seems content with the standard ethical and political content of liberalism. "J. S. Mill's suggestion that governments devote themselves to optimizing the balance between leaving people's private lives alone and preventing suffering seems to me pretty much the last word" ("The Contingency of Community", CIS, 63). His favorite quick definition, following Judith Shklar, is that liberals are people who think "cruelty is the worst thing they do" (see, for example, "Private Irony and Liberal Hope", CIS, 74). More fully, his liberalism is defined by "the sort of social hope which characterizes modern liberal societies – the hope that life will eventually be freer, less cruel, more leisured, richer in goods and experiences, not just for our descendants but for everybody's descendants" (ibid., 86).

Rorty's only major dissent from traditional liberalism is his denial that liberal values are (or need to be) grounded in any philosophical account of the nature and worth of human beings. But this dissent has major ramifications for the central problem of reconciling two apparently opposing poles of modern morality. On the one hand, we are attracted to the ideal of individual self-fulfillment, to an ethics that urges each of us to make the most of our resources and abilities to build a richly satisfying personal life. On the other hand, we feel the pull of the ideal of altruistic amelioration of the human condition, to a morality that calls us to help eliminate human suffering and let everyone live a pleasant and fulfilling life. The first tendency leads toward the purely private project of moral self-creation, a project that may well ignore other people or involve them only instrumentally. The second calls us to the public project of making others free to pursue their own private projects of self-creation, liberating them from the oppression of pain and opening their lives to a maximal range of possibilities.

Traditional liberalism could at least hope for a resolution of the tension between these poles through the foundational role of human nature. It could, for example, be argued that, given the social dimensions of human nature, a life of moral self-fulfillment would also have to be a life of altruistic service to others. Having rejected human nature as the basis of morality, Rorty has no such moves available to him and has to recognize that there may simply be irreducible conflict between the demands of public morality and the demands of personal self-fulfillment.

It is this difficulty that leads Rorty to distinguish "ironism" from "liberalism". As ironists we savor the distinctive moral characters we develop for ourselves, realizing all along that the values they embed are merely ours, with no claim on anyone else. As liberals we see ourselves as bound to work for the good of our entire community. The tension becomes particularly apparent when we notice that the thinkers Rorty sets up as exemplars of ironism – Nietzsche, Heidegger, Foucault – are all fierce opponents of liberalism. Moreover, their opposition is based on ironism: they see the vulgar bourgeois values of liberal democracy as stifling the self-creative efforts of unique individuals.

Rorty's way of overcoming this opposition is to insist on the sharp separation of public and private morality. Nietzsche's *Übermensch*, Heidegger's poet of Being, Foucault's mad artist are all splendid models of private self-creation. But when set up as models of public virtue, they are at best silly and at worst terrifying. What makes for poetry in the soul begets fascism in the city. Correspondingly, an inner life defined by only the liberal virtues of civility, fairness, and moderation may strike many as bland and uninteresting. But Rorty suggests that private irony and public liberalism can coexist provided we insist that each keep to its own sphere. The values we teach everyone for the sake of civil harmony should not be proposed as models of self-creation, and the personal ideals that guide self-creation should not be mistaken for challenges to the standards of public morality. Liberal democracy allows a range of values in the private sphere that it cannot tolerate in the public sphere.

Although Rorty is not always clear on this point, it is important to avoid defining the private sphere in merely individualistic terms. First, even though we each have our own separate ethical space, this space must have a social dimension, since individuals always to some extent understand their innermost selves in terms of connections with others. As we noted earlier, among our deepest, self-defining desires are those that constitute us as social beings. Second, there are many ethically significant social groups intermediate between individuals and the state. For both of these reasons, we need to understand the public sphere as the maximal domain constituted by the most widely shared values that form a liberal state. So construed, the private domain includes not only the moral spaces of individuals but also all social groups less extensive than the full body politic. Drawing the public–private distinction in this way is necessary if we are to avoid the atomistic individualism of the philosophical Enlightenment.

Even when the trap of atomistic individualism is avoided, the effort to separate public and private values may seem doubly naive. It seems naive, first of all, to think that the public virtues of a liberal society merely provide a neutral framework for the self-creation of individuals. Radical critics from Marx to Foucault have shown how this allegedly neutral framework encourages certain forms of self-creation (e.g., the capitalist's accumulation and display of wealth) and stifles others (a poor worker's desire for education). Conversely, it is naive to think that personal self-creation does not involve public action. Since we are social beings, our self-creation will have to involve patterns of relation to other people. A Nietzschean *Übermensch* will not treat *Untermenschen* in accord with liberal ethical norms. A private life not conforming to public morality constitutes a direct challenge to that morality.

The first line of criticism is well formulated by Nancy Fraser, who points out that "the social movements of the last hundred or so years have taught us to see the power-laden and therefore political character of interactions which classical liberalism considered private".[67] Thus, we have learned from Marx that "the economic is political"; from feminism that "the domestic and the personal are political"; and from Foucault that "the cultural, the medical, the educational . . . is political" (312–13). Given this, Fraser maintains that Rorty arbitrarily excludes "radical theory", and hence the marginalized groups for which it tries to speak, from political discussion by relegating anything that strives to be a fundamental questioning of the liberal status quo to the domain of private fantasy.[68] Her quarrel is at root with Rorty's comfortable use of "we", "assuming, tendentiously, that there are no deep social cleavages capable of generating conflicting solidarities and opposing 'we's'" (315). As a result, she says, he makes "non-liberal, oppositional discourses non-political by definition" (315) and falsely assumes that political talk and action can be legitimately concerned only with implementing shared goals,

---

67   Nancy Fraser, "Solidarity or Singularity? Richard Rorty between Romanticism and Technology", in Alan Malachowski (ed.), *Reading Rorty*, 312. Further references will be given in the text.

68   For a similar line of criticism, see Thomas McCarthy, "Ironist Theory as a Vocation", *Critical Inquiry* 16 (1990), 644–55.

not with struggles "over cultural meanings and social identities" (318). Fraser's objection can be nicely crystallized around Rorty's claim that "an ideal liberal society . . . has no purpose except to make life easier for poets and revolutionaries while seeing to it that they make life harder for others only by words, and not deeds" ("The Contingency of Community", CIS, 61). At least with regard to the goals of any serious revolutionary, the recognition given in the main clause is apparently snatched back in the following subordinate clause.

We can, however, formulate an effective response to Fraser's objection by reflecting on the precise import of the consensus (Sellarsian "we"-intentions) at the basis of Rorty's liberal polity. Fraser herself implicitly recognizes the need for such consensus when she emphasizes that "not all radical theorizing is elitist, antidemocratic and opposed to collective concerns and political life" (313). Fraser's remark acknowledges a certain range of views that fall outside the parameters of discussion in our society and so need not be taken seriously except as "private fantasies". She must, then, as seems entirely reasonable, agree that there are political theories we need not take seriously as potential guides of public policy in a democracy. (Our liberal principles of free speech, of course, allow advocacy of these theories, even though we would not tolerate their implementation.) But the issue then becomes simply one of determining the range of theories excluded by a commitment to liberal democracy. Explicitly autocratic and totalitarian views are obviously excluded, but Fraser seems to think that the same must be true of any theoretical viewpoints (including nontotalitarian versions of Marxism, feminism, and New Left radicalisms) that question the benign effect of liberal institutions on human freedom.

But a firm commitment to liberal democracy is entirely consistent with the radical claim that liberal democratic values and institutions are often vehicles of oppression. It is even consistent with the view that these values and institutions have ineliminable features that make them a constant threat to human freedom. Consistent liberal democrats need hold only that there is no practically viable alternative system of values and institutions that is, all things considered, less of a threat to freedom. They cannot accept the extreme (and implausible) radical claim that liberal democracy as such is simply destructive of individual liberty, but they can adopt the Foucaultian attitude that it, like everything else, is dangerous but not necessarily bad. The project then would be to maintain liberalism as the best hope of sustaining human freedom while constantly counteracting its repressive tendencies. On such a view, radical theory would have a continuing role in diagnosing and responding to such tendencies. Only when radical theory refuses to accept the fundamental viability of liberal democracy (as, Rorty thinks, Heidegger and Foucault are sometimes inclined to do) does liberalism restrict it to the private realm.

It is further worth remarking that a commitment to Rorty's principles of liberal democracy does not imply acceptance of any existing political establishment as an adequate instantiation of these principles. Radical critics are disturbed by Rorty's relative contentment with American political institutions, a contentment that leads him to endorse policies of incremental reform rather than revolutionary transformation.[69] But his liberal democratic principles entail nothing regarding the extent to which any existing institutions exhibit them. I might entirely endorse Rorty's conception of democracy and, unlike him, maintain that our current government is so opposed to this conception as to require violent overthrow. There is nothing intrinsically conservative about Rorty's political principles.

There remains the difficulty of separating self-creation from social action. Almost any action, no matter how apparently private, can and often does have social consequences. But Rorty's distinction between the private and public spheres need not deny this. Its point requires merely that we be able, in practice, to separate actions that do not pose a serious threat to the freedom of others from those that do. Democratic societies tolerate a wide range of self-creative activities – all those judged not to interfere with the freedom of others. The problem is with forms of self-creation that overstep the boundaries of even democratic permissiveness. Here Rorty rightly emphasizes that self-creation need not be a matter of literally making one's life a work of art, that is, actually living and relating to others on the basis of some possibly antisocial personal ideals. Self-creation can also be a matter of aesthetic creation in a separate world of imagination. The model then is Wagner's operas, not his anti-Semitism; Proust's novel, not his dandyism. Vermeer, from the little we know of his life, may never have tried to be anyone other than a dutiful father and citizen of the Dutch Republic. He created himself in paintings, not in the real world of social relations. Democracy places no restrictions on artistic expressions of even the most extremely antisocial self-creative visions (e.g., Georges Bataille's fantasy of reviving Aztec human-sacrifice rituals), except in cases where the art becomes a direct threat to publicly recognized goods.

At this point, radical critics may well revive the charge of conservatism, maintaining that Rorty blocks any fundamental transformation of our soci-

---

69   For a thoughtful discussion of this line of criticism, see Richard Shusterman, *Practicing Philosophy: Pragmatism and the Political Life,* London: Routledge, 1997, chapter 2.

ety by relegating revolutionary impulses to the private sphere. But such critics misunderstand Rorty's private–public distinction, which says nothing
about the adequacy of any existing institution to liberal democratic principles and relegates to the private sphere only what genuinely threatens these
principles. The distinction provides no protection for existing public institutions merely because they exist.[70]

So far, then, liberal ironism remains a viable position. But less tractable
difficulties arise when Rorty expands ironism into something more than an
antiepistemological attitude. In his fullest explicit characterization, he tells
us that an ironist is someone who (1) "has radical and continuing doubts
about the final vocabulary she currently uses", doubts arising from ac-
quaintance with alternative final vocabularies that have impressed but not
convinced her; (2) " realizes that argument phrased in her current vocabulary can neither underwrite nor dissolve these doubts"; and (3) "does not
think that her vocabulary is closer to reality than others" or that "it is in
touch with a power not herself" ("Private Irony and Liberal Hope", CIS, 73).
The last two points merely recap Rorty's ethical antifoundationalism. If ironism amounted to nothing else, liberal ironism would simply be traditional
liberalism that denies the need or possibility of a philosophical basis – a view
that, as I have been arguing, makes very good sense. But point (1) of Rorty's
definition leads him in a new and much more questionable direction.

First, we are bound to wonder what could possibly be the source of the
ironist's doubts. Rorty himself suggests a source that sits very poorly with his
ethical naturalism. He describes ironists as people "never quite able to take
themselves seriously because always aware that the terms in which they describe themselves are subject to change" ("Private Irony and Liberal Hope",
CIS, 73–4); and he attributes this self-doubt to a concern that their final
vocabulary is "wrong": "The ironist spends her time worrying about the possibility that she has been initiated into the wrong tribe, taught to play the
wrong language game. She worries that the process of socialization that
turned her into a human being by giving her a language may have given her
the wrong language, and so turned her into the wrong kind of human being" (ibid., 75). But unless the ironist slips back into ethical objectivism,
what sense is there to the worry that her final vocabulary is "wrong"? As final, it expresses what, all things considered, she really does value. The

70 On the political significance of Rorty's private–public distinction, see Simon Critchley,
    "Deconstruction and Pragmatism – Is Derrida a Private Ironist or a Public Liberal?", in
    Chantal Mouffe (ed.), *Deconstruction and Pragmatism*, London: Routledge, 1996, 19–40
    (also, Rorty's reply, 41–6).

"worry" Rorty evokes makes sense only on the assumption of a ethical objectivism that he has firmly repudiated.[71]

The reaction of Rorty's ironist to the diversity of final vocabularies is, despite his misleading language, better construed as a matter of aesthetic fascination than of ethical worry. The ironist constantly seeks intellectual and aesthetic stimulation, the challenging of old vocabularies for describing ourselves and the formation of new descriptions that take account of more and more perspectives. The "worry" then is that the ironist's contingent perspective at a given time will cause her to miss something new and exciting, not that her perspective is wrong. So construed, Rorty's characterization of ironism is quite consistent with his ethical naturalism.

Even so, the characterization remains problematic because Rorty presents it as the only alternative for a liberalism without a supporting metaphysics. He begins with the plausible claim that right-thinking liberals will see no need to ground their liberalism philosophically, that they will use their final vocabulary knowing full well that they cannot establish its superiority to a variety of other final vocabularies. But he then glides without argument (or even suggestion that something more is being asserted) to the claim that there is special ethical value in challenging and enriching one's perspective with those of others.[72] Rorty is, of course, entitled to this view as a basis for his own private project of self-creation. He presents it, however, as part of the commitment of his liberalism. This move is, in particular, behind his characterization of a liberal society as one whose "cultural hero is Bloom's strong poet" ("The Contingency of Community", CIS, 53) or his claim that the only purpose of a liberal society is to "make life easier for poets and revolutionaries" (ibid., 60–1). Here Rorty confuses ironism as a specific private attitude of those especially interested in exploring alternative ways of thinking and living with ironism as an essential component of liberalism. Nothing Rorty says supports anything more than the latter

71   Michael Williams makes a similar point, when he argues that Rorty's "ironism depends essentially on a kind of *nostalgie de la verité*" (*Unnatural Doubts*, Oxford: Blackwell, 1993, 365, n. 51).

72   Consider the following example. Rorty has maintained that "any attempt to drive one's opponent up against a wall . . . fails when the wall against which he is driven comes to be seen as one more vocabulary. . . . The wall then turns out to be a painted backdrop, one more work of man". He goes on to note that "a poeticized culture [the ideal of the liberal ironist] would be one which would not insist we find the real wall behind the painted ones, the real touchstones of truth". Then, in one startling sentence, he makes the leap I am objecting to: "It would be a culture which, precisely by appreciating that all touchstones are such artifacts, would take as its goal the creation of ever more various and multicolored artifacts" ("The Contingency of Community", CIS, 53–4).

merely epistemic ironism; the former, moral ironism is clearly just his own preference.

The ambivalence becomes particularly clear in Rorty's discussions of Freud. He remarks that "after reading Freud we shall see neither Bloom's strong poet nor Kant's dutiful fulfiller of universal obligations as paradigmatic. . . . There is much to be said for both. Each has advantages and disadvantages" ("The Contingency of Community", CIS, 35). However we judge this as exegesis of Freud , it is surely just good liberalism, recognizing that our public morality should have no preference in principle for the sexiness of constant self-re-creation over the dull decency of rigorous character building. But even in this discussion of Freud, Rorty has trouble holding on to the liberal platitude. Immediately after recognizing the rights of Kantian dullness, he assures us that "for Freud, nobody is dull through and through, for there is no such thing as a dull unconscious. . . . Freud's account of unconscious fantasy shows us how to see every human life as a poem". This, he says, allows us to avoid relegating "the vast majority of humanity [e.g., the decent but dull] to the status of dying animals" (35). We can pass over the fact that Freudian unconscious minds are in fact stultifyingly similar and boring in their obsessions with feces and incest. There is in any case no need for a liberal to "rescue" the lives of almost everyone from the moral stigma of dullness because aesthetic stimulation has no privileged value for liberal morality.[73]

Giving up Rorty's fascination with alternative modes of self-creation also makes literature and literary theory less central for liberal sensibilities than he suggests. He maintains that "the rise of literary criticism to preeminence within the high culture of the democracies" ("Private Irony and Liberal Hope", CIS, 82) reflects the dominance among intellectuals of irony over metaphysics. The reason, of course, is not that literary critics have found the deep truths about human nature that philosophers have missed. But ironists "read literary critics and take them as moral advisors" because "they have read more books and are thus in a better position not to get trapped in the vocabulary of any single book" (ibid., 80–1). They are thus far better moral sources for the liberal than the standard wisdom of, say, traditional philosophy.

Lionizing literary theorists in this way is entirely legitimate given Rorty's

---

73 Rorty's insistence on the moral value of perspectival variety leads him to the very strange passage in which he praises Freud for letting us see "sexual perversion, extreme cruelty, ludicrous obsession, and manic delusion . . . as the private poem of the pervert, the sadist, the lunatic: each as richly textured and 'redolent of moral memories' as our own life" ("The Contingency of the Self", CIS, 38). How, in particular, can a liberal, who thinks that "cruelty is the worst thing we do", think there is significant profit in the aesthetic appreciation of "extreme cruelty"?

preferred conception of private self-creation.[74] But pragmatic liberalism as such must equally allow for projects of self-creation that disdain diversity and strive for a deep personal formation in terms of, say, a rigorous system of deontological morality or Christian piety. For such projects, a Kant or a St. Paul will be far more relevant than a Harold Bloom or a Stanley Fish. The centrality of literary criticism is relative to Rorty's own private moral preferences, not a consequence of pragmatic liberalism as such.[75]

It might be argued that, even if Rorty's ethics of diversity does not follow from pragmatic liberalism, it is particularly congenial to it. Those who appreciate the value of alternative ways of thinking and living are less likely to slip back into the mistakes of ethical objectivism. But, conversely, the aficionados of diversity are, as the cases of Nietzsche and Foucault show, more likely to weaken the inevitably jejune public morality of liberalism with injections of private fantasy. In this respect, someone with less exotic private tastes is more likely to be a good liberal citizen. Pragmatic liberalism requires a balanced appreciation of both the mundane and the *outré*, and neither component can claim special privilege over the other.

None of these criticisms affect the core of Rorty's ironism, the claim that liberalism requires no philosophical foundation. But they show that accepting this core does not require us to follow Rorty's suggestion that ironism also include a preference for moral diversity in the private sphere.

I have been discussing Rorty's work as a dialectical means of formulating, in a preliminary way, the position I call pragmatic liberalism. While quite sympathetic to Rorty, pragmatic liberalism eliminates some important failings in his formulations and develops a position that is both more realistic and less decisionistic. It offers an antirepresentationalist view of knowledge,

---

74   In a recent article, Rorty makes it clear that what he endorses is the humanistic literary criticism of people such as Matthew Arnold and Harold Bloom, not the "literary theory" of Paul de Man, Frederic Jameson, et al. ("The Inspirational Value of Great Works of Literature", *Raritan* 16 [1996], 8–17).

75   Rorty also privileges the literary because of the peculiar centrality he gives to humiliation as a source of the pain liberals want to mitigate. He says that "the best way to cause people long-lasting pain is to humiliate them by making the things that seemed most important to them look futile, obsolete, and powerless" ("Private Irony and Public Hope", CIS, 89). The best way to avoid humiliating others is to appreciate their perspectives from the inside by "entering into [their] fantasies" (93). Literary treatments (whether novelistic or journalistic) are a prime source of such appreciation. But humiliating people by making fun of their final vocabularies is quite marginal in the world of pain compared, say, to starving and beating them or curtailing their freedom because of their race or gender. Those who are healthy, well fed, and able to pursue happiness as they see fit are on the whole fairly impervious to what others may think of their fundamental beliefs.

which avoids the standard charges of relativism and skepticism and includes a modest commonsense and scientific realism. It also offers a naturalized ethics that is able to answer the charge that it lacks moral seriousness, and it avoids Rorty's problematic extension of ironism from the epistemic to the moral realm. Pragmatic liberalism retains a commitment to the core Enlightenment project of human autonomy through reason while avoiding both philosophical hubris and self-destructive skepticism.

Pragmatic liberalism is by no means the only alternative available to those dissatisfied with modern epistemology and morality. Those whose dissatisfaction derives from the kind of historical critique Rorty develops in PMN are likely to be particularly attracted to the work of Alasdair MacIntyre and Charles Taylor. Those who, in addition, feel uneasy with the ethical naturalism of pragmatic liberalism may be more inclined to MacIntyre's call for a return to the Aristotelian tradition or to Taylor's development of a modern Augustinianism. The rest of this book further elaborates pragmatic liberalism in the context of MacIntyre's and Taylor's work. The goal is both to defend pragmatic liberalism against objections grounded in their views and to develop and refine its content by coming to terms with these views.

PART II

ALASDAIR MacINTYRE

A MODERN *MALGRÉ LUI*

The expression "pragmatic liberalism" is likely to irritate particularly those who sympathize with the views of Alasdair MacIntyre. Correspondingly, those who defend positions of the sort I have put forward in Part I cannot ignore the shadow MacIntyre's critique of liberalism casts across their path. Like the pragmatic liberal, MacIntyre is particularly concerned with modern philosophy as an effort to replace the Aristotelian worldview, which had been successfully challenged by the new science of Galileo and Newton. Aristotle had seen the world as a system of natures, acting for ends defined by their essences. The new science showed that this teleological view was of no use for the prediction and control of natural phenomena and replaced it with a mechanistic picture of the world that allowed no role for natures or the goals they defined. MacIntyre has little to say about the significance of this development in its original domain of natural science. But he is fully convinced that extending the view to the moral domain was a terrible mistake. His *Geistesgeschichte* of modern philosophy is an account of the failure of efforts to develop an ethical view of human beings without a concept of human nature. This challeges the heart of the pragmatic liberal project.

The difference between MacIntyre and the pragmatic liberal can also be formulated in terms of the "Enlightenment project" of developing a secular liberal view of morality. They both agree that this project failed as an effort to provide philosophical foundations for liberalism. But the pragmatic liberal maintains and MacIntyre denies that there is a viable form of liberalism without philosophical foundations.

At the same time, MacIntyre's dissatisfaction with epistemology after Descartes and his post-Hegelian accentuation of the historical take him along much the same road as pragmatic liberalism in the critique of modern philosophy. Moreover, MacIntyre's subtle treatment of practice and, particularly, his embedding of ethical practices in traditions provide an essential enrichment of pragmatic liberalism's ethical view. Such an enrichment is possible, I shall argue, because, contrary to his own self-understanding, MacIntyre's account retains key modern – indeed, liberal – elements.

In Section 1, I formulate the case MacIntyre makes against modern morality by trying to show the incoherence of the Enlightenment project. Section 2 suggests that this case is effective against only one strand of Enlightenment thought (what I will call the "philosophical Enlightenment") and does not affect another strand (what I will call the "humanistic Enlightenment"), to which pragmatic liberalism belongs. Section 3 responds to MacIntyre's objection that, even if modern morality is logically coherent, it does not provide a concept of the common good sufficient to resolve moral disagreements rationally. The remaining sections examine the Aristotelian tradition that MacIntyre proposes as superior to modern liberal morality. Section 4 explores the attraction of MacIntyre's general idea of philosophizing out of a tradition, and Section 5 assesses the particular tradition, that of Aristotelian virtue ethics, MacIntyre endorses. Section 6 raises some fundamental questions about MacIntyre's defense of tradition but also argues that pragmatic liberalism can learn a great deal from what he has to say on this topic. Finally, Section 7 assesses MacIntyre's claim that his Aristotelian–Thomistic tradition is superior to the rival liberal tradition to which pragmatic liberalism belongs.

1. MacIntyre's Critique of the Enlightenment

In *After Virtue*, MacIntyre develops his historical account in reverse order, beginning with what he sees as the confusion and frustration of modern morality. Modern debates on moral issues are, on his account, paradigms of Kuhnian incommensurability. Proponents of each view offer valid arguments, but from premises "such that we possess no rational way of weighing the claims of one as against the other". It is not just that some parties to the debates irrationally refuse to accept well-supported premises. The premises from which we must argue are simply not open to rational justification and are based on "some non-rational decision" (AV, 8).

This situation explains the central role emotivist metaethical theories have played in twentieth-century discussions. Any claim that the *meaning* of an ethical utterance consists in an expression of feeling (e.g., "Lying is bad" = "I dislike lying") is readily refuted: I may hold lying to be immoral even if I find it very attractive. Such refutation is avoided, however, by the suggestion that, whatever their meanings, moral expressions are *used* to express feelings. So understood, MacIntyre maintains, emotivism is still not a universal metaethical truth; but it is true of our modern moral situation. With no rational basis for our decision to accept a moral position, all we can in fact do by asserting it is to express this nonrational preference.

MacIntyre is prepared to defend his claim that modern thinkers are unable to provide a rational basis for moral judgments by showing just where, for example, Hume or Kant or Gewirth goes wrong in his justification efforts. But he is more interested in understanding why such efforts have to fail. The central reason, he urges, is the absence from modern ethical thought of any normative conception of human nature. For Aristotelians, the ethical project was defined by three elements: (1) human beings as they happen to be in fact, (2) human beings as they would be if they achieved their essential nature, and (3) the ethical rules governing human behavior (AV, 53). The project of Aristotelian ethics was to derive (3) as the necessary means of moving from (1) to (2), a viable enterprise given an adequate normative conception of human nature. Modern ethical theory rejects any such conception and is left the impossible task of deriving (3) from (1) alone.

The impossibility of the modern task – of the Enlightenment project – can be understood both logically and historically. Logically, the impossibility is expressed by the dictum "An 'ought' cannot be derived from an 'is'". As MacIntyre points out, this is not true for the case of objects falling under functional concepts. For example, "This is a watch" does entail "This ought to keep accurate time". However, the modern rejection of normative human nature means that "human being" is no longer regarded as a functional concept. As a result, the basis for an "is"-"ought" inference is eliminated, and the goal of modern ethical theory becomes unattainable.

Historically, the problem is that modern ethical theory begins from incomplete fragments of premodern views. We still accept substantial chunks of the traditional system of ethical rules, particularly as they have been transmitted through Christianity. We also have a body of wisdom, based on perennial experience, about what human beings are, as a matter of fact, like. And, finally, we still acknowledge the need for a rational justification of our moral rules on the basis of what we know about human beings. But, in the course of the modern undermining of Aristotelian science, we have lost any normative conception of human nature. Of course, this is often perceived not as a loss but as a liberation from oppressive moral authority. But, either way, the result is that we find ourselves trying to carry out a traditional project while lacking an element essential for the enterprise.

Given his understanding of the Enlightenment project, MacIntyre's critique is very persuasive. If we must begin with the individual as a moral atom, then morality must be somehow constructed out of that individual's desires and rational capacities. There must, that is, be a way to build a rational bridge from the individual to standard ethical norms. Unless this can be done, we are left with nothing but the individual's desires as arbitrary demands, interminably conflicting with the desires of other individuals (the situation described and accepted by emotivism). Other possible connections – including appeals to deep social origins of values – are excluded by the assumption of atomistic individualism.

Since the atomistic individual is nothing but its egoistic desires and rational capacities, the needed connection to morality must be made in terms of one of these elements. Utilitarianism starts from desires and Kantianism from rationality. MacIntyre points out that the appeal to desires amounts to an effort to restore something like the rejected notion of teleology and that the appeal to rationality amounts to an effort to restore something like universal divine law. Both efforts fail because they are based on moral fictions.

The moral fiction of utilitarianism is *utility*, the characteristic of an action whereby it contributes to the happiness of humankind as a whole. Utility is a fiction for two reasons. First, since there are incommensurably different kinds of happiness, it makes no sense to measure comparatively, as the utilitarian must, the "amounts" of happiness contributed by different actions. Second, there is no way of moving from my motive to achieve my own happiness to an obligation to promote the general happiness.

The moral fiction of Kantianism is the notion of a *right*, the intrinsic entitlement of every rational being, simply as rational, to certain goods or treatment. Kantian justifications of morality – for example, Alan Gewirth's, for which MacIntyre has particular respect – require a move from the (undeniable) claim that I necessarily will my own freedom and well-being to the claim that I must believe that I have a right to these goods. Given this, the Kantian can argue that I must also, on pain of irrationality, believe that everyone else has a right to these goods (since everyone else has the same basis for the right that I do, namely, willing their own freedom and well-being). The trouble, MacIntyre points out, is that there is no reason to say that, simply because I must will some good for myself, I must also believe that I have a right to it. MacIntyre drives this criticism home in two ways.[1] First, there is the logical point that the notion of *thinking-I-have-a-right* is independent of the notion of willing, no matter what the object of the will. Second, there is the historico-conceptual point that rights "presuppose the existence of a socially established set of rules", rules that are contingent and occur only "at particular historical periods under particular social circumstances" (AV, 67). There are societies in which rights do not and cannot exist. Accordingly, the Enlightenment's notion of universal "rights of man", intrinsic to each person as such, is a fiction.

Because we lack the means to justify our moral commitments, they are made simply by arbitrary decision (hence the truth-for-us of emotivism). As a result, the modern self is an isolated moral atom, defined entirely by its own choices. Prior to making these choices, it has no metaphysical or social content. Philosophers such as Sartre have been entirely true to the modern situation in seeing "this capacity of the self to evade any necessary identification with any particular contingent state of affairs . . . [as] the essence of moral agency" (AV, 31).

According to MacIntyre, this situation is reflected in the sorts of moral characters typical of the modern age: the Rich Aesthete, described by Henry James in *The Portrait of a Lady;* the Manager, articulated in Weber's sociology of bureaucracy; and the Therapist, analyzed by Philip Rieff in *The Triumph of the Therapeutic.* The Rich Aesthete typifies modern moral decisionism, devoted to the pursuit of ends set up entirely by his or her own choice. Presumably, if they but had the means, all moderns would lead such lives. The Manager and the Therapist have, as such, no views on ends, but present themselves as experts on the best means to any pregiven end. The Manager's expertise lies in the public domain of organizational (including governmental) ends, whereas the Therapist is our guide to the best means of gaining private goals.

We are now in a position to understand better the chaos of contemporary moral discourse as MacIntyre evokes it at the beginning of *After Virtue.* On the one hand, there are the two conflicting modern fictions of utility and rights, each generating incommensurable pairs of arguments on any controversial topic. Rights arguments take as primary the atomistic individual. Utility arguments privilege the bureaucratic organizations designed to maximize the happiness of individuals. On the other hand, there are remnants of the principles and maxims of the old discarded morality based on a normative human nature, preserved particularly in religious traditions.

---

1 See also Gilbert Harman's critique of Gerwirth's argument in G. Harman and J. Thomson, *Moral Relativism and Moral Objectivity,* Oxford: Blackwell, 1996, 50–2.

These sometimes support utilitarian arguments, sometimes Kantian arguments, sometimes neither; and they are in any case based on principles that modern thought cannot countenance. The result is the babel of our interminable moral arguments.

So far, MacIntyre has exposed the moral fictions that mask modern morality's lack of a foundation and cover up the fact that what it presents as values are nothing but "the preferences of arbitrary will and desire" (AV, 71). But even on the level of will and desire, modern morality is pervaded by yet another moral fiction. One might, after all, think that, even if there is some philosophical difficulty about the foundations of our values, at least, once a given set of values is fixed, modern instrumental reason is unsurpassed in realizing them; that, if we somehow shrug off the philosophical problem of foundations, we can rejoice in a moral system that, particularly through its central character of the Manager, provides an immensely efficient system for satisfying human desires.

But even this instrumental efficiency is, according to MacIntyre, a moral fiction. It is based on the idea that there are established social scientific laws by which managerial experts can predict and thereby control the behavior of social entities such as markets, business organizations, and small groups. In fact, however, "the salient fact about [social] sciences is the absence of the discovery of any lawlike generalizations whatsoever" (AV, 88). Nor is this an accidental or temporary condition. MacIntyre argues that there are systematic reasons why social phenomena will always be essentially unpredictable. These range from the nature of radical conceptual innovation to the ability, recently emphasized by chaos theory, of minute causes to produce large-scale effects. *Fortuna,* Machiavelli's "bitch-goddess of unpredictability" (AV, 91), is ineradicable from human affairs and gives the lie to modern claims of managerial expertise. As MacIntyre puts it:

> I do not of course mean that the activities of purported experts do not have effects and that we do not suffer from those effects and suffer gravely. But the notion of social control embodied in the notion of expertise is indeed a masquerade. Our social order is in a very literal sense out of our, and indeed anyone's, control. No one is or could be in charge. (AV, 107)

There are, of course, modes of instrumental rationality that are effective within certain limited domains (e.g., exit polling as a way of predicting the outcomes of elections). But there is no large-scale ability to control social life that could justify the power and authority modern corporations and government cede to managerial expertise.

MacIntyre concludes, then, that the Enlightenment project fails not only to provide foundations for morality but also to make good on its promise to satisfy, through instrumental reason, the individual desires it must substitute for morality. This leaves us, he thinks, with only two options (AV, Chapter 9). Either we can follow Nietzsche in embracing a life with no meaning beyond that imposed by our choices (an ethics of will-to-power) or we can return to the Aristotelian idea that moral meaning is provided by a normative conception of human nature. The Enlightenment's effort to maintain traditional morality while rejecting human nature has failed. We must either give up the former or accept the latter.

2. Which Enlightenment?

MacIntyre's critique of the Enlightenment is only as persuasive as his portrayal of the Enlightenment project. There is a strand of Enlightenment thought that does correspond to his portrayal and is susceptible to his critique. This is what we might call the "philosophical Enlightenment", that of the modern philosophers who undertook the foundationalist project of grounding morality in the desires of atomistic individuals. But there is another, quite different strand of Enlightenment thought, which we might call the "humanistic Enlightenment" or the "Enlightenment of the *philosophes*".[2] This sees the autonomy following the overthrow of church and king as an independence of the human *community* from allegedly transcendent powers and standards. For it, autonomy does not imply that individuals are isolated moral atoms; they are social beings whose desires are rooted in the practices that define their community and have made them part of it. But there is nothing of moral significance beyond the human community, which is ethically answerable only to itself. This is the view of the less philosophical, more practical and literary-minded early French Enlightenment – of Voltaire, Diderot, and even, to some extent, Rousseau.[3] My pragmatic lib-

---

2 This distinction is drawn by Whitehead: "*Les philosophes* were not philosophers" (*Science and the Modern World*, New York: Macmillan, 1925, 86).

3 This strand of the Enlightenment is emphasized by Peter Gay, *The Enlightenment: an Interpretation*, two volumes, New York: Knopf, 1966, 1969. See also Robert Darnton's excellent brief defense of the Enlightenment in these terms in "George Washington's False Teeth", *New York Review of Books*, March 24, 1997. Richard Rorty offers a similar view through his distinction of the political and the philosophical Enlightenment in "The Continuity between the Enlightenment and 'Postmodernism'", unpublished ms. MacIntyre is far from alone in launching an attack that affects only one version of Enlightenment thought. To cite just one prominent recent example, John Gray's critique is of "the Enlightenment project" construed as centrally concerned with "the rational reconstruction of morality . . . and the assertion by science of authority over all other forms of knowledge" (*Enlightenment's Wake: Politics and Culture at the Close of the Modern Age*, London: Routledge, 1995, 144).

eralism is much closer to this Enlightenment than to that which MacIntyre criticizes.[4]

MacIntyre insists on the general cultural significance of the philosophical Enlightenment's project of justifying morality. He is right that after the sixteenth century morality emerged as a separate domain, not underwritten by religious or political authority, and so in need of another sort of cultural certification (AV, 37). But why think that philosophical theory was the necessary vehicle? MacIntyre himself notes the oddity of this claim, given the marginal role of philosophy in contemporary society. But he maintains that, in the earlier modern period (presumably before the post-Kantian professionalization of philosophy), "philosophy did constitute a central form of social activity". Accordingly, he thinks it is plausible to claim "that the key episodes in the social history which . . . largely displaced morality . . . were episodes in the history of philosophy" (AV, 36).

This is an extraordinary claim, even for cultures – such as Scotland in the eighteenth century or Germany during the Napoleonic period – for which philosophy was a central activity. By its nature as intellectual *reflection*, philosophy cannot ground the social structures that give rise to it. It may – as in Socrates or Marx – profoundly criticize an existing culture and perhaps even have a major role in its revolutionary transformation. But any justification philosophy might provide for its own social matrix could (and need) be only retrospective, an elucidation of or a supplement to whatever ground the society already possessed in the hearts and minds of its members. Otherwise the moral (and cognitive) practices of a society could have no basis prior to the inevitably late emergence of philosophical reflection. And, even after this emergence, there would be no grounding for members who knew nothing of philosophy – always the vast majority.

MacIntyre is right in thinking that the Enlightenment overturned the main traditional underpinnings of society and its morality: religious and political authority. But he is wrong in thinking that there was no alternative but to replace these with yet another external authority – not to say so esoteric

---

4   Bernard Williams has responded to MacIntyre along similar lines: "For some critics, such as Alasdair MacIntyre, the belief in the featureless moral self is a characteristic expression of the Enlightenment and constitutes a major reason why we should abandon its legacy. . . . But the Enlightenment, as representing a set of social and political ideals in favour of truthfulness and the criticism of arbitrary and merely traditional power, has no essential need of such images. . . . [We] need not condemn the ideals of the Enlightenment inasmuch as they are identified with the pursuit of social and political honesty, rather than with a rationalistic metaphysics of morality" (*Shame and Necessity*, Berkeley: University of California Press, 1993, 159).

a one as philosophical reflection. What I have called the Enlightenment of the philosophers did tend to move in this direction, a tendency apparent, for example, in Kant's *Foundations* and Second Critique. But even Kant articulates a very different spirit when he answers the question "What is Enlightenment?" in terms of individuals' courage to think for themselves. Enlightenment means that we are all our own intellectual masters, relying not on the judgment of experts – whether theologians or philosophers – but on our common sense and sensibility. On this view, morality, like any other fundamental commitment, will be warranted not by sophisticated philosophical argument but by the honest judgment of plain individuals.

This understanding is particularly prominent in the early French Enlightenment – a movement to which MacIntyre pays scant attention. Voltaire, in particular, who is not mentioned in AV, denigrates the fruitless technicalities of foundational philosophy and endorses the commonsense skepticism he associates with Locke. In his story "Micromegas", two gigantic travelers, one from Saturn, the other from Sirius, manage to have a conversation with some Earthlings. After listening with amused irony to the pontifications on the soul of an Aristotelian, a Cartesian, a Malebranchian, and a Leibnizian, they welcome the remarks of "a little student of Locke":

> "I know nothing," he said, "of how I think, but I know that I have never thought except at the suggestion of my senses. That there are immaterial and intelligent substances I do not doubt; but that it is impossible for God to communicate thought to matter, I doubt very strongly. I adore the eternal power; it is not my part to limit it. I assert nothing, I content myself with believing that more is possible than people think."[5]

Here we have a very plausible alternative to MacIntyre's insistence on philosophical justification.[6] Voltaire is skeptical about the metaphysical and other transcendental accounts systematic philosophers offer to justify our practical beliefs. But he does not see this skepticism as entailing a skepticism about these beliefs, which are more than adequately grounded in the shared wisdom of our society. As Voltaire says in his *Philosophical Dictionary* entry on "Philosopher": "[Philosophers] might all be mistaken on physics [the nature of reality]; but that is of so little importance to the conduct of life, that philosophers had no need of it. Ages are required to discover a part of the laws of nature. A single day is sufficient to know the duties of man".[7]

---

5 *Candide and Other Writings*, ed. Haskell Block, New York: Modern Library, 1956, 105.
6 As we will see in Part III, there may well be more of Voltaire than of Locke himself in the view evoked here.
7 *Candide and Other Writings*, 429.

Not surprisingly, Voltaire remains unclear as to the precise nature of our common wisdom about morality. Is it some cognitive insight, corresponding to humdrum truths about a moral world in whose grip we find ourselves from the beginning? Or could this wisdom be understood, along the lines suggested in Part I, as the deepest desires hard-wired in us by biology and culture? Voltaire is not theoretically sophisticated enough to provide an answer – or probably even to care. But his example shows that the Enlightenment was not unequivocally committed to the philosophical justification MacIntyre says it was. More important, his position represents a plausible alternative to MacIntyre's thesis that Enlightenment morality inevitably collapses into an irrational decisionism.

MacIntyre might well agree that Voltaire and others like him – *philosophes* but not philosophers – had no stomach for rigorous philosophical argument and so rejected the foundationalist project. But, he might respond, this does not mean that their position did not in itself require the philosophical task of grounding morality. Once we resolve, as the Enlightenment did, to jettison both religion and normative human nature and begin with nothing but our contingent desires, there is no alternative but to provide a philosophical bridge from these desires to moral principles.

But MacIntyre's claim is true only if we insist on beginning from the atomistic individual, whose desires express nothing more than the individual's idiosyncratic preferences. If we instead begin from the desires that make us members of a community, we can argue, as I have in Part I, that these desires themselves form the basis of our morality. MacIntyre sees Enlightenment autonomy as merely a silly exaltation of the individual's desires. But he fails to distinguish desires in the *decisionistic* sense, which are merely what I happen to prefer, from desires in the *constitutive* sense, which make me a member of a moral community. For the humanistic Enlightenment (that of the *philosophes*) I am endorsing, autonomy means the autonomy of the latter desires and of the communities they constitute. This is not the philosophical Enlightenment of atomistic individualism but the humanistic Enlightenment of "the party of humanity".[8]

Someone might, of course, maintain that, even if we are talking about constitutive desires, there is still a need for a philosophical bridge from them to morality, arguing that nothing that is merely part of our contingent historical makeup can ever ground moral standards. But MacIntyre's own ac-

---

8   A phrase of Voltaire's. Speaking of Pascal, he said: "J'ose prendre le parti de l'humanité contre ce misanthrope sublime", *Lettres Philosophiques*, #28, Paris: Garnier-Flammarion, 1964, 160.

count of morality roots it in the contingent practices of historical communities (traditions) and the desires these practices inculcate in us. Nor does he think that members of these communities have no basis for their moral commitments if (as is almost always the case) they lack an adequate philosophical argument for them. MacIntyre cannot consistently require a philosophical justification in the one case but not in the other. Given this, the pragmatic liberal can appropriate MacIntyrean traditions as transmitters of the constitutive desires that make us members of our moral community.

There is, moreover, good reason to think that it is the humanistic rather than the philosophical Enlightenment that underlies modern morality. Had philosophical Enlightenment triumphed, MacIntyre's Rich Aesthete, Therapist, and Manager would exhaust our moral possibilities. But in fact there are many other paradigmatically modern moral characters that express the humanistic Enlightenment. Consider, for example, the Social Activist, the Cultural Critic, and the Novelist. Social activism takes many forms, from the teacher who turns down a safer and higher-paying job in the suburbs to work in an inner-city school, to the leaders of international environmental movements. But in almost every form, it appeals to a set of communal values that are sufficient to motivate individual action. There is no question of the Aesthete's personal indulgence or of the Therapist's or Manager's merely instrumental rationality. The values of the Social Activist are both public and fundamental.

The Cultural Critic is concerned with evaluating specific attitudes and practices on the basis of our fundamental values. Has political advertising corrupted the ideal of informed citizen choice? Are the public schools offering less privileged groups the access they deserve to education? Can high culture be properly given a privileged position (with, for example, state subsidies) in a democratic society? Once again, the Cultural Critic's perspective is that of neither individual predilections nor the neutral attainment of pregiven ends. The Critic speaks from the standpoint of a modern moral heritage judged imperiled by misguided practice.

In the modern world, the novel has been a primary vehicle of moral inquiry, edification, and criticism. Here I do not have in mind only (or even mainly) such social or political tracts as *Hard Times, The Jungle, Grapes of Wrath*, or *Animal Farm;* or the grand philosophical declarations of Dostoyevski or Thomas Mann. I am thinking rather of Flaubert, Proust, and James on sexuality; Nabokov, Calvino, and Kundera on artistic sensibility and political power; Austen, Eliot, and Dickens on family life and friendship. The Novelist is an archetypal figure of the humanistic Enlightenment, ridiculing both traditional authorities and new-fangled philosophies, probing (whether to celebrate or condemn) every desire that drives human lives, exploring every possibility of human achievement and failure.[9] If MacIntyre were right about modern society, all our novels would be bad ones: exercises in aesthetic self-indulgence or fictionalized self-help manuals. Modern novels are worth reading precisely because they offer a vital contact with the moral sources of our humanistic culture. That so distinctively modern a literary genre contains so much moral sustenance refutes MacIntyre's jeremiad on the ethical vacuity of modern life.[10]

3. In Defense of Enlightenment Humanism

I have cited the Social Activist, the Cultural Critic, and the Novelist to show that contemporary culture expresses the humanistic Enlightenment at least as much as the philosophical Enlightenment. This, in turn, shows, given our earlier discussion, that MacIntyre's assertion of our society's ethical incoherence fails. For his critique succeeds only against the atomistic individualism of the philosophical Enlightenment. It does not follow, of course, that humanistic Enlightenment is the ideal of human life or even that it is superior to MacIntyre's own preferred Aristotelianism. It is still open to MacIntyre to maintain that our modern morality of Enlightenment humanism has put us into an intolerable situation, one that would be significantly improved if only we could replace it with an Aristotelian morality of the virtues. But what exactly is so bad about modern morality, and why would a morality of the virtues be better?

MacIntyre's strongest complaint about modern morality is that it cannot provide rational agreement on moral issues. He traces this inability back to the modern world's marginalization of two elements that are essential for a coherent moral life: practices and narrative unity. The participants in modern moral debates are, on the whole, modern selves, defined entirely by their contingent, socially isolated desires. They do not participate in practices directed toward internal goods and lead lives that lack a unifying narrative. As a result, they are unable to agree among themselves on any shared conception of the human good, and this leads directly to an inability to agree on basic moral issues.

It is important to note that the lack of consensus is not primarily a mat-

---

9   See Milan Kundera, *The Art of the Novel,* New York: Grove Press, 1988, particularly the opening chapter, "The Depreciated Legacy of Cervantes".

10 This is not to say that the novel has not also been a vehicle for critiques of Enlightenment humanism in, for example, the writings of Céine and Genet.

ter of there being a number of conflicting moral traditions in modern discussions. There are such traditions, but MacIntyre maintains that fruitful debate among rival traditions is by no means impossible. The problem is rather that so many moderns are "individuals", that is, moral atoms unrooted in any tradition, who therefore come to the debate committed to nothing but their own private interests. This is why the problem of egoism is central for modern moralists. The problem is unsolvable, since there simply is no coherent way to show that selves who are mere congeries of individual passions must agree on any common moral principles.

MacIntyre, of course, insists that the modern concept of the "individual" does not express the essential nature of human beings, but merely the unfortunate situation to which modern society has brought most of its members. This situation has been produced by the modern economy of production (AV, 227). In premodern societies, people worked in their own households, so that their productive efforts (farming, weaving, cooking) were part of the practice of sustaining family life and the life of the larger community of which the family is a part. But the modern economy forced workers from their homes and into shops and factories, where they had to give their efforts to enterprises in which they had no interest beyond the wages they received. The result was lives divorced from the internal goods of practices, goods that alone provide the basis for a life with narrative unity and overall moral significance. So our modern lack of moral consensus is caused by an even more distressing evil: the loss of moral meaning in the lives of isolated individuals.

There are, however, other ways to describe the modern situation that MacIntyre deplores. The break with home- and village-bound practices meant that people no longer had to accept the conception of human life imposed on them by religious and political institutions. They could begin to ask whether the restrictions their priests and feudal lords imposed were really required by human nature and divine law or rather just represented the self-interest of the priests and lords. They could even begin to formulate their own ideas, based on personal experience and inclinations, of what a good life would be. At the same time, the new economic system provided many more people with the material resources they needed to make a start on realizing the sort of lives they preferred. The result is a world – at least in the rich democracies – where there is incomparably more freedom and prosperity (meaning basic material well-being) than there has ever been before. Widespread freedom and prosperity do not themselves make for general happiness, but we cannot imagine a world without them in which more than a small elite could ever hope to be happy.

Nothing MacIntyre says denies this positive description of the modern situation, and there is no reason to think he favors renouncing our freedom and prosperity for the sake of reviving premodern practices. I myself would go further – perhaps MacIntyre would as well – and maintain that preserving the modern achievement of widespread freedom and prosperity is a sine qua non for any human future that we envisage. Perhaps MacIntyre is right that we moderns suffer because we lack the unifying practices and shared moral vision of premodern times. But there can be no question of compromising what modernity has achieved for the sake of filling this lack. At the worst, then, we might have to accept the moral loss MacIntyre laments as the price of our freedom and prosperity.

The real issue is whether the liberal arrangements (social, economic, and political) that sustain our freedom and prosperity can allow for MacIntyre's ethical communality. Can a liberal society allow for a shared commitment to the common good that will support consensus on major moral issues?

The question of whether there is a liberal conception of the common good is equivalent, in MacIntyre's terms, to the question of whether liberalism is a tradition. For, on his view, a tradition is precisely the sociohistorical vehicle of such a conception. In *After Virtue* he certainly gives the impression that liberalism is not a tradition. He says, for example, that "the individualism of modernity could of course find no use for the notion of tradition within its own conceptual scheme except as an adversary notion" (AV, 220). And, in the one place where he does mention a "modern tradition", it is to refer to a view that "the variety and heterogeneity of human goods is such that their pursuit cannot be reconciled in any single moral order", a characterization that denies the conception of a common good essential to MacIntyre's own notion of tradition. Moreover, the very idea of the liberal atomistic individual seems to be an idea of someone without any moral tradition.

However, in *Whose Justice? Which Rationality?* MacIntyre explicitly recognizes that liberalism is a tradition: "Liberal theory is best understood, not at all as an attempt to find a rationality independent of tradition, but as itself the articulation of an historically developed and developing set of social institutions and forms of activity, that is, as the voice of a tradition". As a tradition, liberalism has, even if somewhat reluctantly, a conception of the common good: "Liberalism, while initially rejecting the claims of any overriding theory of the good, does in fact come to embody just such a theory". It also has other central features of a tradition:

> Like other traditions, liberalism has internal to it its own standards of rational justification. Like other traditions, liberalism has its own set of authoritative texts and its disputes over their interpretation. Like other traditions, liberalism expresses itself socially through a particular sort of hierarchy". (WJWR, 345)

This is an important clarification on MacIntyre's part. If liberalism is in fact a tradition with a conception of the general human good, then one of the major arguments against it is eliminated. For then liberal debates about morality are not merely the clash of opposing individual wills. There is a shared conception of the good to which participants in such debates can appeal and hence a possibility of resolving these debates in a rational way. This shared conception is not any traditional notion of a specific substantive goal (e.g., adherence to a particular code of law, the practice of a certain set of virtues). It is, rather, simply the idea that everyone should have the maximum amount of freedom consistent with a similar degree of freedom for everyone else.

MacIntyre's acceptance of liberalism as a tradition need not be fatal to his critique. For one thing, as we shall see, he is prepared to argue philosophically for the superiority of his Aristotelian tradition to the liberal tradition. Moreover, I suspect that he would not even regard his recognition that liberalism has a conception of the common good as saving the liberal from the problem of interminable moral disagreement. For, he would surely maintain, this conception is too thin to provide a rational resolution to moral disputes within the liberal tradition.

This is particularly apparent in the discussion of modern debates about justice in the penultimate chapter of *After Virtue*. MacIntyre asks us to reflect on a typical modern disagreement between A, who thinks raising taxes to support welfare programs is unjust because it takes from him money he has legitimately earned, and B, who thinks tax increases are necessary to overcome obvious injustices in the distribution of resources and opportunity. As MacIntyre sees it, this very common sort of disagreement is irresolvable in modern liberal society because each side invokes "considerations which are incommensurable with those advanced by the adversary party" (AV, 245). He formulates the conflict between A and B as follows:

> A holds that principles of just acquisition and entitlement set limits to redistributive possibilities. If the outcome of the application of the principles of just acquisition and entitlement is a gross inequality, the toleration of such inequality is a price that has to be paid for justice. B holds that principles of just distribution set limits to acquisition and entitlement. If the outcome of the application of just distribution is interference . . . with what has up till now been regarded in this social order as legitimate acquisition and entitlement, the toleration of such interference is a price that has to be paid for justice. (AV, 245–6)

Given this understanding of the disagreement, MacIntyre maintains that our liberal society has no way of adjudicating the conflicting claims of earned entitlement and basic needs. "Our pluralist culture possesses no method of weighing, no rational criterion for deciding between" these claims (AV, 246).

MacIntyre has, however, misstated the nature of the disagreement. He presents it as a radical clash of fundamental principles: a principle of earned entitlement that overrides claims of basic needs versus a principle of basic needs that overrides claims of earned entitlement. This is why he thinks the nature of the disagreement is illuminated by the debate between Rawls and Nozick over the correct philosophical theory of justice. Both Rawls and Nozick try "to provide rational principles to which appeal may be made by contending parties with conflicting interests" (AV, 246), with Nozick providing a philosophical basis for A's position and Rawls for B's. What this misses is that the dispute between A and B, at least as it is typically carried out in American politics, does not go nearly so deep. Generally, A and B will agree that both earned entitlement and basic needs have a significant claim on decisions about how to allot resources. Neither is holding that the one value trumps the other in principle. The issue between them is not of principle but of judgment: what is the best way of taking account of both values in a particular context? Liberal communities resolve such issues every day, deciding, for example, that a new park in the inner city is worth an increase in the local income tax or that property taxes should not be raised to expand arts programs. The rhetoric of each side in such disputes, naturally enough, evokes the general principle (accepted by both sides) that supports its own view. But the resolution of the issue will often depend on specific facts about just what will be gained and lost by the action in question.

Note that rejecting an understanding of the dispute as being over philosophical issues does not turn it into a mere clash of individual interests or wills. A and B may each stand to benefit if their position wins the day. But they are each able to appeal to specific facts – the burden a new tax will impose on homeowners, the outrageous conditions of ghetto life – that can and do move those on the other side of the debate. Such appeals do not, of course, provide an algorithm for resolving the issues under dispute. In this sense, MacIntyre is right that liberal morality has no "rational criterion" for ending discussion. But this is a feature of all rational discussions. In the end, they all must come down to our judgments of how the relevant values apply to a given situation. The point is that, within the liberal tradition, we do regularly and routinely agree on such judgments.

This fact is obscured by our understandable focus, first, on particularly vexing issues, such as abortion and affirmative action, which have remained intractable even after the most extensive discussion; and, second, on cases in which the exercise of unprincipled power, from sheer personal willfulness to bribery and blackmail, determine political outcomes. But this focus ignores the numerous daily cases in which the institutions of liberal democracy routinely generate quite sensible conclusions – about the placement of stop lights, the relative priority of educational needs, the comparative seriousness of foreign crises – about how we should conduct our common lives.

In sum, MacIntyre ignores the middle ground, between philosophical principle and personal interest, in which democratic politics is typically carried out. He misreads disputes about the best way to implement principles as disputes over the principles themselves and insists on treating political disagreement as philosophical rather than pragmatic. (This perhaps reflects a typically European rather than a typically American view of politics.) Not that disagreements over philosophical principle do not exist. But the genius of liberal politics has been to provide a framework in which even those who disagree about substantive conceptions of the human good can engage in fruitful political discussion, provided they agree on the necessity of preserving minimal liberal freedoms. The liberal tradition is dominant precisely to the striking extent that citizens of Western democracies have found in it the resources for effective political discussion and action, even in contexts of deep disagreements about substantive human goods.

Here it is important to note, contrary to MacIntyre and many other critics of liberalism (as well as some of its proponents), that considerations based on appeals to substantive goods need not be entirely excluded from discussions within a liberal society. This might be required by a liberalism that demands a philosophical foundation for all moral principles and finds one only for the principles defining minimal liberal freedom. But for pragmatic liberalism, such principles reflect merely the core agreement necessary to sustain a liberal society. The parties to any given ethical or political discussion may – and often will – agree on far more than this core. This will be most obviously true for discussions among members of subgroups within a liberal society (e.g., members of a church or political party) defined by commitments to substantive goods that go beyond the liberal freedoms. But it may, on a given issue, also be true of a liberal society as a whole. Pragmatic liberalism allows us to operate with whatever level of moral agreement we can muster in a given situation, provided this agreement does not put in jeopardy the core liberal freedoms.

The preceding discussion leads us to a principle that is at least implicit in the practice of all liberal states. This is the acceptance of what we might call a range of "secondary public goods", beyond the primary public good of freedom, that are properly supported by the state. Unlike the primary goods, these are not built into the constitution as "inalienable rights" of citizens. Rather, they correspond to further goods that the community as a whole endorses through its mechanisms of public decision making (in principle, this implies, in some sense, majority support for the goods). Such support goes beyond the commitment to the primary public good, and it may well not accord with the private preferences of a significant minority of the citizenry. The principles of the liberal state forbid it to compel dissenting citizens to engage in activities opposed to their basic private values, but it may compel them to support such activities on the part of others. Thus, we may vote to build highway systems, sports stadiums, or symphony halls; and, although we may not force those opposed to automobiles, athletics, or classical music to use these facilities, we may force them to support them. (Of course, a liberal community may decide, in a given case, that even though its majority favors a certain activity – say, religion – it should not require everyone to support it.) In this way, liberalism allows for public support for what would otherwise be entirely private goods and rejects an absolute subordination of private to public goods.

I conclude that MacIntyre's case in *After Virtue* against liberalism does not succeed against our pragmatic version of it. He first tries to show that the liberal understanding of human beings as atomic individuals simultaneously requires and makes impossible a philosophical justification of morality. But, as we have seen, liberalism need not and often has not understood human beings in this way. He then tries to show that liberalism cannot support genuine ethical commitment because it does not allow for the shared values characteristic of a moral tradition. But, by his own eventual admission, liberalism is a moral tradition and so it can, in principle, sustain ethical commitment. Finally, he argues that the liberal tradition cannot, at any rate, provide sufficient ethical commitment to allow rational resolution of moral disagreements. But we see that this is not so once we realize the pragmatic rather than the philosophical nature of moral disagreements within a liberal society. Despite the attacks of *After Virtue,* liberalism remains a coherent ethical standpoint, quite capable of sustaining a shared moral life. MacIntyre has to accept it as a genuine competitor with his Aristotelian tradition. He cannot, as he seemed to hope, simply eliminate liberalism for reasons internal to it. He may still be able to show that Aristotelianism is superior, but this will require a vindication of this superiority in a direct confrontation with the liberal tradition.

4. The Lure of Tradition

After Virtue and *Whose Justice? Which Rationality?* define the terms of engagement, as MacIntyre sees them, between the Aristotelian tradition and the liberalism and Nietzscheanism opposed to it. He explains the sharp ("incommensurable" in his Kuhnian language) differences that separate them and develops a method by which one tradition may be vindicated over an incommensurable rival. His Gifford Lectures, *Three Rival Views of Moral Inquiry*, go on to apply (or, at least, sketch the application of) this method to show the superiority of Aristotelianism. But, quite apart from the success or failure of this enterprise, MacIntyre's work is important for the new life it has given to the very idea of philosophizing out of a tradition. In this section, I pause to reflect on the attractiveness of this idea.

On MacIntyre's understanding, a philosophical tradition is not merely a chain of philosophers who have read, commented on, revised, and extended the work of their predecessors. The chain must itself be embodied in an enduring community, with a full range of the practices and institutions needed to sustain meaningful human life. Further, this community must recognize and support the work of its philosophical subgroup as an essential contribution to its own life. A philosophical tradition in MacIntyre's sense is a historically extended process of reflection inextricably tied to the practices and institutions of a human community. MacIntyre is primarily concerned with the Aristotelian tradition that came to maturity in fourth-century Athens and the Augustinian tradition of medieval Europe. These two traditions were, moreover, united by Thomas Aquinas and other philosophers in the Catholic tradition. It is to this Aristotelian–Thomistic tradition that MacIntyre holds allegiance.[11]

As we have seen, it is also possible to speak of a "liberal tradition" and even, I would suggest, of a "pragmatic liberal tradition" from the humanistic Enlightenment through Richard Rorty. But pragmatic liberalism cannot assign philosophy anything like the role it has in MacIntyre's Aristotelianism. Where Aristotelianism sees philosophy as achieving a body of objectively rational truth that any reflective person should accept, pragmatic liberalism rejects the project of grounding basic truths about human beings through rational insight and argument. Rather, it maintains that, since there is no such grounding, everyone should be free to pursue the human good as they understand it, provided this does not interfere with others' similar pursuit. Pragmatic liberalism emerged from the failure of modern philosophers, beginning with Descartes, to provide a generally compelling "traditionless"

---

11 MacIntyre variously characterizes his preferred tradition as "Augustinianism", "Aristotelianism", "Aristotelian–Thomism", and "Thomism". I use the expression "Aristotelian tradition" but ask the reader to recall that, for MacIntyre, this means the synthesis of Aristotelianism with Augustinian Christianity effected by Thomas Aquinas.

grounding for philosophical truth. It reads the interminable disputes of modern philosophy as proof that at least that philosophical project is vain and should not be expected to provide a basis for our shared life in the secular democracies that have replaced the Christian society of medieval and early modern Europe. Pragmatic liberalism is still a "philosophy", at least in the minimal sense that it rejects, rather than simply ignores, the claims of previous philosophers and asserts, though without inconsistently venturing an objective grounding, the ethical view that freedom is the only fundamental human good.[12] If the philosophical content of pragmatic liberalism is weak in comparison to Aristotelianism, its social penetration is still strong. It is deeply embedded in the practices and institutions of the rich North Atlantic democracies.

But for the moment, let us ignore liberal alternatives to tradition in the philosophically strong sense and reflect on what seems to be the special opportunity such a tradition offers for philosophical inquiry. It would seem that tradition in MacIntyre's sense is the best hope of achieving the goal of philosophical inquiry as it has been understood since Plato. Philosophy seeks reflective, rational answers to the most fundamental questions about how a person should live. It is possible to live without attempting any such search; one can simply follow the direction of life ordained or most encouraged by one's social environment. Local traditions, accepted without question, will determine most choices that confront us. Apart from passing moments – in adolescence or at later times of crisis – most people take this route. The philosophical temper, however, fears being radically misled by simply playing out the hand we have been dealt. Why think that the mode of life implicitly endorsed by the particular tradition into which we have been born is anything like the right one? Far better, the philosopher (and the spirit of Enlightenment) in us says, to think things through for ourselves, to decide how to live on the basis of rational reflection rather than to follow contingent convention.

But just as the refusal of rational reflection leaves me trapped within what seems right to my society, so embracing it leaves me trapped within what seems right to me. The philosopher's hope is to find answers to the deepest questions so well grounded that any rational inquirer will agree with them. The premises from which we begin should be uncontroversial and the reasoning from them unquestionable. But the history of philosophy is a history of failures to attain this goal. The strong agreement associated with rational

---

12   In my conclusion, I discuss further ways in which pragmatic liberalism allows a signficant role for philosophical reflection.

knowledge – as in the natural sciences – has eluded philosophy. As a result, we seem to be left with three equally unpalatable alternatives: return to an unquestioning acceptance of the "philosophy" implicit in the tradition we were born to, persist in the fruitless attempt to find rational consensus about answers to philosophical questions, or maintain our own individual perspective on philosophical questions, admitting, however, that it is just one view, with no privileged status.

MacIntyre's concept of philosophical tradition suggests a way out of this disconcerting impasse. It suggests that the impasse arises from the assumption that there is a sharp division between conformity to social norms and the search for philosophical truth. This assumption ignores the reality of social traditions that themselves embody philosophical inquiry. In such traditions we find a solid consensus about fundamental questions that is based not on blind contingencies but on centuries of careful philosophical reflection. Becoming a philosopher is not, as moderns typically conceive it, a matter of working from my own "intuitions" to construct a system of my own. Instead, it involves apprenticing myself to masters who represent the current achievement of a long line of interacting philosophers. Further, this line of reflection has itself been embodied in the practices and institutions of a historical community, which it has informed and which inform it. As a result, inquiry within a tradition is enriched and tested by the lived experience of many generations. Such inquiry is the best way to answer the question of how we should live on the basis of an overall rational understanding of what human beings are and what place they have in the universe.

Once we have opted for philosophizing within a tradition, MacIntyre's Aristotelian tradition becomes very attractive. It is one of the oldest and intellectually richest traditions, ripe with deep and subtle philosophical ideas. It embodies 2,500 years of practical applications of philosophical thought; its concepts have guided millions of lives, and these lives have in turn affected the tradition's conceptual formulations. And the tradition is informed by religious experience and aspiration, something that no responsible reflection on fundamental questions can ignore. No matter what its limitations and vicissitudes, religion has a substantial prima facie claim to wisdom about the human condition. Philosophical thought outside the Aristotelian or some similar tradition will be severely limited in historical perspective, practical involvement, and religious sensibility.

On the other hand, each of these distinctive advantages of philosophizing within a tradition has a corresponding disadvantage. The very antiquity of a tradition makes it likely that it contains much that is outdated and ossified; embodiment in practices and institutions makes philosophical thought dependent on their interests, which are never simply those of objective truth; and whatever religious wisdom there may be in any tradition is diluted with superstition and wish fulfillment.

The Aristotelian tradition has, moreover, specific deficiencies that limit its philosophical resources. Its metaphysical core (i.e., its doctrines of God and of the soul) have never solidly met the challenge of the modern natural sciences, with the result that the tradition has simply not been a significant force in general philosophical discussions since Descartes. Nor is it still obviously a dominant factor in even Catholic thought, where metaphysics is now often either entirely ignored or else formulated in terms of existential phenomenology. Even the tradition's still significant ethical impact has been increasingly separated, in many pastoral contexts, from its intellectual content, more and more reflecting less Aristotelian virtue ethics than the therapeutic morality of the dominant liberal society.

On a more fundamental level, there is a tension between the total commitment demanded by a religious tradition and the intellectual openness and flexibility required of serious philosophizing. This is apparent in MacIntyre's own account. On the one hand, he insists on the open, developmental nature of philosophical thought within the Aristotelian tradition. Thomas Aquinas, he points out, sees "a variety of writers . . . as contributing to a single ongoing enterprise of enquiry". His discussion of truth in *De Veritate* "summarizes the outcome of that enquiry so far, advances it one stage further, and leaves the way open for the proponents of yet further considerations to continue beyond that point" (TRV, 74). More generally, Aquinas employed "a method which required that his own work should be essentially incomplete" (TRV, 124). This requirement follows from Aquinas's view of truth as a standard outside all inquiry by which that inquiry can always be judged and found wanting. According to MacIntyre, the Aristotelian tradition's commitment to this notion of truth "opens it up to radical judgments of its own success or failure" and makes it exhibit "the kind of intellectual vulnerability which is the mark of all worthwhile theorizing" (TRV, 125). Because of this openness and vulnerability, "no thesis or argument or doctrine is better than the best grounds proposed for it by those who adhere to it" (TRV, 201).

But at the same time, inquiry within a tradition involves for MacIntyre unswerving acceptance of the tradition's fundamental doctrines. Such inquiry requires "membership in a particular type of moral community, one from which fundamental dissent has to be excluded" (TRV, 60). As a result, the openness of tradition is limited by the core doctrinal commitment. Aquinas's method always "leaves open the possibility of a return to [the]

question with some new argument. . . . there is and can be no finality" –
except, MacIntyre adds, "for the finality of Scripture and dogmatic tradition" (TRV, 125). But how can MacIntyre reconcile this exception – quite
massive, when one realizes the extent to which papal and conciliar pronouncements have defined the limits of orthodox belief – with the openness
of philosophical inquiry? It is one thing to realize that inquiry cannot start
from zero, that rational thinking must always begin with some substantive
commitments. It is quite another to accept the full weight of a tradition requiring core commitments as extensive as those of Aristotelianism and to
insist that these commitments are excluded, in principle, from rational critique and possible rejection. MacIntyre's claim that "no doctrine is better
than the best grounds proposed for it" is contradicted by the "finality" he
accords Scripture and dogmatic tradition.[13]

None of this undermines our earlier case for the value of tradition – and
specifically the Aristotelian tradition – for philosophical inquiry. But it does
suggest that we might do better to appreciate and appropriate traditions –
at least those that involve substantive core commitments – from a bit of a
distance. MacIntyre himself emphasizes that those who do not belong to a
tradition can nonetheless attain something close to an "inside" grasp of it,
learning to speak rather than merely translate its language. Given the philosophical limitations of a full commitment to so demanding a tradition – and
particularly given that the tradition's past is far more impressive than its
present – there is little advantage and much disadvantage to philosophizing
literally from within it.

The preceding discussion is not intended primarily as a criticism of Mac-
Intyre, whose main case for tradition is not the sort of a priori one I have allowed to tempt me. Rather, it is intended to show the powerful initial lure
of a philosophical tradition as MacIntyre characterizes it, while also suggesting that the lure is not entirely compelling. I also want to suggest that
an Enlightenment commitment to rational autonomy can consistently take
a much more favorable view than it typically has of the great philosophical
traditions. It might accept, for example, MacIntyre's Aristotelianism as a significant resource, even if not as a decisive norm. MacIntyre, of course, will find
this sort of acknowledgment of Aristotelianism inadequate, maintaining, as
he does, the clear superiority of his tradition to its liberal and Nietzschean

13 Scripture, of course, is open to interpretation and dogmatic tradition to development.
But, if religious faith is to involve any serious intellectual commitment, there will be a core
of truth not subject to interpretation, development, or rational rejection. In the Catholic
tradition that MacIntyre embraces, this core is very extensive.

rivals. The following sections formulate and evaluate his effort to make this case.

5. The Tradition of the Virtues

MacIntyre opposes to liberal morality an ethics of the virtues. Ethical views built around a set of virtues, rather than rules, have their Western origin in ancient Greece. The archaic period presents (through Homer's epics) a heroic version of such an ethic. But the great flowering of the fifth and fourth centuries in Athens offered a range of competing accounts of the ethics of virtues, particularly in the work of Plato, the sophists, Aristotle, and the tragedians (especially Sophocles). MacIntyre himself endorses the virtue ethics of the "Aristotelian tradition". By this he does not mean a view that preserves all the essential features of Aristotle's account. His notion of a tradition allows for (indeed, requires) continual rethinking and significant revision of the tradition's previous formulations. He proposes an Aristotelian view that incorporates both major transformations introduced by medieval thinkers and important changes of his own.

His view is authentically tied to Aristotle's by, first of all, its rejection of the Homeric and Platonic alternatives. Whereas the Homeric world saw virtues as qualities associated with particular social roles (e.g., the warrior, the housewife), MacIntyre follows Aristotle in seeing them as qualities of human beings as such. And, whereas Plato thought that virtue could be achieved only in the ideal social structure described in his *Republic,* MacIntyre and Aristotle hold that virtue is possible in this world.

More important, MacIntyre accepts Aristotle's core formulation of the nature of the ethical and of the role the virtues play in it. He begins with Aristotle's idea that every activity aims at some good and that, accordingly, the activity of human life as such aims at what can be called unqualifiedly "the good" (AV, 148). This thesis is understood in terms of a human nature that we all share and that specifies the good as the ultimate goal (*telos*) of human life. This goal is *eudaimonia* (roughly, happiness or well-being, but, as MacIntyre notes, this name alone leaves much of the content of *eudaimonia* unspecified). The virtues enter in as enduring qualities ("habits") that are necessary for humans to attain *eudaimonia.*

This much constitutes the Aristotelian core of MacIntyre's position. But, as he points out, he also deviates from Aristotle in three fundamental respects (AV, 162–4). First, he rejects the "metaphysical biology" on which Aristotle bases his conception of human nature. Second, he denies Aristotle's assumption that the ethical life can be led only in a *polis.* Third, he follows Sophocles in rejecting Aristotle's view that to possess one central virtue is to possess all of them, with its consequence that there can never be genuine conflicts between equally compelling goods. These are in addition to the "metadeviation" introduced by MacIntyre's subjecting Aristotle's ethics to the development and correction of a tradition, something Aristotle himself would have never countenanced (AV, 146).

Given his Aristotelian foundation, MacIntyre proceeds to set forth an understanding of the virtues that, he maintains, preserves the core of the Aristotelian tradition as it has developed from its Homeric beginnings through the Middle Ages and up to its eclipse in the modern age. This core will, he maintains, provide a formulation of virtue ethics, based on the most cogent results of different stages of the Aristotelian tradition, for which we will be able to give "a more compelling account than any of the other accounts so far" (AV, 186). As such, it will be the most effective challenge to the modern liberal conception of morality.

MacIntyre's account of the virtues embodies them, successively, in specific practices, in "the narrative order of a single life", and in a "moral tradition" (AV, 187). Each of these three stages introduces essential elements of the virtues as the central characteristics of an ethical life.

A practice, for MacIntyre, is not just any activity, but a specific sort of communal activity. Whereas any activity has goals, a practice has goals that are internal to it as an activity. That is, achieving (to some extent) the goals is part of what it means to engage in the activity; attaining the goals is not contingently (externally) related to the activity. Thus, playing the violin is a practice because it is impossible to engage in it without to some small extent realizing its goal (the production of music); whereas investing in the stock market is, presumably, not a practice, since we can engage in it without attaining its goal of making money. Further, as MacIntyre understands a practice, it is not content with achieving goals fixed ahead of time by means already available. Rather, it is carried out in such a way that "human powers to achieve excellence, and human conceptions of the ends and goods involved, are systematically extended" (AV, 187). This, it seems, is why merely throwing a football back and forth is not a practice, whereas the game of football is; and why architecture but not bricklaying is a practice.

Given this understanding of a practice, MacIntyre is able to characterize a virtue as "an acquired human quality the possession and exercise of which tends to enable us to achieve those goods which are internal to practices and the lack of which effectively prevents us from achieving any such goals" (AV, 191). Many virtues will be specific to a given practice (for example, skill in the end game is a virtue specific to chess). But there are some virtues characteristic of all practices. MacIntyre cites, in particular, justice, honesty, and courage. These three virtues are essential for acquiring competence in any practice. Becoming competent requires that we give other practitioners, particularly our superiors, the respect and recognition they deserve (justice), that we forthrightly acknowledge our shortcomings (honesty), and that we make whatever sacrifices are necessary to achieve competence (courage).

The essential role of virtues in practices is not, however, enough to establish an ethics, since specific practices themselves have full ethical significance only in the context of an entire human life. MacIntyre supports this claim by arguing that a human life involving the virtues only in terms of specific practices would be defective in three ways (AV, 201–3). First, it would involve "too many conflicts and too much arbitrariness", since there would be no way, except arbitrary choice, to decide our allegiance to incompatible virtues of conflicting practices. I could not choose between cultivating the aggressiveness needed to make me a successful public prosecutor and the gentleness needed to make me a successful friend and lover. Second, certain important virtues, such as justice, can be completely understood only in relation to a conception of the good of a human life as such. Justice, for example, is owed to those who deserve it not because of their contribution to the goods of some specific practice but because of their contribution to the common human good. Indeed – and this is MacIntyre's third reason – at least one virtue, purity of heart (understood in the Kierkegaardian sense of "willing one thing"), makes sense only in relation to an entire life.

The next question, therefore, is, How are we to understand the idea of "an entire human life"? What is the unity that constitutes a "life" as a meaningful whole? MacIntyre argues at length that the unity of a life is that of a *narrative,* a story in which each stage is fully intelligible only in relation to what has preceded and what follows and which, as a whole, has a meaning beyond that of any of its parts. The heart of his elaborate argument is the claim that there is no way of understanding an action apart from locating it in a causal and temporal sequence of actions. Of course, the same action is often simultaneously characterizable in a variety of different ways. But each of these ways is justified only because there is a true story (narrative) in which the action so characterized is embedded. My turning on a light may be a signal to a friend if there has been prior agreement between us that this will mark the time to act; it may also be an act of terrorism if what the friend is supposed to do is detonate a bomb; and it may be the beginning of a revolution if the bomb is in the presidential palace. But in every case, the correctness or incorrectness of a description of an action depends on its place in a narrative sequence.

With this understanding of action, MacIntyre's line of argument is straight-forward: a life is a sequence of actions; hence, the unity of a life must consist in the unity of a sequence of actions, which must itself take the form of a narrative. But just what sort of narrative is a human life? One of heroic achievement, tragic conflict, comic irony? MacIntyre has a quite specific answer: the narrative of a human life takes the form of a medieval quest (AV, 219). My life as a whole must be a quest because it must be directed to asking and answering, "in both word and deed", the question "What is the good for me?" This question must direct my life as a whole because otherwise I have no way of placing the internal goods of different practices in relation to one another, thereby providing a basis for resolving conflicts among them. It is only by knowing what my (overall) good is that I can order and adjudicate the various goods I seek. (For reasons that will soon be clear, I must also connect this question with its generalization, "What is the good for man?")

It follows that my life quest has one of the features of a medieval quest: it is guided by a preliminary conception of the human good that provides the quest with its goal (telos) from the very beginning. But the initial conception of the good is merely preliminary. Also in the manner of a medieval quest, my search for the good life is not guided by a complete understanding of just what I am searching for. Rather, one essential part of the goal is simply to understand what the goal is: "the good life for man is the life spent in seeking for the good life for man" (AV, 219). Of course, this is not all the quest seeks. To the extent that I learn what the content of a good life is, I must also form myself in accordance with this content. The virtues needed to carry out both aspects of this quest will be moral virtues, that is, not virtues leading to the internal goods of one or another practice but to the good for man as such.

To sum up MacIntyre's argument so far: he has begun with the obvious fact that our lives are made up of various practices in which we engage. Each separate practice has its own internal goods and concomitant virtues necessary to achieve them. But anyone who engages in a variety of practices will encounter problems of how to relate the goods (and virtues) of different practices, particularly when these conflict with one another. I need, accordingly, a conception of my life as a whole as a basis for ordering the goods and virtues of particular practices. Given MacIntyre's understanding of action, this conception must be that of a narrative unity. Further, since this narrative unity must resolve questions about the ordering of particular goods within the context of my entire life, the narrative must take the form of a quest for an answer to the question "What is the overall good of a human life?" This question needs to be answered in both word and deed; that is, I

must both find out what the good life is and carry out this answer by actually leading the good life. The quest-narrative that is my life must be guided
throughout by a normative conception of the human good. Initially, this will
be a quite thin conception, perhaps amounting to little more than the need
to search for a fuller, more adequate conception of the human good. But, to
the extent that my quest is successful, I will arrive at ever "thicker" conceptions of the human good. The moral virtues are precisely those qualities required for me to carry out my quest.

So far, however, we have discussed only the first two stages in MacIntyre's
development of virtue ethics: that of virtues as embedded in practices and
that of virtues as part of a unified life narrative. The third stage locates the
virtues within a moral tradition.

Tradition enters the picture because no one is capable of carrying out a
quest for the good of his life as an isolated individual. This is not merely a
practical point (it's too hard a job to do alone) but also a conceptual one. I
necessarily take the stage of my life as a character in a story that has been
going on for a long time. I am the child of a certain family, the citizen of a
certain state, the member of a certain church. This, as MacIntyre says, gives
my life "its own moral particularity" (AV, 220), a specific standpoint from
which I must begin. Having such a specific starting point is what MacIntyre
means by belonging to a tradition. A tradition, in other words, is the communal counterpart of the narrative of an individual life. It is a narrative involving many characters extended over a long period of time. But, like the
lives of the individuals it includes, it is a quest for the human good, an effort to understand and actualize this good. Since a tradition involves many
individuals, its concern cannot be the good for just any one individual.
Rather, it must be concerned with the intersection of all these individual
goods, that is, the good for human beings as such. It is because I am necessarily part of such a tradition that, as mentioned earlier, my quest is not only
for my own good but for the general human good.

MacIntyre's understanding of a moral tradition is distinctive in at least
three major respects. The first is a point that he makes but does not especially emphasize: that an individual life is typically embedded in more than
one tradition: "the history of each of our own lives is generally and characteristically embedded in and made intelligible in terms of the larger and
longer histories of a number of traditions" (AV, 222). So we do not typically
find ourselves limited by the specificity of a single tradition. Second – a point
MacIntyre does emphasize – individuals are not required to "accept the
moral *limitations* of the particularity" of a tradition into which they are born
(AV, 221). There is no escaping entirely from the traditions with which we

begin. But our quest for the human good may well (and typically will) involve transforming and going beyond the understanding of the human good we received at our beginning. Finally, MacIntyre's traditions combine social and cultural immersion in a way of life with a high level of intellectual reflection. They are not alternatives to critical rationality; rather, they are the only means whereby such rationality can be integrated into concrete human existence.

MacIntyre's understanding of tradition is, accordingly, very different from that of Burke, with whom the notion is most often associated in intellectual and political contexts. For Burke, tradition is opposed to both reason and conflict. It is the locus of an emotional allegiance that goes so deep as to preclude serious dissent or discussion. For MacIntyre, tradition is precisely the locus (the only possible locus) of rational thought. And a primary function of thought within a tradition is to transcend "through criticism and invention the limitations of what has been previously reasoned within that tradition" (AV, 222). Moreover, as we would expect from MacIntyre's account of the moral quest, one major occupation of rational discourse within a tradition is to argue about the conception of the good that should guide the tradition. A tradition, accordingly, is the opposite of the mere preservation (or revival) of the past that Burke and most modern conservatives have made it. For MacIntyre, traditions are, unless they are dead or dying, essentially dynamic, respectfully beginning from but always questioning and revising what has been handed down. "A living tradition then is an historically extended, socially embodied argument, and an argument precisely in part about the goods which constitute that tradition" (AV, 222).

Finally, how do the virtues enter into a tradition? Precisely as the qualities needed by its members if the tradition is to be sustained. Just as justice, honesty, and courage are needed to support any practice, they are needed to carry out a tradition's moral quest. Moreover, since a tradition essentially involves an effort to know the human good, it requires distinctively intellectual virtues. One further virtue that MacIntyre emphasizes without giving it a name is "that of having an adequate sense of the traditions to which one belongs or which confront one" (AV, 223).

6. MacIntyre and Modernity

We have now seen the main elements of MacIntyre's sketch of "the rational case that can be made for a tradition in which the Aristotelian moral and political texts are canonical" (AV, 257). This is, however, a rather misleading way of formulating what his argument has achieved. For the most striking feature of MacIntyre's case is that the Aristotelianism it defends is much more a metaethics than a normative ethics. If successful, his argument shows that human ethical life is a matter of thinking and acting, in accord with appropriate virtues, within traditions dedicated to understanding and realizing the nature of the good for man. This result is Aristotelian in that it requires ethical thought and life to be centered on a conception of the general human good and in that it gives a major role to the virtues. But such a result is neutral among an entire range of ethical traditions and a corresponding range of particular conceptions of the human good. There has been no vindication or even discussion of the specific content of the sorts of normative ethical views typically defended by Aristotelians (e.g., Aristotelian views on just what it is to be a human being, what the precise nature of happiness is, which virtues – and how understood – are central to the moral life). At best, MacIntyre has shown that ethics requires *a* tradition, with *a* conception of the human good and of the virtues. He has offered no defense of the specifically Aristotelian views on the human good and the virtues. As far as his discussion goes, the Platonic, Stoic, Augustinian, civic humanist, or even liberal traditions might be preferable to the Aristotelian.

There is, moreover, reason to doubt that MacIntyre has fully established his Aristotelian metaview. The Aristotelian view is universalistic. It insists that ethical life and inquiry has the whole of a human life as its domain and is guided by a conception of the human good in general. But, given MacIntyre's starting point in specific practices, it is impossible for him to achieve such universalism. Consider first the transition from the goods of a variety of specific practices in which an individual is involved to a conception of the good for the individual's life as a whole. MacIntyre says that a move to such a conception is necessary to provide a basis for ordering the specific goods. But logically, all that is needed is a conception of the good sufficiently general to subsume and order just those particular goods that I have found to be in conflict. There is no need to seek anything so general as a good for my life as a whole. Indeed, as we have seen, an individual can belong to more than one tradition, a situation likely to be very common in our pluralistic modern world. It would seem impossible for such a person to have a meaningful ethical conception of "my life as a whole", since on MacIntyre's own account, as long as both traditions remained vital for an individual, there would be no way to unify their incommensurable goods and virtues. Nor is it clear that such a situation would have to involve net moral loss.

A similar point applies to MacIntyre's transition from the good for my life as a whole to the good for human beings in general. He presents the latter notion as what is common to the answers to *all* questions of the form "What is the good life for me?" (AV, 218). But the need for an individual to generalize from the question about his or her own good comes from the fact that, as MacIntyre puts it, "the story of my life is always embedded in the story of those communities from which I derive my identity" (AV, 221). But these communities are always made up of some specific subset of human beings; they do not compose the human race as a whole. Accordingly, my situation requires a generalization to what is common to the question "What is the good for me?" for only the members of the communities to which I belong. There is, then, no need to follow Aristotle in insisting on an entirely general conception of the human good. This would make sense only if MacIntyre had an ahistorical source for an understanding of human nature in general, as Aristotle thought he did in his metaphysical biology. MacIntyre's historicism gives him no such source, with the result that his ethical traditions can never reach anything more than a conception of what is good for the communities associated with them.

My conclusion, then, is that the ethical position MacIntyre defends in *After Virtue* is much less Aristotelian than he allows. It lacks the thick normative content as well as the universalism of the Aristotelian tradition. When we take account of these qualifications on MacIntyre's case for tradition, the notion becomes one more suited to enrich than to undermine pragmatic liberalism. Pragmatic liberals can, for example, appeal to tradition as the most plausible vehicle for the inculcation of the deep desires that constitute our fundamental epistemic and ethical orientations. They can also appropriate MacIntyre's arguments for the necessity of an ethical tradition, pointing out that his case merely establishes the need for some tradition and maintaining the preferability of liberalism over Aristotelianism. In this way, liberalism is enriched with a notion of tradition that makes no concessions to Burkean conservatism. On the contrary, as explicated by MacIntyre, tradition is precisely a source of anti-Burkean critical rationality. Thus, MacIntyre shows liberals how to incorporate a much needed historicist perspective without compromising their commitment to the autonomy of human reason.

The critical historicism that makes MacIntyre's account of tradition a resource for modern liberalism also creates a major tension in his conception of a tradition. The tension arises from his effort to combine a historicist understanding of tradition with an emphasis on its specific cultural location, particularly with regard to language and social practice. "Every tradition is embodied in some particular set of utterances and actions and thereby in all the particularities of some specific language and culture" (WJWR, 371). The high degree of particularity is apparent from, for example, MacIntyre's insistence that the "conception of language presupposed" by his account "is that of a language as it is used in and by a particular community living at a particular time and place with particular shared beliefs, institutions, and practices" (WJWR, 372–3). On this view, we should not speak of "Latin" or even "classical Latin" but rather of "Latin-as-written-and-spoken-in-the-Rome-of-Cicero" (WJWR, 373).

At the same time, MacIntyre's traditions are sweepingly historical, existing over centuries and requiring, at each point, a deep and lively sense of their past. In particular, such a sense is required for judgments of truth and justification. The first principles (both metaphysical and practical) of a tradition "are justified insofar as in the history of this tradition they have, by surviving the process of dialectical questioning, vindicated themselves as superior to their historical predecessors" (WJWR, 360).

This combination of locality and historicity is very unstable. Thomas Aquinas, for example, is supposed to be a member of the same tradition as Aristotle. How can this be, given that the two, separated by 1,500 years, shared almost nothing in the particularities of their lives? Even on the key point of language, Aquinas was quite ignorant of Greek, not to mention "Greek-as-it-was-written-and-spoken-in-the-Athens-of-Aristotle". MacIntyre ridicules "the confident teaching of texts from past and alien cultures in translation not only to students who do not know the original languages but by teachers who do not know them either" (WJWR, 328). But this was precisely the situation of Aquinas lecturing on the texts of Aristotle to his students at the University of Paris.

Even if we assume that Aquinas and Aristotle were somehow in the same tradition, what sort of justification of the tradition's first principles was available to Aquinas? Many readers of Aquinas have had the clear impression that he believed these to be grounded in self-evident insights available in principle to any rational being. MacIntyre denies this, maintaining that Aquinas, like any member of a tradition, saw the principles as vindicated by their success in a historical dialectic.[14] Even if we grant this assumption, Aquinas was not capable of more than a woefully inadequate historical justification of his first principles. Such a justification, recall, requires evidence that the principles have been shown to be superior to alternatives in the historical process of dialectical questioning. Aquinas, however, knew very little about this historical process. He had minimal access to the debates over Aristotle in the later Academy and other ancient schools, since the relevant texts

---

14   For an effective critique of MacIntyre's interpretation of Aquinas on self-evident principles, see Nicholas Wolterstorff, *John Locke and the Ethics of Belief*, Cambridge: Cambridge University Press, 1996, 225, n. 29.

were either permanently lost or not yet discovered. Even if he had had access to an adequate body of texts, he could not, on MacIntyre's account, have understood them properly, since he did not know Greek. How, then, could Aquinas have a solid basis for believing that Aristotle's first principles had withstood the dialectical assaults, over many centuries, of Platonists, Skeptics, Stoics, and Epicureans? Modern scholars, with far more textual and linguistic resources than Aquinas, are in no position to make such a judgment. On MacIntyre's account, Aquinas was surely not justified in accepting Aristotelianism.

If this is so for an intellectual of Aquinas's caliber, it is enormously more so for ordinary members of a tradition. They, of course, have essentially no access to their tradition in its historical sweep, only to its particular local manifestation. Medieval peasants may have been connected to the Greeks of Aristotle's time, to the early Christians, or to the Church of Augustine by complex causal links. But they were in no position to make any reliable judgments as to whether the beliefs and practices transmitted by those links represented the best that had been thought in the past or a sad distortion of the truth. For almost all members of any major tradition, the authority behind what they are taught does not lie in the great figures of the past but in the say-so of their local superiors. These superiors will, of course, claim to be presenting the truth as it has endured (or, as MacIntyre would have it, dialectically won out) over the centuries. But, once again, hardly anyone is in a position to make an informed judgment of the validity of this claim.

We might appeal to the authority of intellectuals who are in a position to appropriate a tradition's history in the way MacIntyre's view of rationality requires. But this would be to misunderstand the limits of both intellectuals' access to their history and their influence on society. Even the best trained and historically attuned intellectuals do not have sufficient access to the "historical dialectic" to ground more than speculations about its significance. Further, the most important figures are far more concerned with their own creative constructions than with a nuanced reading of the past. But even supposing that intellectuals were able to achieve the kind of understanding of their antecedents that MacIntyre's account of rationality in a tradition requires, there is no reason to think that most members of the tradition would absorb anything close to this understanding of it. They would receive the tradition from sources at best remotely and very partially influenced by the best thinkers of the tradition.

MacIntyre rightly disdains Burke's conception of tradition, which makes it a vehicle of unreflective emotional commitment rather than rational judgment. But his own effort to introduce rational judgment requires a breadth of historical awareness that is incompatible with what he rightly sees as the local situatedness of any tradition. Our locality means that we absorb a tradition as part of our immediate environment and have little sense of the complex historical process whereby what we absorb came to us. Lacking such sense, the history of our tradition, beyond our encounters with its immediate manifestations, is an opaque causal vehicle, not an intentional object of rational evaluation. MacIntyre speaks of the past of traditions being "encapsulated in the present and not always in fragmented or disguised form" (WJWR, 391). But he gives us no account that would make plausible how this could happen for traditions that span, over many centuries, diverse languages and forms of life.

The instability of MacIntyre's concept of tradition no doubt helps explain why this concept is deeply at odds with the very Aristotelian tradition for whose sake he invokes it. He himself has admitted (AV, 146) that Aristotle himself was no Aristotelian on this point, but who in the Aristotelian tradition was – until perhaps Newman, if he can be regarded as an Aristotelian? The Catholic Church – certainly the primary institutional vehicle of MacIntyre's Aristotelianism – has a strong commitment to tradition, but not with the historicist emphasis essential to MacIntyre's view. Catholic philosophers and theologians have typically presented their first principles as either self-evident or accepted on faith. They have not regarded them as vindicated by historical dialectic. And they have certainly not agreed that their Catholic tradition could "at some future time . . . fall into a state of epistemological crisis" from which it might not emerge intact (WJWR, 364).

In the face of such difficulties, the best way to salvage MacIntyre's very valuable notion of a tradition is to loosen the rigid locality that fits so ill with its essentially historicist nature. Such a move well comports with liberalism, which, as I have suggested, prefers an appreciation of more substantive traditions from a bit of a distance. Once we give up the idea that living reasonably requires the full constraint of living out a specific tradition in all its local particularity, we free ourselves to appreciate the intellectual and social resources offered by any of the traditions with which we are significantly involved. Once again, the pragmatic liberal is able to make better sense and use of tradition than is MacIntyre.[15]

The modernism latent in MacIntyre's position becomes most apparent when he tries to apply his concept of tradition to the modern situation. As

---

15   For an excellent discussion of how liberalism can appreciate – both morally and politically – the value of other traditions, see Charles Larmore, *The Morals of Modernity*, Cambridge: Cambridge University Press, 1996, especially chapters 2 and 6.

we have seen, he acknowledges the variety of conflicting traditions that confront members of modern society. Most of us naturally see ourselves as heirs to a variety of traditions, which inform our religious, ethical, political, and scientific practices. I may quite properly see myself as a complex combination of my mother's pacifism, my grandfather's Catholicism, my father's trade unionism, and my favorite university professor's liberalism. Although MacIntyre, as we have seen, acknowledges this plurality (cf. AV, 222), he also insists that rational inquiry is impossible outside some specific tradition. "There is no standing ground, no place for enquiry, no way to engage in the practices of . . . reasoned argument apart from that which is provided by some particular tradition or another" (WJWR, 350). Moreover, he holds that "genuinely to adopt the standpoint of a tradition thereby commits one to a view of what is true and false and, in so committing one, prohibits one from adopting any rival standpoint" (WJWR, 367).

Combining the preceding elements, we encounter a major tension in MacIntyre's position. According to him, a rational inquirer must belong to just one tradition. But most of us clearly belong to more than one and even – which MacIntyre says is impossible – to mutually inconsistent rivals. The tension becomes particularly intense in MacIntyre's explanation of how modern individuals might come to accept a given (premodern) tradition. He distinguishes three cases. The first is that of a person who, "upon encountering a coherent presentation of one particular tradition . . . experience[s] a shock of recognition". Such a person realizes that the tradition in question "is a scheme of overall belief within which many, if not all, of his or her particular established beliefs fall into place" (WJWR, 394). The second case is that of someone "who finds him- or herself an alien to every tradition . . . and does so because he or she brings to the encounter with such tradition standards of rational justification which the beliefs of no tradition could satisfy" (WJWR, 395). Such a person – who MacIntyre suggests may be only an ideal limit – can be brought into a tradition only by a nonrational conversion, for the person's unrooted situation allows inquiry to terminate only by "expressions of will and preference" (WJWR, 397).

The third and most typical modern case is that of individuals who belong to no particular tradition but "tend to live betwixt and between, accepting usually unquestioningly the assumptions of the dominant liberal individualist forms of public life, but drawing in different areas of their lives upon a variety of tradition-generated resources of thought and action" (WJWR, 397). According to MacIntyre, this sort of individual needs to "test dialectically the theses proposed to him or her by each competing tradition, while also drawing upon these same theses in order to test dialectically those convictions

and responses which he or she has brought to the encounter". The idea is
that such an individual has an incoherent set of beliefs (derived from conflicting traditions) and needs to determine in which tradition these inco-
herences will be best "characterized, explained, and transcended" (WJWR,
398).

These three possibilities sit very ill with MacIntyre's understanding of the
epistemic role of traditions. All of them require that, contrary to MacIntyre's
account, individuals exist as rational inquirers without a full commitment to
any tradition. In the first case, those who "recognize" their commitments in
a given tradition – for example, someone with an entirely secular upbringing who comes to see Catholicism as an appropriate home for his convictions – have obviously come to a coherent intellectual and practical position
without immersion in and formation by the tradition in question. (Otherwise, there would be no sense to the "shock of recognition".) They have been
engaged in rational inquiry without commitment to a specific tradition and
in fact judge the tradition acceptable by the standards of that inquiry.

The second case shows that, at least in principle, individuals can have a
commitment to standards of rationality without attachment to any tradition.
MacIntyre paints an epistemically horrifying picture of such people, claiming that they "can belong to no linguistic community" and that for them "no
set of beliefs proposed for acceptance is . . . justifiable" (WJWR, 395). But
all this really means is that, since they belong to no tradition, they have no
traditional "first-language" and accept no overall conception of the human
good. They do speak what MacIntyre calls "the internationalized languages
of modernity" (WJWR, 398), languages able to describe and evaluate from
the outside any tradition encountered; but, of course, such individuals have
no interest in knowing a tradition from the inside. They are also able to
make rational decisions about what MacIntyre calls "pragmatic necessities"
(WJWR, 397), which are, after all, the only issues they find meaningful. Mac-
Intyre's rhetoric may suggest that those who entirely lack a tradition fall into
some sort of skeptical incoherence, caught between the alternatives of inconsistency or avoidance of all thought and speech. But in fact they merely
lack traditional modes of thought, speech, and action – modes *their* rational
standards judge to be groundless and arbitrary.

The third case seems to correspond to the situation of those who find
themselves within the modern liberal tradition. MacIntyre places such people in an intermediate space "betwixt and between" all traditions. But they
accept "the assumptions of the dominant liberal individualist forms of life"
and, in good liberal fashion, lead private lives based on views drawn from a
variety of traditions. Given that MacIntyre allows the existence of a liberal

tradition, it is hard to see how such people would not belong to it. If so, there is no reason that they should, as MacIntyre suggests, seek out a further tradition that will give coherence to the diversity of their private beliefs. There is no formal or practical inconsistency in acting for quite different goods as long as each good corresponds to a separate aspect of my life. I may, however, have an interest in overall coherence, and then it might make sense to seek this from some available tradition. (Alternatively, it might make more sense to construct my own distinctive conception of an overall good.) But my acceptance of a tradition would have derived from a judgment based on my own liberal standards of rationality and would at best result in my integrating the relevant tradition into my overall liberal commitment. This is what liberals typically do with religious, ethical, and many other beliefs of theirs that go beyond their public commitment to the liberal tradition. MacIntyre offers no reason for thinking that this is incoherent or otherwise inappropriate.

We see then that MacIntyre's own application of his concept of tradition to the modern world implicitly takes back his strong claims about the impossibility of rational thought and coherent ethical action outside of the traditions that the modern world rejects. On his own account, modern individuals do think and act apart from these traditions, either within the liberal tradition alone or even without a full commitment to any single tradition. In describing the modern situation, MacIntyre himself implicitly adopts the liberal view of individuals who, employing their own criteria of rationality, confront and evaluate the substantive concepts of the good put forward by premodern traditions. This is just what liberalism has in mind when it celebrates human autonomy.

Modern individuals need not, as we have seen, be understood as isolated atoms. Their criteria of theoretical and practical rationality may well – no doubt do – derive from social practices that have formed them from birth. But these practices have not made them part of a (premodern) tradition in MacIntyre's sense, for they have not committed them to a substantive conception of the general human good. Modern individuals are free to adopt one of these conceptions, the thinner liberal conception, or none at all. It is clear that MacIntyre is not happy with this situation. But he has not shown that the modern situation is epistemically or morally untenable .

The root problem with MacIntyre's conception of tradition is that, although it is intended as the vehicle of his rejection of modernity, it is itself in many ways a modern notion. The modernity is most apparent in its strong historicity. As we have seen, MacIntyre's effort to combine this strong historicity with strong locality destabilizes his concept of tradition and makes it inapplicable to his own paradigm case of Aristotelianism. Moreover, applying his concept of tradition to the modern world involves MacIntyre in an implicit acceptance of the modern concept of the individual as nonatomistic but autonomous, that is, as deeply formed by social forces but not thereby committed to a substantive conception of the human good. This is why, as I have argued, pragmatic liberalism is able to endorse the viable core of MacIntyre's account of tradition.

This endorsement requires, first, that pragmatic liberalism recognize itself as a tradition, distinguished, however, from most others by its lack of a full-blown conception of the common good. This reflects merely the core liberal conviction that our shared (public in the widest sense) commitment can be to no more than the human freedom of self-creation and to the procedural requirements for allowing everyone as much freedom as possible without interfering with the freedom of others. But adopting MacIntyre's view also requires pragmatic liberals to recognize – as liberals often have not – that the private sphere of self-creation should not be understood as merely a domain of unconstrained choices by isolated individuals. Self-creation is not typically ex nihilo; it is rather a project within a given tradition in which individuals find and develop their identities.

Liberal society is populated by a variety of subtraditions – sometimes overlapping, sometimes contending, sometimes mutually irrelevant – in which its members seek their fulfillment. Moreover, different members of liberal society will have different attitudes toward the dominating liberal tradition itself. There are those who fully accept the tradition in the sense of subordinating their commitment to any other traditions to fundamental liberal values. This will often require significant transformations in the meaning of traditional views and in the manner of commitment to them. (The vicissitudes of liberal religious belief provide a good example of the complexities that arise.) But there are also those whose overriding commitment is to one or another subtradition (say, a religion or a traditional ethnic form of life). Such people may accept the liberal tradition only as a necessary modus vivendi, as a way of living with others with whom they deeply disagree.[16] In one way or another, however, all members of a liberal society accept in some way the dominant liberal tradition.

Pragmatic liberalism need not, then, reject MacIntyre's notion of tradi-

---

16   In some cases, of course, a subtradition may significantly overlap with the liberal tradition, which itself has arisen from elements of, for example, Christian religious traditions. In other cases, the mere willingness of members of a subtradition to live with those who disagree with them represents a significant transformation of the subtradition.

tion. It can use it to explicate, while avoiding naive decisionism and atomistic individualism, the ways individuals relate to both liberalism itself and to the diverse modes of self-creation for which liberalism wants to make room. But even if pragmatic liberalism in this way can become stronger by coming to terms with MacIntyre's challenge, it will not yet have met MacIntyre's claim, to which we now turn, that he can establish the superiority of his Aristotelian tradition to alternatives such as pragmatic liberalism.

7. MacIntyre versus Pragmatic Liberalism

MacIntyre's account of the clash of traditions is broadly Kuhnian.[17] Like Kuhn, he regards rival traditions as incommensurable, where this means that there are no neutral criteria to appeal to in deciding between them. Also like Kuhn, he speaks of epistemological "crises", which occur within a tradition when, by its own standards, its intellectual goals are not being achieved.[18] However, regarding two key points on which many readers have found Kuhn ambivalent, MacIntyre is unequivocal: rival traditions are logically inconsistent with one another, and it is possible to establish rationally that one tradition is preferable to another.

The latter point is, of course, the crucial one, since many have argued that there can be no rational decision between incommensurable alternatives. This follows, however, only on the assumption that rationality requires neutral decision criteria. MacIntyre rejects this assumption, arguing, first, that a tradition can be shown to be inadequate by its own standards. Once this is established, it is possible to show that a rival tradition both succeeds where the defeated tradition failed and explains precisely how and why the failure occurred. Given this (and no offsetting inferiority of the rival tradition), it is clearly rational to prefer the rival tradition.

MacIntyre has never explicitly made the case for his Aristotelian tradition against a pragmatic liberalism developed in the spirit of Rorty's work. His argument is directed, on the one hand, against the modern rationalism of the philosophical Enlightenment from Kant through Sidgwick (the tradition he calls "Encyclopedia") and, on the other hand, against the postmodern

---

17 There are ways in which MacIntyre's account is even closer to Imre Lakatos' "methodology of scientific research programmes", particularly in its emphasis on competition between rival approaches. But MacIntyre typically develops his view in Kuhnian terminology.

18 See MacIntyre's "Epistemological Crises, Dramatic Narrative, and the Philosophy of Science", *The Monist* 60 (1977), 453–71, reprinted in Gary Gutting (ed.), *Paradigms and Revolutions: Appraisals and Applications of Thomas Kuhn's Philosophy of Science*, Notre Dame, IN: University of Notre Dame Press, 1980, 54–74.

antirationalism of Nietzsche and Foucault (the tradition he calls "geneal-ogy"). Although pragmatic liberals set themselves apart from both of these traditions, their position overlaps with that of the genealogists at the focal point of MacIntyre's attack: the conception of self-identity required for a meaningful human life. MacIntyre's core claim is that genealogy's concep-tion of the self is inadequate to make sense of the very project of genealogy: "Make of the genealogist's self nothing but what genealogy makes of it, and that self is dissolved to the point at which there is no longer a continuous genealogical project" (TRV, 54). Understanding this critique requires un-derstanding what MacIntyre thinks genealogy "makes of the self", that is, its concept of personal identity, and what he means by the "genealogical project".

The genealogical view of personal identity is best understood by contrast to a standard conception, asserted by Aristotelianism but also implicit (even if not philosophically explicit) in many human societies – "perhaps in all traditional societies" (e.g., American Indian, Celtic, African) and "in urban political societies with a shared religion" (e.g., the Greek *polis*, the Islamic caliphates, the Mayan empire) (TRV, 198). On this standard conception, personal identity has "three central dimensions". The first is bodily identity: "I am and do not merely have a body" (TRV, 196). The second is the "con-tinuing accountability" of an agent: "being continuously liable to account for my actions, attitudes, and beliefs to others within my communities". The third is unity of life as a quest, where the quest is "to discover that truth about my life as a whole which is an indispensable part of the good of that life" (TRV, 197).

To say that I am a self in this sense is to say that I make "the nature of my life and the good of that life the objects of my enquiry". But such an inquiry presupposes that there is a truth about my life for me to discover, "a truth beyond and ordering all particular truths" (TRV, 200) by which my life as a whole can be judged. Truth in this sense cannot be merely the "truth-from-a-perspective", the truth of how things might appear from some position within my life. What is at stake is the truth about my life as a whole, and this must be a truth independent of any perspective I may happen to occupy; in-dependent, in particular, of the ethical perspective defined by my contin-gent beliefs and desires. Pragmatic liberals agree with Nietzsche and Fou-cault that there is no such truth about my life.

It follows that pragmatic liberals, according to MacIntyre, are not entitled to the standard conception of self-identity. They, of course, will not resist this conclusion, since they explicitly reject the idea of a substantial self that defines a moral center deeper than my beliefs and desires. But MacIntyre would ask pragmatic liberals (as he asks Nietzsche and Foucault) whether their moral project does not require the standard conception of self-identity.

Pragmatic liberals acknowledge that I may play any number of roles (child, parent; conformist, rebel; believer, skeptic) in the course of my life. Which roles dominate at a given time depend on what sort of self I am trying to create, but no role ever has the absolute significance of what I really am. MacIntyre, however, insists on raising the question of the status of the key project of pragmatic liberalism, the project of free creation of myself. Surely, he says, this very project requires the sense that I am a substantial self committed to living as a pragmatic liberal; that, for example, I credit myself with the achievement of freely creating my self and not succumbing to the bad faith of accepting some externally defined identity.

There is no doubt that pragmatic liberals, like everyone else, think of themselves as enduring persons, responsible for their pasts, planning for their futures; they treat their lives as wholes. But how does this convict them of self-contradiction? Here we need to distinguish two sorts of criticism, which MacIntyre does not clearly discriminate. Although pragmatic liberals hold views about the self that are in some sense skeptical, it is crucial to be clear about the precise sense of this skepticism. Skepticism can take the radical form of questioning beliefs so fundamental to human life that there is no way to live without implicitly accepting them. The radical skeptic questions such things as whether the past is a guide to the future, whether any objects exist outside the mind, and whether persons have some sort of enduring identity. We might call such beliefs "Humean" because Hume emphasized both the impossibility of grounding them rationally and the impossibility of giving them up. As Hume noted, radical skeptics fall into at least pragmatic contradiction anytime they leave the rarefied atmosphere of philosophical speculation and take part in the human world. But pragmatic liberals should not be read as skeptics of this sort. They question not inevitable commonsense truths but philosophical theories posited to explain (or explain away) such truths. They are, we might say, not radical but theoretical skeptics, questioning not common sense but philosophical theories.

This clarification does not refute MacIntyre's criticism, but it does show just how it needs to be formulated. The point must be not that pragmatic liberals deny Humean truths about personal identity, but that they implicitly accept philosophical views about personal identity that they explicitly deny. Is this a plausible claim?

In terms of MacIntyre's critique, the implicit assertion would have to be rooted in the fact that pragmatic liberals have a sense of their lives as wholes, seeing them as defined by their projects of self-creation in a liberal society. Now merely seeing my life as a whole is simply admitting what no one can deny: that I am in some sense a continuously existing entity, with memories of a past and expectations of a future. Beyond this banal truth, the substantive philosophical (specifically, ethical) issue is whether this continuity is due to my having a nature in virtue of which I have duties and obligations independent of my beliefs and desires. Is there, in other words, any moral authority, outside of myself, to which I must defer?[19] This is the question that pragmatic liberals answer in the negative. The validity of MacIntyre's challenge turns on whether their liberal project itself is inconsistent with this answer.

How, then, might the claim that there is no moral authority to which I must answer outside myself be inconsistent with a life project? The idea, no doubt, is that a project involves a goal against which the success or failure of my life must be measured. What happens to me and what I do will be good or bad, depending how it relates to the goal. In the pragmatic liberal's case, for example, to be taken in by claims of absolute philosophical truth is bad and to break free of such claims is good. But, MacIntyre will argue, such a standard of good and evil is independent of what I desire. For I may desire to believe absolute claims. In that case, the pragmatic liberal must insist that such a desire is wrong; I ought not to have it. But then we are obviously dealing with an obligation (and a good, from which the obligation derives) independent of the desires it regulates. A good that can contradict what I desire cannot itself be a function of what I desire.

The preceding argument does show that a standard of achievement, a good in terms of which my desires can be evaluated, must exist independently of the desires for which it is a standard. But, as we saw in our discussion of Rorty's ethical naturalism (Part I, Section 7), one desire (or set of them) can provide the standard for other desires. There are, that is, certain relatively enduring, fundamental desires against which less fundamental desires – from passing whims to longer-termed lapses – can be evaluated. The pragmatic liberal position remains coherent as long as it admits a hierarchy of desires that allows us to evaluate what we desire now (or for some restricted period) on the basis of what we desire in a more enduring way. In this way, pragmatic liberalism can avoid the internal contradiction MacIntyre thinks undermines it.

---

19 Here it is important to keep in mind that the pragmatic liberal self referred to here is not the atomistic self of philosophical modernity but a being constituted by strongly social desires.

Even if he could successfully show that a given rival tradition is inadequate in its own terms and that Aritotelianism overcomes and explains these inadequacies, MacIntyre would still face what we can call the "problem of the counterattack". It might be that Aristotelianism too is inadequate in its own terms and that the rival tradition overcomes and explains *its* inadequacies. How, for example, does MacIntyre's Aristotelianism meet the challenge of modern science to the hylomorphism that seems essential to it? How does it respond to the charge that its theological dogmatism (the "finality of Scripture and dogmatic tradition" that MacIntyre acknowledges, TRV, 125) is untenable in a world of religious pluralism? Even if they faced no other problems, MacIntyre's arguments would have to be supplemented by answers to such questions. He acknowledges this need (TRV, 181) but does little or nothing to suggest how to satisfy it.

In a similar vein, there is a serious question as to whether MacIntyre's approach to the rational evaluation of rival traditions is consistent with his own tradition. He claims his conception of rational superiority is "implicit and sometimes explicit in the Aristotelian–Thomistic tradition" (TRV, 180), that, in particular, this tradition insists on "identifying and characterizing the limitations of [a] rival tradition as judged by that rival tradition's own standards" (TRV, 181). But this seems directly contrary to Aquinas's understanding of his own practice in the *Summa contra Gentiles,* his major effort to refute nonbelievers. At the beginning of that work (I, 2, 3) he comments on the difficulty he faces in trying to refute erroneous views, noting, first of all, that "the sacrilegious remarks of individual men who have erred are not so well known to us so that we may use what they say as the basis of proceeding to a refutation of their errors". He contrasts his situation to that of "the ancient Doctors of the Church", who had either themselves been "Gentiles" (pagans) or at least had "lived among [them] and had been instructed in their teaching". He further notes that, while we can refute heretics by arguments based on the New Testament and Jews by arguments based on the Old Testament (since they share our acceptance of these authorities), the refutation of Mohammedans and pagans is more difficult. Since they accept none of our Scriptures, "we must have recourse to the natural reason, to which all men are forced to give their assent".

Here Aquinas clearly rejects MacIntyre's claim that successful refutation of a rival view must be based on internal considerations and goes on to assert the universal authority of natural reason. Presumably, MacIntyre would argue for a revision of this view as an appropriate development within his own tradition. But it is not at all clear how such an argument would be consistent with the Aristotelian doctrine of a shared human nature, which is surely essential to MacIntyre's ethical position. It is worth noting, moreover, that MacIntyre does not allow for a parallel line of development within Enlightenment thought. Deriding the contributors to the ninth edition of the *Encyclopedia Britannica* – for MacIntyre, a quintessentially Enlightenment enterprise – because "it never even occurred [to them] to enter imaginatively into the standpoint of those allegedly primitive and savage people they were studying" (TRV, 182), he gives no credit to later developments within the Enlightenment that led to less ethnocentric attitudes.

For all its power and perceptiveness, MacIntyre's traditionalism does not support a successful challenge to pragmatic liberal morality. His efforts to show that such a morality is incoherent or leads to interminable ethical disagreement fail, as does the argument for the superiority of Aristotelianism to pragmatic liberalism. There are, moreover, serious questions about the internal coherence of MacIntyre's own effort to oppose tradition to modern liberalism. As we have seen, this incoherence arises because MacIntyre's call for a return to tradition is in fact based on modern presuppositions of historicity and individual autonomy.

But pragmatic liberalism has much to learn from MacIntyre. He provides it with an anti-Burkean account of tradition that is not available from standard liberal sources. This allows a positive understanding of human community that rejects decisionism and atomistic individualism and accepts the historicity of reason, all without compromising a fundamental liberal commitment. MacIntyre's powerful reflections on tradition and modernity provide essential resources for a viable pragmatic liberalism.

PART III

CHARLES TAYLOR

AN AUGUSTINIAN MODERN

Alasdair MacIntyre regards our contemporary situation as one of interminable disagreement about moral values, a disagreement that derives from the ethical inadequacy of the modern conception of the self. Charles Taylor, by contrast, thinks there is considerable agreement about moral values but considerable confusion and disagreement about the sources of these values, where "sources" are whatever it is that accounts for the unquestionable hold morality has on us. Further, although he agrees with MacIntyre that the moral sources tapped by the Enlightenment project of modern philosophy are ultimately inadequate, he has a far more favorable view than MacIntyre of their richness, power, and even inevitability.

My focus will be primarily on Taylor's *Sources of the Self*.[1] Critical reflection on its *Geistesgeschichte* of modern thought will reveal pragmatic liberalism's seventeenth- and eighteenth-century roots. Taylor will also help us deepen pragmatic liberalism's view of the self with the resources of nineteenth-century romantic naturalism and twentieth-century literary modernism. But

---

1 *Sources of the Self* will be my focal point because it parallels *Philosophy and the Mirror of Nature* and *After Virtue* by developing Taylor's position through a *Geistegeschichte* of modern philosophy. This position is consistent with that developed less historically in his *Philosophical Papers* (Volumes 1 and 2, Cambridge: Cambridge University Press, 1985), although there are different emphases. For reactions to *Sources of the Self* by Rorty and MacIntyre, along with Taylor's response, see the symposium on the book in *Philosophy and Phenomenological Research* 54 (1994).

the book also poses a major challenge to ethical naturalism by its strong argument against any account that does not find sources of morality beyond human beliefs and desires. Reflection on Taylor will lead pragmatic liberalism to a much more nuanced view of ethical objectivity.

Sections 1 through 3 offer an analysis and critique of Taylor's history of Enlightenment thought, and Section 4 continues the discussion into the Romantic reaction to the Enlightenment. Throughout, I not only criticize Taylor's perceptive analyses but also use them to improve the pragmatic liberalism I have developed in Parts I and II. Finally, in Sections 5 and 6, I defend a version of ethical naturalism against Taylor's criticisms.

1. Taylor's Historical Project

Unlike MacIntyre but like Rorty, Taylor is willing to begin from "the moral imperatives which are felt with particular force in modern culture" (SS, 495). These imperatives follow from the central modern values of "freedom, benevolence, and the affirmation of ordinary life". From these values derive the characteristically liberal moral concerns that most of us share: "we . . . feel particularly strongly the demand for universal justice and beneficence, are peculiarly sensitive to the claims of equality, feel the demands to freedom and self-rule as axiomatically justified, and put a very high priority on the avoidance of death and suffering" (SS, 295). Taylor's question is about the sources of these shared values, in the sense of both their historical origin and their philosophical basis.

The largest division of Taylor's history is that between an ancient/medieval period in which the sources of morality flow from the cosmic order external to the self and a modern period in which these sources flow from this very self. But there is also a fundamental division within the modern development. First, the idea of the self as source of morality is successively radicalized, until it reaches the extreme of the totally autonomous atom of the radical Enlightenment. Then, particularly via the Romantic reaction, the self is enriched through a relation to nature that provides it with a specifically modern depth and complexity.

The baseline for Taylor's story is Plato's morality of the mastery of reason. It is all too easy to read Plato in a misleadingly modern way. When he says that the good person is one in whom reason rules, we tend to think he means that morality is a matter of making decisions on the basis of the best evidence and arguments available and sticking to them, regardless of our feelings or desires. Depending on our conclusions about what sorts of decisions are rational, such a view could be either utilitarian or Kantian – in any case, it would be distinctively modern. But, Taylor points out, this distorts Plato's view, since for him rationality requires less adherence to procedural rules of evidence and argument than attainment of a correct vision of moral truth. Moreover, this moral truth, in sharp contrast to modern conceptions, is not separable from cosmic truth. The moral order is included in the order of the world as a whole, and knowledge of the Forms comprises simultaneously an understanding of both metaphysical and ethical truth. The Delphic injunction, "gnōthi seauton", does not tell us to explore the inner depths of our personalities but rather to locate human nature in the grand cosmic scheme.

The move to modernity is a move away from morality nourished by such external sources as Plato's Forms to morality nourished by the inner resources of the self. A crucial first step is Augustine's development of a Christian interiority. He makes what becomes the standard Christian identification of the Forms with the divine Ideas that are the archetypes of all creation. This is not, however, the mere transfer of cosmic order from one external location to another. A personal God, whose love of the self has both created it from nothing and redeemed it from sin, has an intimacy with the self far beyond even Plato's erotic union of the soul with the Forms. This intimacy is such that our only access to divine truth is through the inwardness of the self: "Noli foras ire, in teipsum redi; in interiore homine habitat veritas" (*De vera religione*, XXXIX, 72; cited, SS, 129). Augustine's synthesis of Christian theology and Platonic philosophy gives the inner world of the self a role quite foreign to the ancient world.

This is not, of course, to say that the ancients were incapable of reflecting on the self. There was a long tradition among ancient moralists, recently highlighted by Michel Foucault and by Pierre Hadot, of the "care of self", a project that involved close awareness of the self as the proper object of moral concern, as opposed to other possible objects such as power or wealth. But this ancient concern is still with the self as a third-person object, even if one with a privileged position in the moral world. The concern is reflexive because the self for which I care is *my* self. But the concern does not see the self as an object that can be properly understood only as the distinctive subject of my unique experiences (i.e., from a first-person standpoint). An outsider (e.g., a spiritual guide or advisor) may lack no knowledge relevant to the self's care. This is not so for Augustine, for whom the self can be understood only from my own unique first-person standpoint, the standpoint of what Taylor calls "radical reflection". Self-knowledge in this radical sense requires the new genre of spiritual autobiography, of which Augustine's *Confessions* is the paradigm.

Modernity begins with Descartes's mutation of Augustinianism. Taylor emphasizes that "Descartes is in many ways profoundly Augustinian" (SS, 143), particularly in his emphasis on radical reflexivity, apparent in the fundamental place he gives the cogito and in the move to God from his idea of God. But Descartes's Augustinianism had to incorporate the new vision of nature provided by modern science. This vision rejected the teleological view of nature and saw the material world as a purely mechanistic system. The result was a dissolution of the Platonic and Augustinian connection between cosmic and moral order. The natural world was no longer a moral source. But precisely to the extent that the world ceases to be a moral source, the self becomes one.

This transition derives from the new representationalist epistemology that Descartes sees as required by modern science. For the ancients and medievals, knowledge resulted from the mind's union with the forms that provided the structure and intelligibility of the world. Rejecting any such forms, modern science reconceived knowledge as a matter of the mind's determining that certain representations accurately corresponded to a world that remained in principle external to it. The function of reason (the means by which we attain knowledge) was no longer the ultimately passive acceptance of a verific union but the active construction and verification of representations. This meant that rationality could now be understood in a purely procedural way, that is, as the proper following of the rules of evidence and argument.

Descartes, of course, maintained that following such procedures would lead to knowledge of reality. But, in contrast to the Platonic–Augustinian view, there was now a conceptual space between ideal rationality and truth. For Augustine, the progression of reason is a series of increasingly full sightings of Truth, from glimpses of it in the material world, through a sharper sense of it in our own souls, to a full vision in God. To be fully rational is simply to know the Truth. For Descartes, the progress of reason is a matter of constructing arguments from which we infer the truth. Even in the ideal limit, what we have is a maximally clear and distinct perception of our ideas, from which we infer their truth, not a direct vision of their truth.[2] Rationality no longer *means* seeing the truth. Rather, it means judging evidence and arguments according to the appropriate formal canons, a process that, if carried out properly, should result in knowledge of the truth.

The epistemic fulfillment of reason, accordingly, is no longer a transforming experience of external reality but a successful construction of a correct representation of that reality. Given the new procedural conception of

---

2   Thus Descartes's need to vindicate even truths evident by "the natural light of reason" by an appeal to the divine guarantee.

reason, the same holds for the ethical realm. Although, as commentators often note, Descartes' ethics is similar to that of the Stoics, there is a fundamental difference. For the Stoics, "the hegemony of reason was that of a certain vision of the world, in which everything which happens comes from the providence of God. . . . For Descartes, the hegemony means what it naturally tends to mean to us today, that reason controls, in the sense that it instrumentalizes the desires" (SS, 147). Just as reason employs our perceptions to achieve its goal of truth, so it employs our desires to achieve its goal of happiness. In both cases, this new role for reason arises because there is no longer a directly available source of the true and of the good. The self, through its procedures of rational control, necessarily becomes the proximate source of truth and goodness.

Of course, as in Augustine, God and not the self remains the ultimate source of truth and goodness. The difference is that now the activity of the self has become essential for us to reach the divine source, which indeed remains known only indirectly, via representation. In a fundamental sense, this should not matter. After all, Descartes winds up affirming the same basic set of religious and ethical truths as Augustine. But, although Taylor does not emphasize the point, Descartes's modification of Augustinianism to accommodate the new science makes the position vulnerable in new ways. Now our rational access to the divine source requires the autonomous internal activity of the self, not merely the self's proper orientation to what is outside of it. Suppose it turns out to be impossible for the self to carry out the Cartesian project; suppose, for example, that criteria for clear and distinct perceptions are not forthcoming or that there is no sound argument for God's existence. For Augustine, since God is at every point directly involved in the life of the self, such failure can be due only to the perversity of a self that will not see what is overwhelmingly there. For Cartesianism, however, there is at least the possibility that the project fails because there is nothing for it to discover. Atheism has become an intellectual possibility.[3] Descartes himself, as the Letter of Dedication prefaced to the *Meditations* shows, regards faith as a safety net against such failure: "It is of course quite true that we must believe in the existence of God because it is a doctrine of Holy Scriptures".[4] But, once faith becomes detached from the best results of rational inquiry, its authority is much more open to challenge.

---

3 See the classic discussion of Lucien Febvre, *The Problem of Unbelief in the Sixteenth Century: the Religion of Rabelais,* tr. Beatrice Gottlieb, Cambridge, MA: Harvard University Press, 1982 (original French publication, 1942).

4 *The Philosophical Writings of Descartes,* tr. J. Cottingham, R. Stoothoff, and D. Murdoch, Cambridge: Cambridge University Press, 1984, Volume 2, 3.

But just how did modern thought move from Descartes's Augustinian accommodation with modern science to a full-scale rejection of any religious vision? The bulk of Taylor's historical analysis is an effort to track two different paths in this direction. One goes through Locke to the utilitarianism of what Taylor calls the "radical Enlightenment". This leads to the total contraction of the self into the ahistorical atom MacIntyre regards as typical of modernity. The other path is in quite another direction, moving from early Protestant "affirmations of everyday life", through Rousseau, to the Romantics. This leads to an expanded self, with inner depths nourished not by God but by nature. Corresponding to these two paths are the two major modern alternatives to God as the ultimate moral source: the autonomous individual and the expressive self.

Taylor himself in the end suggests that modernity needs to find God as its moral source ("great as the power of modern naturalist sources might be, the potential of certain theistic perspectives is incomparably greater", SS, 518). But *Sources of the Self* is not designed to make the moral case for theism. Taylor is Augustinian in his emphasis on inwardness and in his hope that God can be seen as our ultimate moral source, but he admits that he is not ready to offer a philosophical articulation and defense of this hope (SS, 517–18). His main claims are that conceptions of ourselves as autonomous individuals cannot sustain moral life and that even the richer expressive self of modern romanticism is morally inadequate without a relation to objective values independent of even its deepest beliefs and desires.

2. Locke and the Radical Enlightenment

As Taylor sees it, Descartes's legacy as the father of modern philosophy is the focus on the self, understood as the agent of the project of procedural rationality. This project is a consequence of the scientific revolution, which discredited the ancient idea that reality could be grasped directly by a properly disposed mind. Reality, it turned out, was of difficult and only indirect access. The self has to start from its own ideas (representations) and then, by a rigorous process of methodological evaluation, determine the truth. According to Taylor, this process is simultaneously one of disengagement and objectification. We have to withdraw from every alleged source of epistemic authority and put it under critical scrutiny. This obviously applies to purely external claimants to authority such as Aristotle's philosophy or the pope's dogmas. But it also applies to allegedly internal authorities, such as the innate ideas that Descartes thought conveyed self-evident truths. Locke saw no reason to trust these "intellectual instincts" as infallible indicators of truth.

So even the self, regarded as a bearer of substantive truth, has to be an object of our disengaged scrutiny. This, Taylor says, leads to Locke's central conception of the "punctual self", which is the self withdrawn from every substantive assumption, the purely formal locus of inquiry that rigorously excludes any unexamined cognitive content, the intellectual equivalent of a point. This point consists simply of a consciousness scrutinizing its experience.[5]

Locke's approach can also be understood as the outcome of his comprehensively antiteleological view. Just as the new science had excluded final causes from the operations of material bodies, so Locke refused to acknowledge any innate tendencies of the mind toward truth. This meant that no cognitive inclination of ours (an innate idea, intellectual intuition, self-evident truth) could be taken at face value. What authority it might have could derive only from the disengaged investigations of purely procedural reason.

Reason must, then, begin by clearing the cognitive ground of everything that might lead us away from truth. This had been, of course, a common philosophical intent from Plato through Descartes. But, according to Taylor, Locke is distinctive in the extent of the disengagement he undertakes. Not only do we undermine all external authorities, "The demolition is not stopped in principle by our placing trust in any of the prereflective activities of the mind" (SS, 166). What then keeps Locke from a total, self-annihilating skepticism? Only the fact that eventually we reach "the particulate ideas of experience, sensation, and reflection [which] are to be taken as rock bottom, because they aren't the product of activity at all" (SS, 166). We accept these ideas as our starting point simply because we have no alternative. As Locke himself says, "In this part the understanding is merely passive; and whether or no it will have these beginnings, and as it were materials of knowledge, is not in its own power" (*Essay*, 2.1.25, cited, SS, 166). To these foundational ideas reason applies the procedural rules (e.g., of logical deduction and probable evidence) that allow us to construct the truth about the world and ourselves. In this way, "we wrest the control of our thinking and outlook away from passion or custom or authority and assume responsibility for it ourselves" (SS, 167).

---

5 For a vigorous critique of Taylor's interpretation of Locke, see Nicholas Wolterstorff, *John Locke and the Ethics of Belief*, Cambridge: Cambridge University Press, 1996, 233–44. Wolterstorff maintains that Locke is committed neither to a purely procedural concept of reason nor to the punctual construal of the self. He suggests that Taylor reads back into the beginnings of modern philosophy themes that in fact emerge only much later, perhaps with Hegel. In a similar vein, I suggest later that Locke's "affirmation of ordinary life" is not consistent with the radical project of disengagement Taylor attributes to him.

In the domain of ethics, the equivalents of foundational simple ideas are our basic aversion to pain and our desire for pleasure. Many of us, of course, are committed to "higher" ideals of good such as benevolence, but our inclination to these may well be imposed by external authorities. The only utterly unavoidable moral orientation is that of hedonism. This, accordingly, is where Locke's ethics begins.

In Locke, then, Taylor finds a philosophy beginning quite radically from an entirely disengaged, autonomous self. He thinks Locke sees such a view of the self as the only alternative if we want to take with full seriousness and consistency the antiteleological viewpoint of the new science. However, like Descartes, Locke maintains that this rigorously scientific starting point does not cut us off from the moral sources of Christianity. Properly followed, the rules of procedural rationality will, he maintains, lead us from the ideas and desires of the punctual self to the essentials of religion and morality.

Eventually, the primary heirs of Locke's project were the philosophers of the radical Enlightenment. They sharply separated, in a way quite foreign to both Locke and his medieval predecessors, the religious from the ethical aspects of Locke's project. They concluded that the religious claims were incapable of rational support and argued for their abandonment. But they acknowledged the necessity of avoiding ethical skepticism and offered derivations of (generally utilitarian) moral principles from Lockean premises. The radical Enlightenment has pretty much won the day regarding the impossibility of deriving religion from the punctual self. There are very few, whether believers or nonbelievers, who think such an enterprise has prospects of success. By contrast, the ethical project of deriving a morality from the punctual self, though not quite dead, has surely fallen on hard times. But the strongest contemporary criticisms of Locke's legacy attack not specific efforts to carry out the program but the very program itself. In particular, they reject the necessity (or even the coherence) of beginning with the punctual self and deriving all relevant truth by the canons of procedural rationality. Given this rejection, our discussion turns to the significance of the Lockean failure. Does it, as MacIntyre claims, show the need to return to premodern ways of thought; or, as Rorty maintains, the foolishness of continuing the search for deep philosophical truth; or, as Taylor will suggest, the need to philosophize from an enriched understanding of the modern self and its moral sources?

But before we move on to assess the consequences of Locke's failure, it is worthwhile to think a bit harder about the motives for Locke's enterprise and the strength of the claim that it had to fail. Taylor sketches two lines of criticism that seem to catch the crucial points. With regard to motivation, he argues that "the option for an epistemology which privileges disengagement and control isn't self-evidently right" (SS, 164), since it is itself based on assumptions that can readily be questioned. With regard to the inevitable failure of Locke's project, he notes the extreme tension it creates by asserting a "radical objectivity [that] is only intelligible and accessible through radical subjectivity" (SS, 176).

There is no doubt that the triumph of the new science was the primary intellectual motive for Locke's view of the self. It is easy to see this view as simply an unjustified extrapolation. Even granted that the external material world has been revealed as nothing but a mechanistic system, devoid of intrinsic natures and purposes, it surely does not follow that the same is true for the inner world of the self. As Taylor puts it, "the move to self-objectification requires more than a belief in mechanistic physics". Leibniz and the Cambridge Platonists accepted a mechanistic view of nature "while trying to retain or rebuild a teleological view of the subject". Locke's "disengagement from self involved a rejection of all such attempts". But what could justify this "radical rejection of teleology, of definitions of the human subject in terms of some inherent bent to the truth or to the good" (SS, 164)?

Taylor, of course, is not suggesting a dualism that would reduce the world to a mechanistic system, exhaustively knowable by the new scientific method of disengagement, and leave the self to be known by the nonempirical methods of, say, philosophy. His point is rather that, for all the power of disengagement, there are limits to what it can reveal about both the world and the self and that, when proposed as the sole means of knowing, it collapses into incoherence under the burden.

On the other hand, we should not assume, as Taylor seems to, that anywhere disengagement fails, engagement will succeed. That would be a plausible suggestion if the failure of the old science had been only metaphysical, if all that Galileo and Newton had called into question had been a certain picture of the material world. But the scientific revolution was methodological and epistemological as much as it was metaphysical. The ontology of forms was correlated with a view of knowledge as a matter of, in Taylor's words, "engaging more fully with this order [of forms], turning the eye of the soul towards it. . . . The picture of our attaining knowledge is that of our coming to discern the pattern through careful attention. . . ." (SS, 164). The new science triumphed precisely because it rejected this method of engagement in favor of disengaged scrutiny. But the method of sympathetic engagement had not failed simply because it had not been adequate to material reality. It not only failed to see the truth but also "saw" as obvious what was in fact false. This was because the intellectual vision touted as a pure unveiling of truth was in fact a vehicle for centuries of prejudice and distortion. Engaged attention brought with it the epistemic baggage of the ages. Disengagement had proved to be the effective way to overcome the ancient errors embodied in our "intuitions". If this was so for knowledge of nature, how much more likely that it would be so for matters directly concerned with human interests, such as morality. One did not have to be a Foucaultian *avant la lettre* to conclude that the interests of truth required an extension of the scientific revolution to the moral sciences. Accordingly, the limitations and failures of disengagement by no means imply the cognitive reliability of engagement.

Modernity also involved a new moral orientation that raised questions about the status of engagement as a way of knowing. This orientation is associated with the "affirmation of everyday life" that Taylor rightly cites as a major source of modern morality and that we discuss more fully in the next section. Citing Francis Bacon's insistence on the priority of practical daily life to elitist theoretical contemplation, Taylor notes that, in the modern view, "science is not a higher activity which ordinary life should subserve; on the contrary, science should benefit ordinary life" (SS, 213). He concludes that "the Baconian revolution involved a transvaluation of values. . . . What was previously stigmatized as lower [ordinary life] is now exalted as the standard, and the previously higher [theoretical contemplation] is convicted of presumption and vanity" (SS, 213–14). Taylor fails to note that such a reversal of traditional values raises questions about the traditional methods of engaged knowing that supported the old hierarchy. Moreover, the new standpoint tends to make moot the deep traditional questions about how we should live, the very questions that might seem to require engaged inquiry. Accepting the priority of everyday life means accepting the everyday values (roughly, individual and communal happiness through work and love) that give our lives meaning. The really significant ethical questions then become the instrumental ones of how best to make these values realities. Which sorts of activities are best suited to simultaneously fulfill individuals and make them useful contributors to their communities? What sorts of political communities are most conducive to such activities? What methods of child raising are most likely to produce good citizens of such communities? Such questions are not – contrary to our social scientists – likely to be answered by the objective inquiries of disengaged reason. But they are even more unlikely to be answered by traditional engaged reflection in the manner of Plato or Augustine.

None of this supports the radical program of total disengagement that Taylor attributes to Locke. A self that is reduced to nothing more than its superficial and momentary desires, for example, would be impoverished even by the modest standards of an ethics of ordinary life, which takes as given a self with inclinations to communal virtues such as loyalty and benevolence. Just as we cannot reach the physical world if we insist on starting from minimalist sense data, we cannot reach the moral world from a minimalist conception of the self. Radical foundationalism, whether in epistemology or ethics, is self-destructive and, as Hume saw, must yield before the inevitability of accepting basic humdrum beliefs.

But it is likewise a mistake to think that radical foundationalism is the only alternative available to proponents of modern disengagement who reject the traditional teleological ethics grounded in an intellectual vision of the good. Here Taylor tends to collapse two different distinctions involving the modern stance of disengagement. Sometimes disengagement contrasts with the classical philosophical project of turning and opening the self to the ontological truth of a world of forms. Such disengagement was, as we have noted, plausibly seen as required by the triumph of modern science and by the related affirmation of ordinary life. But at crucial points Taylor identifies disengagement with its most radical form, which withdraws not only from the classical project but also from even the epistemic and moral commitments of everyday life. This occurs, for example, when he contrasts disengagement with what he calls "engaged exploration" of our moral reactions (SS, 164). Perhaps some modern thinkers – and Locke, at least in some moods, may be an example – pushed disengagement to this radical limit. But there is no basis for assuming, as Taylor often does, that disengagement in the first sense is equivalent to or entails disengagement in the second sense. In particular, anyone who is serious in affirming the values of ordinary life can hardly take a totally disengaged attitude toward these values. Insofar as a commitment to the cognitive methods of modern science was combined with the affirmation of ordinary life (and Taylor shows that this was typically the case), it must be understood simply as a disengagement from the classical teleology of forms.

The distinction of two forms of disengagement provides a response to Taylor's suggestion that modern philosophy collapses under the paradox (ultimately contradiction) involved in its concluding to a radically objectivist view of human beings from a radically subjectivist starting point. If its idea is to attain radical disengagement by objectifying everything, including the objectifying self, then modern philosophy is left with the terminal embarrassment of accounting for the inevitably subjective self that does the objectifying. The point, however, is that nothing in the modern project of rejecting classical teleology (and hence the classical transcendent sources of morality) commits it to this kind of incoherence. Disengagement can stop at the commonsense limit of the objects and values of everyday life. David Hume's "academic skepticism" is one version of such nonradical disengagement. Pragmatic liberalism is another.[6]

3. The Primacy of Everyday Life

Most ordinary people have no doubt always had a firm if only implicit commitment to the worth of the ordinary life that they, by definition, lead. Traditional moral ideals, however, typically subordinate the ordinary to some higher good to which our humdrum, workaday goods are means. The point is clear in Plato's and Aristotle's distinction between "living" and "living well", with the former merely a necessary condition for the latter. However, with the advent of modernity, according to Taylor's persuasive argument, ordinary life itself becomes a central moral value. Work (production) and family (reproduction) are affirmed, typically in opposition to allegedly "higher" ideals of, say, aristocratic honor or philosophic contemplation.

Taylor notes that this moral affirmation of the ordinary derives from both the new science and the new religion that inform early modernity. On the one hand, Baconian science originated in experiment and culminated in technology, both domains of the mundanely practical in contrast to the a priori theorizing of traditional science. On the other hand, Protestant theology rejected the conception of the sacred as something reached only through the mediation of a priestly elite and by a renunciation (e.g., in celibacy) of profane life. Instead, "the fullness of Christian existence was to be found within the [ordinary] activities of this life, in one's calling and in marriage and the family" (SS, 218).

Correlative to the affirmation of ordinary life was a new conception of the world as an ordered whole. We have already seen how modern science's rejection of the ontology of forms led to a mechanistic conception of nature. Nature so conceived did not, of course, lack all order, just the order of intuitively intelligible substantial forms. It remained a system of efficient causes, lacking intrinsic meaning but disposed by God for providential purposes. This system is what Taylor refers to as the "interlocking order" of the world. Modern thinkers, Deist and Protestant alike, interpreted this order

---

6   David Hiley offers a perceptive reading of critiques of traditional philosophy – including those of Hume and Rorty – in terms of the ancient school of Pyrrhonian skepticism. See his *Philosophy in Question: Essays on a Pyrrhonian Theme*, Chicago: University of Chicago Press, 1988, especially chapters 1 and 6.

as ordained to the fulfillment of ordinary human life. Indeed, after Darwin, even the atheistic Enlightenment could understand humans as specially adapted to the surrounding world by natural selection.

The affirmation of everyday life is strikingly central for Christians, Deists, and atheists, all of whom have distinctive reasons for according it a special place in their worldviews. But, although Taylor is on target in emphasizing the pervasive importance of this affirmation, he ignores the fact that, in the long run, it supports the secular tendencies of modernity and poses problems for traditional Christianity.

Taylor takes great pains to show that the affirmation of ordinary life has a theological basis, not only in new Protestant theologies but even in the (properly understood) tradition that they rejected. This might seem odd, since Christ emphatically proclaimed his kingdom to be "not of this world". Taylor, however, points out that Christianity (and Judaism before it) has always been characterized by its assertion of the goodness of the world as the creation ex nihilo of an all-good God. (This was one reason that Augustine's break with the Manichees was so crucial for his conversion.) Taylor makes his point by contrasting Stoic (and Socratic) renunciation with Christian renunciation:

> The great difference . . . is this: for the Stoic, what is renounced is, if rightly renounced, ipso facto not part of the good. For the Christian, what is renounced is thereby affirmed as good – both in the sense that the renunciation would lose its meaning if the thing were indifferent and in the sense that the renunciation is in furtherance of God's will, which precisely affirms the goodness of the kinds of things renounced: health, freedom, life. (SS, 219)

It is, of course, important to recognize the Christian doctrine of the goodness of all reality, from the highest to the lowest. But, as this formulation suggests, the doctrine also involves a hierarchical ordering of goods. In this ordering, not only are some goods recognized as far superior to others; lesser goods are also presented as important primarily as means to the higher goods. Ordinary life is undeniably good in its own right. But it is also undeniably infinitely less good than the happiness God has prepared for us in heaven. Given this, the moral logic of Christianity requires the subordination of happiness in this life to happiness in the life to come. Christians could and did disagree on the extent to which renunciation of lesser goods was necessary to attain the bliss of salvation. But such disagreements had to be contained within the limits set by the need to renounce any earthly happiness that leads us into sin. Further, whatever the force of Protestant arguments against monastic vows, it was very hard to deny that Christian perfection required renunciation of some intrinsically innocent goods. Otherwise, there was no way to make sense of key biblical injunctions to "sell all you have and give it to the poor", "leave mother and father for my sake", and "take up your cross".

For Christians, then, any affirmation of ordinary life will require careful qualification. Our mundane life is good, but it cannot be our ultimate good. Moreover, there is always the very real possibility of conflict between worldly goods and our ultimate supernatural good. Heaven is not just icing on the cake of a life entirely fulfilling in purely natural terms. The life we lead in hope of everlasting reward is not the life we would, even at our best, lead without such hope.

The difficulty is particularly apparent in Taylor's explanation of how the Protestant rejection of the hierarchism of medieval Catholicism led to an affirmation of ordinary life. Given their conviction that salvation had to be entirely due to God, the reformers could allow no priestly class, no special rites, no heroic mode of life to take the place reserved for grace alone. This led them, as Taylor says, to a denial of "the very distinction between sacred and profane" and to a corresponding "affirmation of ordinary life as more than profane, as itself hallowed and in no way second class" (SS, 217–18). But ordinary life is "hallowed and in no way second class" only in comparison with other modes of life in this world. It is distinctly second class in comparison to the afterlife for the sake of which it is led. Christianity is nothing if not an ethic of perfection. For such an ethic, what matters is not what is good but what is best.[7]

Taylor rightly points out that the ultimate subordination of worldly goods to heavenly ones does not require "conceiving the hallowing of life . . . as something which takes place only at the limits" (SS, 221). Even though salvation goes beyond temporal goods, Christianity can understand it as including, not abandoning, them. This is the ultimate significance of the doctrine of the resurrection of the body. The afterlife does not abandon but transforms our earthly life. None of this, however, affects the fact that Christianity requires a choice between God and creatures as our ultimate end. There are naturalistic reductions of God to creatures and idealistic identifications of creatures with God that eliminate the need for a choice. But Christianity insists on the transcendence of God and so calls for a genuine decision.

Accordingly, a Christian emphasis on the intrinsic value of ordinary life will always risk colliding with the more central claim that our ultimate goal

---

7   As Peter Brown remarked (in an informal discussion) of the attitude of early medieval Christians, "Being alive makes it hard to be holy."

is not in this world. The more we are impressed with mundane values and become content with the life they define, the less we will be moved by the Christian call to something better. It is no accident that Nietzsche regards saying yes to the world as the ultimate expression of his anti-Christianity.

The problem I am posing is not a conceptual one. There is no doubt that Christianity has the intellectual resources to understand ordinary life coherently as both intrinsically valuable and subordinated to eternal life. The problem is rather motivational – in both a moral and an epistemological sense. Our appreciation of the intrinsic value of ordinary life can readily lead to a contentment with this value as an adequate aspiration for human life. A heart fulfilled by human labor and love may lose its Augustinian restlessness. Once this happens – as it has pervasively in the modern world – Christianity loses a major source of its affective power. The case for it will then become increasingly epistemological, overcoming an indifference of feelings by convincing the mind. It is often said that the Enlightenment emphasis on intellectual justification of religious belief misunderstands the nature of faith. But once an appreciation of temporal values has sufficiently weakened the affective appeal of religion, there is no alternative. The Enlightenment demand for convincing apologetics flowed not only from nonbelievers' commitment to procedural reason but also from believers' affirmation of everyday life. It is in this context that the generally acknowledged failure to meet this demand had a devastating effect on religious belief.

The affirmation of ordinary life has quite a different effect on the project of radical Enlightenment. The danger of this project is that it will collapse into a self-defeating epistemological or moral skepticism. This is inevitable unless there is some way of preventing the total collapse of the self, no longer sustained by cosmic truth, into an irremediably subjective atom.

The affirmation of everyday life provides a way to stop the radical Enlightenment's slide to skepticism. This affirmation is, in effect, equivalent to a realization that we are, inexorably and from the beginning, committed to a set of humdrum truths. This commitment defines our fundamental loyalty and sets a limit to skeptical critique. At the same time, it involves no commitment to anything beyond the commonsense world unless a rational case is made for a transcendent reality. As Taylor points out, Hume seems to have held this sort of position:

> He denies the entire providential view of the world. But in spite of the fact that he takes over the Lockean way of ideas so wholeheartedly, in spite of the fact that some of the later utilitarian writers professed to be inspired by him, he doesn't take up a thorough stance of disengagement. (SS, 344)

This is the view summed up in Hume's famous aphorism, "Be a philosopher; but, amidst all your philosophy, be still a man".[8] More fully, the idea is that extreme skepticism (e.g., about the existence of an external world, the reality of causal connections, the significance of moral values), no matter how well supported by theoretical argument, simply collapses in the face of our natural inclinations:

> The great subverter of . . . the excessive principles of scepticism, is action, and employment, and the occupations of common life. These principles may flourish and triumph in the schools; where it is, indeed, difficult, if not impossible, to refute them. But as soon as they leave the shade, and by the presence of real objects, which actuate our passions and sentiments, are put in opposition to the more powerful principles of our nature, they vanish like smoke, and leave the most determined sceptic in the same condition as other mortals.[9]

This position obviously involves the sort of humdrum realism about the external world that I put forward in my discussion of Rorty's attack on representationalism. (Reflection on this discussion, however, might lead us away from Hume's willingness to accord skepticism even a theoretical victory.) Morally, as Taylor points out, the view puts Hume in the camp of Hutcheson rather than Locke and his utilitarian followers. The reduction of the self to a moral atom of individual desires is avoided by our simple inability to disengage ourselves from moral sentiments such as benevolence. Hume "anatomizes" these sentiments but, as Taylor says, this project "is not undertaken in order to free ourselves of them . . . , noting their ultimately arbitrary nature in order to be able to suspend them or change them". Hume's aim was rather "to show the house that as humans we had to live in. We anatomize the moral sentiments, in all their ultimate metaphysical arbitrariness . . . in order to accept them, endorse them, know the address we are living at. Even the disengagement serves the end of an ultimate engagement" (SS, 344–5).

As Taylor, following Peter Gay,[10] points out, Enlightenment humanism construed along these lines can be plausibly read as a revival of a pagan tradition, one in which Epicurus and Lucretius were leading figures. He also notes the similarity of this tradition's basic philosophical stance to Wittgenstein's (in, for example, *On Certainty*). Taylor, however, seems interested in this view mainly as an anticipation of and a transition to the later Romantic fusion of naturalism and expressionism that is the theme of the last part of

---

8 *An Enquiry Concerning Human Understanding*, Indianapolis: Hackett, 1977, 4.
9 Ibid., 109–10.
10 Peter Gay, *The Enlightenment: an Interpretation*, two volumes, New York: Knopf, 1966, 1969.

SS. I would rather emphasize the intrinsic plausibility and attractiveness of Hume's position (which, incidentally, I find far more explicit in his writings than Taylor does). Taylor himself gives an eloquent summary of this "neo-Lucretian" view:

> We explore from within the human life form. We find that within this form, humans are irresistibly given to accord certain things significance. . . . It used to be thought that without some kind of ontological warrant in the very fabric of things, this significance would be illusory; and now it looks as though the universe cannot provide such a warrant. . . . But this doesn't matter. We don't need it. What is important is to recognize this form and accept it, cherish it, and learn to live with it. (SS, 347)

Hume's view no doubt will profit from some contemporary enhancement. As we have already noted, it need not yield even abstract intellectual hegemony to representationalist skepticism. Also, residues of Hume's political and social conservatism need to be precipitated out of our conception of the moral sentiments, along with the naive tendency to universalize the sentiments. Finally, as we shall see, we must make room for the new vistas of Romantic expressionism, not as part of our core public morality but relocated in a Rortyan domain of private self-creation. But the heart of Hume's neo-Lucretian vision, itself perhaps just a thoroughly consistent affirmation of ordinary life, is very similar to the heart of pragmatic liberalism. Taylor's discussion thus has provided us with at least one major historical root of the position I have been developing and defending in this book. Moreover, tying pragmatic liberalism to the modern affirmation of ordinary life is an excellent way of guarding the position against the temptation, to which we have seen Rorty sometimes succumbing, to push its skeptical spirit too far.

4. Beyond the Enlightenment: Evil, Romanticism, and Poetic Truth

Pascal planned to begin his *Apology* for the Christian religion with a description of the human condition as a combination of *grandeur et misère* – the wealth of thought and the poverty of frailty and sin. The first step in winning over nonbelievers was to get them to realize that Christianity, with its teaching about our Fall from a heavenly destiny, offers an excellent sense of what it means to be human. The second step was to have nonbelievers see that the Christian doctrine of redemption through grace should be the hope of anyone who appreciates the human condition. Through these two steps, nonbelievers would be prepared for faith by coming to see that Christianity was a teaching that might be true and that they hoped was true. (The final step, less congenial to modern ears, seems to have been a demonstration of the actual truth of Christianity from miracles, particularly prophecies.)

A reading of Pascal's *Pensées* is likely to make even the most enlightened modern uneasy. Where, in our secular vision, can we find anything like the profundity of his Christian dialectic of sin and redemption? The Enlightenment's message is that the old bogeys are dead and that our fate lies in our own hands. In Kant's phrase, all we need to do is "dare to know" (*sapere aude*) and we will be able to take control of our lives and march to a humanistic heaven on earth. Critics of the Enlightenment have a ready supply – from Condorcet, Marx, and others – of naively utopian projections of what we will be able to achieve once we break the chains of ignorance and superstition. The naiveté lies in the idea that our misery is all external and contingent, the connivance of tyranny abetted by priestcraft. It ignores the terrible and plausible possibility that the root of our sorrow may be our own perversity. It is, after all, hard to read history and not come away with the thought that there is something horribly wrong with human beings. This led Chesterton to remark that original sin is the one Christian doctrine for which there is overwhelming empirical evidence.[11]

The typical optimism of the Enlightenment ignored, then, the centrality of sin in our existence. Moreover, even if it had recognized sin, the radical Enlightenment's commitment to the autonomous self could allow no hope of salvation. We are nothing but our desires; and, if these turned out to be evil at the root, there would be no grace to redeem us. Following Taylor, we can characterize this failing of the Enlightenment in Augustinian terms as an inadequate account of the human will. The point is made by what Taylor calls the "anti-leveling objection", which opposes the Enlightenment's "one-dimensional picture of the will" for ignoring the fact that "good and evil are in conflict in the human breast" (SS, 355). We might also apply here a generalization of William James's terminology of "once-born" and "twice-born" religious views.[12] The Enlightenment holds an optimistic but ultimately superficial "once-born" view, which sees mankind as basically good and evils as temporary setbacks due to eliminable external factors. Reality accords much more with the "twice-born" view of Augustinian Christianity, which recognizes the imbrication of evil in the very core of human existence.

Rousseau endorses this objection and so is a major critic of the Enlight-

11   G. K. Chesterton, *Orthodoxy*, Garden City, NY: Doubleday, 1959, 15.
12   See William James, *The Varieties of Religious Experience*, New York: New American Library, 1958, Lecture IV.

enment. As Taylor puts it, he "brought back in to the world of eighteenth-century Deism the fundamentally Augustinian notion that humans are capable of two loves, of two basic orientations of the will" (SS, 356), one toward good, the other toward evil. But at the same time, he supported Enlightenment secularism by offering a non-Christian account of the origin of evil and of our salvation from it.

In the Christian story, the original evil is a corruption of an initially good nature through human disobedience to God. The result is a loss not only of happiness but also of the means to regain it. Left to ourselves, we humans remain morally crippled. The unmerited intervention of divine grace restores us, and not merely to natural integrity but also to a new supernatural life. Rousseau's account maintains the Christian notion of our beginning in a natural state of goodness and of a human fall from it. The fall, however, is no longer a matter of disobedience to an apparently arbitrary divine command. It derives rather from the development of artificial social structures and practices that destroy our natural goodness. In contrast to the Christian narrative, there are humanly intelligible mechanisms that explain the corruption. It is, accordingly, possible for us to know why things have gone wrong and how to go about setting them right. In this regard, Rousseau originates a powerful modern tradition of human self-redemption, leading, for example, to Marxism. But what ensures that we are capable of carrying out our redemption ourselves, that the corruption has not gone so deep as to have crippled our capacity to cast it off? Here Rousseau introduces another counter-Christian assumption: that there remains in us a "voice of nature" (conscience), which is a reliable and effective guide to salvation.

Rousseau offers, then, what we might call a "naturalist" account of original sin. He accepts the Christian view that our will is divided between the good for which we are made and the evil is to which we are disposed by a primal fall. But the good is to live according to the honest feelings of our natural selves, and the evil to live according to the pride and hypocrisy encouraged by the artificial inequalities of society. In contrast to Christianity, both the source and the remedy of radical evil lie in this world. In this sense, the core of Christian doctrine – sin as disobedience to God and redemption as requiring divine grace – is eliminated.

It is, of course, hardly a criticism of Rousseau to point out that his understanding of evil differs from that of orthodox Christians. But it would matter if this difference made his account less adequate to our experience of evil, to the Pascalian phenomenology of our *grandeur et misère*. Here one possibly crucial issue is Rousseau's insistence on the essential innocence of human nature. Although we find ourselves enmeshed in evil, we also have, in our very nature, the means to escape from it. Christians might maintain that this essential innocence is belied by the depth of human evil as we encounter it, that the ever recurring and accelerating horrors of history make entirely implausible the thought that we could ever on our own escape our evil. Indeed, Christians are not alone in arguing that it has been precisely the triumph of Enlightenment nonbelief, proclaimed as our salvation, that has produced in the twentieth century the worst form of evil: mass annihilation by deliberately invented technologies of destruction.

It is, however (*pace* Chesterton), very hard to see how truths about the nature and amount of moral evil perpetrated by humans support the conclusion that we are beyond self-redemption. This conclusion would require evidence that, appearances to the contrary, we all lead wicked lives; or at least that we all would lead wicked lives if given the opportunity. Despite all the evils, from the monstrous to the petty, perpetrated by humans, there is no such evidence. Believers will, of course, maintain that the evidence is not there only because God has intervened to save us from what we would otherwise do. But where is the evidence of such intervention? It is hard enough to make a plausible case for the overall positive moral effect of religion, let alone for the claim that all instances of human virtue are due to its influence.

It seems, then, that a naturalist account of evil – an account that finds the source of evil in deviations from nature and its remedy in a return to what we "really" are – need not be inferior to the Christian as an account of the Pascalian phenomenology. It does not, of course, follow that Rousseau's (as opposed, for example, to Darwinian, Marxist, Nietzschean, or Freudian alternatives) is the best version of naturalism or that the best naturalist account is superior to those of allegedly revealed religions. What does follow is that "deep accounts" of human existence – accounts incorporating the moral complexity of a will divided against itself – are possible in naturalistic terms. The Enlightenment is capable of moving from a once-born to a twice-born vision.

And, in fact, from Rousseau on, modern secular thought shows its ability to go beyond the impoverished punctual self – and even the humdrum self that is the agent of ordinary life – to an experience of inwardness with its own distinctive depth and complexity. As Taylor shows, this experience is understood in a variety of philosophical ways, from Rousseau's own deistic "voice of nature", through various forms of romantic pantheism, to Schopenhauer's atheistic pessimism. In each case, nature replaces the Christian God as the higher reality in relation to which the drama of our inwardness unfolds.

This is not to say that nothing essential has been lost in the transition from the traditional Christian to the modern experience of the self. Notably, the traditional claims of objectivity and public validity have disappeared. Of course, Rousseau regarded "the voice of nature" that spoke through conscience as a source of universally valid truths, and the great idealists, culminating in Hegel, were not reluctant to make claims of "absolute truth" for their systems. But the heady mixtures of refined intellectual insight and complex emotional sensitivity that precipitated modern conceptions of the self were hardly open to public scrutiny and objective validation. It is not surprising that, as Taylor's discussion implicitly shows, the modern exploration of the self becomes increasingly a matter of literary perception and expression. Baudelaire's "post-romantic visions" of evil, Proust's transforming memories, and the modernist epiphanies of Joyce, Eliot, and Pound are not merely idiosyncratic, but neither are they competing systems of universal truth. Each offers a way of entering (or constructing) the self to which many readers have strongly resonated. The best of them are worthy competitors with the great religious visions of Augustine and Pascal. But there is no reason to suggest that any one way should exclude the others. Modern experience has no place for a "religion of the Book"; its moral and religious sensibilities are nourished by many – conflicting and incommensurable – books.

Taylor's tracing of the irreducible varieties of modern experiences of the self in effect provides the historical basis for Rorty's division between a public ethics of liberalism and private moralities of self-creation. Private moralities are nourished by diverse literary, philosophical, and religious probings of our inwardness, but they can claim no more than a personal validity. Public ethics achieves intersubjective validity but at the price of moral thinness. The thinness does not amount, however, to a reduction to the punctual self. The agent of Rorty's public ethics is a socially connected, benevolent self, both a subject and an object of our affirmation of ordinary life. Further, although this self cannot, for the purposes of public morality, be characterized in terms of any of the specific "deep" accounts that sustain private self-creation, it can be publicly recognized as having the right to development on the basis of such accounts. There is no need for public morality to value the self only as a seeker of the common-denominator goods we all acknowledge, however much the "leveling" ideology of some democracies might encourage this.

Taylor seems, to an important extent, sympathetic to Rorty's distinction between the public and the private. He too insists that beyond the shared values (equality, benevolence, etc.) that define our public domain, there is a crucial realm of "personal resonance" (SS, 510). Here we explore and make mythic, metaphysical, or theological commitments of the sort that in premodern times asserted "the publicly established order of references". Now, however, such commitment "comes indexed to a personal vision, or refracted through a particular sensibility". As with Rorty, this personal commitment is closely tied to literature and art; Taylor is thinking of "the mythology or metaphysics or theology of Yeats, Mann, Lawrence, or Eliot" (SS, 491).

Taylor, however, insists that this domain, though private or personal, is not subjective. He rejects, for example, I. A. Richards's "psychologistic view of modern poetry" (SS, 490), which Stephen Spender summarizes as the view that poetry "is a means of arranging the order of our internal lives by making a harmonious pattern of extremely complex attitudes, once thought to refer to an external order of metaphysics but now seen to be a symbolic ordering of our inner selves" (cited, SS, 490–1).[13]

How can a domain be personal but not subjective? Taylor's point is that, even though our mode of access to values is unavoidably individual, the values themselves may be encountered as objective realities. Proust's vision of involuntary memory (of, for example, the taste of a cookie his aunt gave him or the unevenness of a pavement in Venice) as embracing and sustaining a life that would have otherwise been lost or wasted is not just a way of re-ordering his psyche. It is a vision of the metaphysical structure of reality:

> The truth surely was that the being within me which had enjoyed these impressions had enjoyed them because they had in them something that was common to a day long past and to the present, because in some way they were extra-temporal. . . . This explained why it was that my anxiety on the subject of my death had ceased at the moment when I had unconsciously recognised the taste of the little madeleine, since the being which at that moment I had been was an extra-temporal being and therefore unalarmed by the vicissitudes of the future.[14]

Proust has not *decided* to think of his memories and himself as extratemporal; he has *seen* them to be such. His vision is not subjective because it does not flow from him, is not just an expression of what he feels or wants to be true. Contrary to Rorty, we are dealing not with self-creation but self-discovery. "We know that the poet, if he is serious, is pointing to something – God, the tradition – which he believes to be there for all of us" (SS, 492).

---

13   Rorty cites Taylor's claim that the view expressed in this text "manifestly will not do" and counters: "I think it will do admirably" ("Taylor on Truth", 20.)

14   Marcel Proust, *Time Regained*, tr. C. K. Scott Moncrieff, T, Kilmartin, and D. J. Enright, New York: Modern Library, 1993, 262.

This is an important correction of Rorty's tendency to decisionism. However, we need to be leery of speaking unqualifiedly of "objectivity" in this context. The objectivity of Proust's vision does not give it universal validity in the ordinary sense. It is a valid perspective on reality, but it is still *Proust's* perspective. Taylor acknowledges this when, in speaking of the object of the poet's vision, he says: "We also know that he can only give it to us refracted through his own sensibility. We cannot just detach the nugget of transcendental truth; it is inseparably embedded in the work. . . ." (SS, 492). Because of this, poetic objectivity is quite different from mathematical or scientific objectivity, where we have no sensible alternative to accepting the truth presented. This is not to say that poetic truths have no sort of universal claim. They demand recognition as valid from a given viewpoint; and this is not trivial, since the viewpoint is not one that we can simply ignore. But, on the other hand, the viewpoint is just one of many and cannot itself determine how it should be related to other equally valid viewpoints. It may, for example, need to be subordinated to a more comprehensive vision or reinterpreted in the light of complementary insights. And, of course, in the realm of art, we can never definitively assess the place of any given perspective, since we have no access to an absolute standpoint (an aesthetic view from nowhere) that could see clearly and wholly all perspectival truths.

There is a somewhat similar perspectival character to scientific and mathematical truths, but with the crucial difference that, in these domains, there is typically no synchronic proliferation of different perspectives. At least in conditions of Kuhnian normal science, we have only one vision of scientific truth presented to us at a given time. (I would suggest that this is due to the nature of scientific reality, in contrast to what we might call "moral reality".) Diachronically, of course, we do encounter differing scientific perspectives, but here we have good reasons for judging new perspectives as superior to and inclusive of the old. Indeed, it is often precisely because the previous perspective was inadequate that we are led to develop the new one.

Accordingly, in contrast to the scientific case, the existence of objectively valid artistic perspectives on morality does not provide us, even at a given time, with a single compelling artistic vision. Individuals have the right to follow their own visions. But personal visions, even if objective in some sense, remain in the private domain and are not normative for public morality. Moreover, objectivity in this sense is compatible with a naturalistic view of morality as the formation of desires through complex processes of social development. Our experience is that certain values are given to us, not the product of our personal choices. But what is not the product of my personal choice may still be internal to me, rooted in the causal processes that have made me who I am.

We return to the question of objectivity in the next section, where I suggest that ethical views may have the sort of perspectival objectivity I have here attributed to artistic visions. For now we can, in any case, note that Taylor provides us with an extremely important deepening of pragmatic liberalism's ethical viewpoint. He shows the way to a "twice-born" naturalistic awareness and account of evil. He also provides the means for understanding private self-creation as having a basis that is objective, even if not transcendent, and thus as corresponding to much more than arbitrary taste or whim.

5. Taylor's Critique of Naturalism

So far, we have been discussing Taylor's *Geistesgeschichte*, arguing that it does not undermine key positions of pragmatic liberalism but rather enables us to increase its scope and plausibility. I now turn to the detailed and explicit critique of ethical naturalism with which Taylor opens *Sources of the Self*.

Pragmatic liberalism, as I have been formulating it, includes an assertion of the ethical naturalism Taylor opposes. This naturalism holds that any claims to "ethical knowledge" need be grounded only in the psychological and social processes that lead us to make ethical judgments, not in any objective truth independent of these processes. Such judgments need not, as Taylor maintains, be about a distinctive realm of moral truth or derived from any special moral experience. It is, however, important to realize that the pragmatic liberal version of naturalism is not based, as ethical naturalism sometimes is, on a scientistic conception of knowledge. It does not, that is, reject a distinctive realm of objective ethical knowledge on the grounds that the practice and achievement of modern science define objectivity, truth, and reality for all domains of human thought and experience. The point is not that objective ethical values are excluded a priori because they could not be the object of scientific scrutiny, or even that we have no good reason to think that such values, however they might be discovered, exist. The ethical naturalist's claim, as I defend it, is simply that the validity and viability of ethical judgments do not require their grounding in a domain of nonnatural truth. When I judge that an action or state is good, for example, I may think I am acknowledging some intrinsic feature of that action or state that requires my acceptance of it as good.[15] But in fact there is no need to posit

---

15   This "intrinsic feature" need not belong to some additional domain of peculiar metaphysical entities. Like Thomas Nagel, the ethical objectivist may merely claim that "the objective badness of pain, for example, is not some mysterious further property that all pains have, but just the fact that there is reason for anybody capable of viewing the world objectively to want it to stop" (*The View from Nowhere*, Oxford: Oxford University Press, 1986, 144).

such intrinsic features, and my judgment may be ultimately understood as an expression of my favorable attitude (albeit one deeply and complexly rooted in a moral tradition) toward the action or state.

Taylor opposes ethical naturalism in three major ways. Each appeals to an aspect of our moral experience for which, he claims, naturalism cannot account. The first aspect is *strong evaluation,* the second *moral frameworks,* and the third *hypergoods.*

Strong evaluations, which Taylor places at the heart of moral experience, are "discriminations of right or wrong, better or worse, higher or lower, which are not rendered valid by our own desires, inclinations, or choices, but rather stand independent of these and offer standards by which they can be judged" (SS, 4).[16] As a clear example of a strong evaluation, he cites the respect for other humans (all or at least some subclass) found in every society. On the one hand, this respect (and similar "moral intuitions") are so "uncommonly deep, powerful, and universal . . . that we are tempted to think of them as rooted in instinct. . . . Culture and upbringing may help to define the boundaries of the relevant 'others', but they don't seem to create the reaction itself" (SS, 4–5). But the fact that, for example, our strong disinclination to kill or injure others has a different "shape" in different cultures – applies to different classes of people and is explained in different ways – also shows that our instinct for respect is "inseparable from an account of what it is that commands our respect" (SS, 5). So Taylor concludes that our moral reactions must be described in a dual way:

> On the one hand, they are almost like instincts, comparable to our love of sweets, or our aversion to nauseous substances, or our fear of falling; on the other, they seem to involve claims, implicit or explicit, about the nature and status of human beings. From this second side, a moral reaction is an assent to, an affirmation of, a given ontology of the human. (SS, 5)

This second aspect of our moral reactions is the objective basis of our strong evaluations.

Ethical naturalists need not deny Taylor's account as a description of how we in fact think about morality, but they will have to maintain that the first,

---

16 Taylor offers a fuller discussion of strong evaluations in "What Is Human Agency?" in *Philosophical Papers, Volume I: Human Agency and Language,* Cambridge: Cambridge University Press, 1985. Here I am concerned only with Taylor's use of strong evaluation to make claims about the objectivity of values. For a critique of other aspects of strong evaluation, particularly its implications for the psychology of identity and the role of reflection in ethical agency, see Owen Flanagan, *Self Expressions: Mind, Morals, and the Meaning of Life,* Oxford: Oxford University Press, 1996, chapter 9.

"instinctual" dimension is, by itself, somehow able to speak to the realities of the situation. As Taylor rather sternly puts it, they give in to "the temptation . . . to rest content with the fact that we have such reactions, and to consider the ontology which gives rational articulation to them to be so much froth, nonsense from a bygone age" (SS, 5). According to Taylor, the naturalist's claim is that moral reactions should be treated on a par with physical attractions and aversions, such as our taste for sweets and distaste for the smell of rotting meat. Taylor maintains that there is a difference. Both moral reactions and physical aversions are reactions to a certain property of an object, "but in one case the property marks the object as one meriting this reaction; in the other the connection between the two is just a brute fact" (SS, 6). This, however, is precisely what naturalism denies, since it holds that "the belief that we are discriminating real properties, with criteria independent of our de facto reactions" has no rational basis (SS, 6).

Taylor maintains that this naturalist denial is inconsistent with "the way we in fact argue and reason and deliberate in our moral lives" (SS, 6). Consider the case almost all of us would make against racists (those holding that people with, for example, skin colors different from theirs are not worthy of the same moral respect as other humans). We would point out that skin color is simply not a feature relevant to the question of whether a person is worthy of respect. Moreover, even racists will not maintain that other races are inferior simply because of their color and other physical features. They will argue that they are genetically less intelligent, more prone to immoral behavior, and the like. Thus, the entire discussion is based on the assumption that qualitative judgments of moral worth cannot be just a matter of reactions that we happen to have, but require grounding in relevant properties of the objects our judgments are about.

Taylor is right that a moral argument has to appeal to features that are relevant to moral judgments. Racists must not merely express their negative attitude toward other races; they must justify that attitude by citing attributes that support it. This requires that racists – and those with whom they are arguing – agree that the attributes in question are relevant to moral judgment and that they can give reasons for thinking that those about whom they are making the judgment have those attributes. Racists may, for example, believe (as the rest of us do) that a certain level of intelligence and moral sensibility is relevant to being worthy of certain sorts of moral respect. Their argument will be as good (or, in this case, as bad) as the plausibility of denying that level of intelligence and moral sensibility to other races.

But even if we all agreed that our beliefs about the connection between intelligence and moral sensibility to worthiness of respect were merely matters of affective attitude, it would still be possible for us to engage in moral argument. Argument of any sort requires only shared premises and ways of arguing from those premises to relevant conclusions. It does not require any particular justification (or any justification at all) for the shared premises.

We can, of course, point out that most people do not think the premises of their moral arguments are merely expressions of affective attitudes; they think they are, for example, self-evident or revealed by God. But Taylor's point is not that the naturalist's position is not widely held but rather that it makes moral argument impossible. He might maintain that, if we all agreed with the naturalist, we would see no point to moral argument. But this is extremely unlikely, since we frequently argue even about claims that we think are ultimately matters of just personal taste. Suppose, for example, we are sharing a bottle of Lafite '61 and you venture the judgment that this is a rather ordinary wine, without the special combination of power and finesse typical of great vintages of Lafite. I might respond that you're right about the atypical nature of the wine but urge that the subtlety of its bouquet and the lingering finish make up for any other lacks and support the conclusion that this is a great even if atypical bottle. There is no doubt that all the gustatorially favorable terms used in this discussion ("power", "finesse", "subtle bouquet", "lingering finish") are merely things that we happen to like in a wine. There is nothing, apart from our attitudes, that makes a wine intrinsically great no matter what we think. But even so, given a set of attributes that we happen to agree are relevant to a wine's being great, we can argue meaningfully and effectively about its greatness. The same will be true of moral attributes on the naturalist's account of them.

In a similar vein, Taylor attacks ethical naturalism on the grounds that it can make no sense of the fact that we demand consistency of one another in ethical discussions. Even naturalists make this demand, "but the issue of consistency presupposes intrinsic description. How could anyone be accused of being inconsistently nauseated?" (SS, 7). Inconsistency, however, is a matter of the relation of two statements to one another. I cannot be "inconsistently nauseated" because "This is nauseating" is a single simple sentence, lacking the internal complexity needed to admit of contradiction. But it is entirely possible for two different affective expressions to contradict one another, as is the case with "This is nauseating" and "This is delicious".

Taylor's second line of attack deploys the notion of moral frameworks. As he uses the term, a framework incorporates a crucial set of qualitative distinctions. To think, feel, judge within such a framework is to function with the sense that some action, or mode of life, or mode of feeling is incomparably higher than the others which are more readily available to us. (SS, 19)

Examples of moral frameworks are the Homeric (and other versions of an "honor ethic"), for which "the life of the warrior, or citizen, or citizen soldier is deemed higher than the merely private existence" (SS, 20); the Platonic, for which "the higher life is that ruled by reason, and reason itself is defined in terms of a vision of order, in the cosmos and in the soul" (SS, 20); and the modern scientific, with its "ideal of the disengaged self, capable of objectifying not only the surrounding world but also his own emotions and inclinations . . . and achieving thereby a kind of distance and self-possession which allows him to act 'rationally'" (SS, 21).

One mark of the modern world has been the undermining of traditional moral frameworks. This has led to the naturalist suggestion that frameworks are entirely contingent human interpretations. For the naturalist, "frameworks are things we invent, not answers to questions which inescapably pre-exist for us, independent of our answer or inability to answer" (SS, 30). Taylor rejects this suggestion on the grounds that our very identity as persons requires a moral orientation that, in turn, requires a moral framework. "To know who you are is to be oriented in moral space, a space in which questions arise about what is good and bad, what is worth doing and what is not, what has meaning and importance for you and what is trivial and secondary" (SS, 28). Further, this orientation must occur in a "moral space" that is not my own creation. "One orients oneself in a space which exists independently of one's success or failure in finding one's bearings, which, moreover, makes the task of finding these bearings inescapable" (SS, 30). Presumably, this is so because, without a preliminary orientation in a pregiven space, there would be no "I" to choose its own viewpoint.

We may, however, wonder why naturalists must reject such claims. They certainly could agree that my identity as a person requires that I have an orientation in the sense of an overall view of what is good and bad, important and unimportant. At a minimum, they could maintain that I achieve an identity by inventing a framework that provides such an orientation. Taylor, of course, insists that it makes no sense for me to invent such a framework out of whole cloth. But even here naturalists need not disagree. They can, for example, allow (with a bow to MacIntyre) that I have no choice but to begin from the moral orientation of the community into which I have been born. The naturalist is committed to understanding morality solely in terms of human attitudes, but surely these can be the attitudes an individual has in virtue of membership in a community. As I have often emphasized, there is no reason that a naturalist has to view moral agents as isolated atoms.

We need, therefore, to distinguish two sorts of naturalism. One, which Taylor successfully attacks, regards morality as simply an illusion, with no reality beyond what individuals happen to desire. Such a view ignores the fact that morality is given to individuals, that it is real in the sense of being part of "what you have to deal with, what won't go away just because it doesn't fit with your prejudices" (SS, 59). But there is another sort of naturalism, one that regards morality not as an illusion but rather as an intersubjective reality. This view accepts values as part of the furniture of the world, but only of the social world. Values are fixed in the face of the desires of individuals simply as individuals; but they do depend on the desires that derive from the fundamental orientation of individuals as members of social groups.

Taylor himself seems to admit that his defense of strong evaluations and moral frameworks has not refuted the second sort of naturalism.[17] He notes that, "even when one gets beyond the cruder reductionist theories, . . . there is still room for a more sophisticated naturalism", one that "would understand our valuations as among the perceptions of the world and our social existence which are inseparable from our living through and participating in our forms of life" (SS, 67). Taylor cites Bernard Williams as a proponent of this sort of naturalism. This is also the naturalism of pragmatic liberalism. Before we discuss Taylor's third line of criticism, it will be helpful to develop a fuller naturalist view of ethical objectivity by some reflection on Bernard Williams's work.

6. Williams and Objectivity

Williams sees ethics as dealing with the question of Socrates in the *Republic:* "How should one live?" He does not pretend that philosophy can answer this question – even suggests that he would be amazed if it could (ELP, 1–2) – but acknowledges that it would be "silly to forget that many acute and reflective people have already labored at formulating these questions". Nonetheless, he thinks much of this labor has been misdirected and proposes, to the extent possible, "to go back now to Socrates' position and to start again" (ELP, 2). So it's important to realize that, for all his critique of the

---

17 For a good sense of Taylor's hesitation in the face of a social version of naturalism, see his ambivalent response to Michael Rosen's "Must We Return to Moral Realism?", *Inquiry* 34 (1991), 183–94. Taylor's response is on 245–6.

enterprise of moral philosophy, Williams does see himself as engaged in it. His historical critique is in fact an instance of the enterprise he is criticizing. He further sees his engagement in moral philosophy as a means of discovering just how much moral philosophy might have to contribute to answering Socrates' question. The picture then is this: Williams is trying to answer the question "How should one live?" and, moreover, trying to answer it philosophically; that is, by "discursive methods of analysis and argument, critical discontent, and an imaginative comparison of possibilities", which, he says, are what philosophy "most characteristically tries to add to our ordinary resources of historical and personal knowledge" (ELP, 4). In carrying out this project, Williams remains aware that there are other, nonphilosophical ways of dealing with the question (he notes that "almost all books . . . which are any good and which are concerned about human life at all" are about this question [ELP, 1]). His enterprise operates at both the object level of trying to find a philosophical answer to his question and at the metalevel of trying to find out just what philosophy has to contribute to answering the question. In this regard, Williams is in accord with Taylor, and both seem more open than Rorty to a role for philosophy in the elucidation of ethics.

Williams is also in accord with MacIntyre in at least one crucial respect. As we have seen, modern ethical discussions center on either the concept of "duty" (among deontologists) or the concept of "the best" (among teleologists, who often but need not follow the utilitarian route of understanding "best" in terms of happiness). But Williams, like MacIntyre, emphasizes the traditional role in ethical thought of "virtue," which he understands as "a disposition of character to choose or reject actions because they are of a certain ethically relevant type" (ELP, 8–9). Reference to virtue becomes of marginal interest if, as for many moderns, the only ethically relevant description of an action is that it conforms to duty or aims at achieving the best. But the language of virtue becomes central once we recognize, as Williams thinks we should, the irreducible importance of thicker ethical descriptions, such as honesty, honor, or courage.

Williams's *bête noire* is ethical theory, particularly in its modern manifestations. One common failing of ethical theory is reductionism, the effort to distill all ethical considerations into one abstract concept, such as duty or happiness. He maintains that the reductive enterprise "has no justification and should disappear" (ELP, 17). Williams is particularly insistent on the failings of ethical theory regarding the justification of ethical life. He allows a legitimate philosophical concern with providing reasons for behaving ethically. He interprets the Socratic "How should one live?" as "How has one most reason to live?" and even allows for a properly understood "refutation" of ethical skepticism. But he offers a highly nuanced account of the limits of any such refutation, noting the restricted extent to which there can be rational argument with those outside of any ethical standpoint at all and, especially, rejecting the foundationalist project of deriving ethics from an Archimedean point from which we could exert compelling argumentative force on any rational agent (ELP, chapter 2).

The latter project is that of what we might call ethical "super-theories", that is, theories purporting to offer not only a comprehensive account of the ethical domain but also a justification of ethics valid for everyone, even those not already committed to an ethical way of life. Williams attacks two major super-theories, the Aristotelian and the Kantian. But he also severely criticizes approaches that, while giving up the foundationalist project and beginning from "within" the ethical, still seek the goal that defines the project of ethical theory: an account providing "a general test for the correctness of basic ethical beliefs" (ELP, 72). Here Williams's focus is on twentieth-century contractarian and utilitarian theories, neither of which, he maintains, can be adequately supported by our "ethical experience".

None of this means that Williams rejects any and all philosophical thinking about ethics – and, particularly, about Socrates' question. He emphasizes that he does not say that "philosophy cannot offer any critique of ethical beliefs and ideas" (ELP, 17). His enterprise is to think philosophically about ethics without falling into the characteristic mistakes of ethical theory.

Rorty might well – at least in some moods – advise Williams to forget about Socrates' question, and MacIntyre would try to convince him that Aristotelianism has resources to overcome the inadequacies of modern ethical theories. But Williams remains committed – with Taylor and the pragmatic liberal – to finding a way of making sense of our ethical life that requires neither extraethical foundations nor general philosophical criteria for its values. This commitment puts him face to face with the question of ethical objectivity. Without the resources of ethical theory, is there any way to construe ethical judgments as objective? And if not, can we really make sense of our ethical lives?

Discussions of the objectivity of ethics frequently focus on comparisons of ethics with science, which is our paradigm of objectivity, or at least our best candidate for objective knowledge. Williams maintains that this comparison is the best way of expressing the polarity that is less felicitously formulated by such distinctions as those between the theoretical and the practical, and the factual and the evaluative (ELP, 135). He further suggests that the best way of understanding the distinction of science and ethics is through the notion of convergence (the eventual agreement of all inquirers on a given body of knowledge). But the notion needs to be carefully deployed. The distinction does not turn on any actual convergence, which may or may not occur in either science or ethics. Rather, according to Williams, the distinction is based on the fact that the convergence to scientific conclusions could occur because scientific inquiry has been guided by the way things are, whereas convergence to ethical conclusions could not be explained in this way.

Williams discusses two fundamental objections to this use of convergence to distinguish science from ethics. The first, which Williams finds in Rorty, denies that there is any content to the notion of convergence being guided by the way things are. The second allows Williams's notion of convergence but maintains that ethics, as well as science, can converge in virtue of the way the world is.

Rorty's objection can take two forms, attacking either the notion of convergence or the notion of a world that could guide convergence. Rorty pursues the first line when he claims that the alleged convergence of science is merely "a cultural artifact, a product of the way in which we choose to narrate the history of science" (ELP, 137; see PMN, 344–5). He allows that we choose to present science rather than, say, morality or poetry as converging because it is "overwhelmingly convenient" to do so. To this Williams objects, first, that Rorty needs some explanation of why the picture of converging science is so compelling, and any such explanation would need to "assume an already existing physical world in which human beings come into existence and develop their cultures" (ELP, 137). Williams also argues that Rorty's position is self-defeating. If, as Rorty thinks, it is so convenient to accept the convergence of science (and there is no place for deep philosophical reasons that would overrule our doing what is convenient), then there could be no reason for rejecting, as he wants us to do, the convergence picture. Pragmatic liberalism, of course, will reject this version of Rorty's objection as based on his unwarranted aversion to scientific realism.

Williams finds the second form of the objection more significant. He formulates it as a dilemma. If by "world" we mean simply the object of our commonsense beliefs (about "stars, people, grass, or tables"), then it is a trivial truth that all of our beliefs (including those of both science and ethics) are "guided by the world". (This sense of "world"corresponds to what I have called humdrum realism.) If, on the other hand, we take "world" to mean something prior to all our systems of belief, which these systems are trying to represent accurately, then we have "the empty notion of something completely unspecified and unspecifiable" (ELP, 138) (the equivalent of the thing-in-itself of metaphysical realism). Williams agrees that, if these are the only two ways of understanding "world", then the claim that there is knowledge guided by the world is either trivial or senseless.

He suggests, however, a third alternative, one that regards the world as neither the object of the totality of our representations nor an in-itself beyond this totality. The idea is to begin with the world that is "there *anyway*, independent of our experience" (that is, the world of humdrum realism, corresponding to the first meaning of "world") and then notice that some of our beliefs about this world "we can reasonably claim to represent the world in a way" that is "to the maximum degree independent of our perspective and its peculiarities" (ELP, 138–9).[18] This subset of our beliefs allows us to form what Williams calls the "absolute conception" of the world; that is, the world independent of experience, the world that would figure in the truthful account of any inquirers, no matter what their mode of epistemic access to it. There is knowledge that is not of the world in this absolute sense – essentially perspectival knowledge. But it is the distinctive feature of scientific knowledge that it is about the world in the absolute sense, and the convergence of scientific knowledge is due to its being "guided" by the world in the absolute sense. Thus, Williams claims to have presented a conception of the world (the absolute conception) that is neither trivial (the object of any knowledge at all) nor empty.

Given his notion of convergence, Williams next turns to the second objection, that ethics is as capable as science of convergence in the relevant sense. The case for this claim is best made in terms of the "thick" ethical concepts central in ethical experience. We say such things as "I can't marry him because he is a *brutal* man" or "We avoid them because they are *cowards*" or "I am kind to her out of *gratitude*." In each such statement the italicized ethical term seems to be both descriptive and prescriptive. As descriptive, its use is guided by the world: "a concept of this sort may be rightly or wrongly applied, and people who have acquired it can agree that it applies or fails to apply to some new situation" (ELP, 141). As prescriptive it is action-guiding, providing good reasons (even if these reasons can be overridden by other considerations) for acting in one way rather than another. As both world-guided and action-guiding, such judgments seem to support, contrary to Williams, the claim that ethical judgments are objective in the same sense that scientific judgments are.

Williams offers an ingenious line of thought to counter this claim.

18 The pragmatic liberal will, of course, take this talk of representation as just an expression of the humdrum truth that knowledge is of the world, with no commitment to philosophical accounts of what this might involve.

Schematically, he argues that (1) ethical judgments involving thick concepts can express knowledge; (2) if these ethical judgments were objective, then they would not constitute knowledge; (3) therefore, these ethical judgments are not objective. Less paradoxically, his suggestion is that there may be such a thing as ethical knowledge, but that the conditions under which such knowledge could emerge are inconsistent with the sort of disengaged critical reflection needed for that knowledge to be objective.

To establish the possibility of ethical knowledge, Williams begins from the standard analysis of knowledge as justified true belief.[19] He thinks that, at least in some cases, ethical judgments are clearly justified beliefs. In, for example, a society "that is maximally homogeneous and minimally given to reflection" (a "hypertraditional society"), people will have ethical beliefs and, lacking any outside challenges to them, will be justified in these beliefs. Accordingly, the only question remaining is whether these hypertraditional beliefs can be true. If they can, then they can constitute knowledge (appropriately justified true belief).

A natural reaction to this question is to say that the beliefs will be true only if they have an objective status – that is, only if they are about an absolute reality that could be known by others, outside the hypertraditional society. Williams, however, points out that, if this were so, there would be no possibility of hypertraditional ethical knowledge. For then such knowledge would require for its justification a critical defense of the concepts in terms of which it is formulated, as opposed to alternative concepts, such as those used outside the hypertraditional society. Such a critical defense would require a level of reflection that is, by definition, excluded from a hypertraditional society. To use Williams's example, "if what a statement expresses is an opinion about the stars, it follows that it can be contradicted by another opinion about the stars" (ELP, 147). Since stars are objective realities, there are opinions about them that can be formulated outside of the hypertraditional society. Justification (and hence knowledge) of claims about stars therefore requires a reflective standpoint from which the validity of such alternative opinions can be assessed. Hence, hypertraditional judgments about stars must remain unjustified and so cannot constitute knowledge.

On the other hand, the condition of reflective justification need not be met for judgments that are not about objective realities but instead concern

---

19   Actually, acknowledging the Gettier problems afflicting the traditional definition, Williams replaces talk of justification with talk of "tracking" (in Nozick's sense). I ignore this refinement in my discussion, but the main point should survive any plausible alternative definition of knowledge.

what can be posited only in terms of the concepts of the hypertraditional society. Such judgments can be known entirely within the hypertraditional framework. This, in fact, Williams thinks, is the situation of ethical judgments in a hypertraditional society. Such judgments are "part of their way of living, a cultural artifact they have come to inhabit (though they have not consciously built it)" (ELP, 147). Their ethical concepts are, in the deepest sense, part of their world but not anyone else's; and, for this reason, they are entirely capable of knowing truths formulated in their terms.

The Homeric hero Ajax, for example, after he has slaughtered a herd of oxen under the delusion that he was destroying the Greek leaders who had denied him Achilles's armor, knows, in virtue of the sense of honor by which he leads his life, that he must commit suicide. We, of course, do not and cannot know this because our lives are not informed by the Homeric code of honor. Ethical theory will insist on asking whether Homeric honor *should* guide Ajax's life: Is it the right ethical standard for a human being (or a rational agent)? To this the proper response is that, apart from his code of honor, Ajax simply can have no ethical life – indeed, no human life at all. To raise the question of moral theory for him is to assume a level of reflection that is not part of his world. Accordingly, Ajax does know that he has to commit suicide.

But the condition of this knowledge is the nonobjectivity of the judgments that express it. For if the hypertraditionalists move to a level of reflection that causes them to think of their traditional concepts as describing an objective world – say, the world also described by the concepts of newly arrived explorers – then their ethical claims will no longer be justified. They will, that is, lack the resources to show the preferability of their ethical lives to the alternatives of which they are now aware. Thus, Williams says, "we reach the notably un-Socratic conclusion that, in ethics, *reflection can destroy knowledge*" (ELP, 148). Moreover, it seems that we moderns are no better off than the newly reflective hypertraditionalists. Despite centuries of ethical theory, we still lack foundational arguments or general criteria that would show that *our* ethical way of life, as opposed to the alternatives of which we are aware, is the proper answer to Socrates' question, How should one live? We live, of course, neither in a hypertraditionalist nor in a fully reflective condition. Insofar as there are corners of our moral world that are sufficiently nonreflective, we may have ethical knowledge, but it will lack objectivity. And the effort to achieve objectivity through reflection will almost surely destroy this knowledge.

Despite the preceding line of argument, Williams still allows the possibility of some sort of objectivity in ethics. For the sake of consistency, it would have to be an objectivity other than that of science; that is, it could not involve convergence to a body of absolute ethical truths. One thing this means is that there will be no ethical truths that any inquirer, even one outside any ethical life (i.e., outside any social world), will inevitably reach. At the very best, our question will have to be: "Granted that human beings need to share a social world, is there anything to be known about their needs and basic motivations that will show us what this world would best be?" (ELP, 153). Williams's suggestion is that there just might be something of an answer from scientific accounts of human nature. We might, in particular, come to know that the best social world for us to live in is one that involves certain thick concepts and certain beliefs formulated via these concepts. We might, for example, learn that it is best to live in a world where people believe that lying is cowardly and slavery is brutal. This would be objective knowledge – based on scientific truths about human nature – relevant to ethics. But even this, Williams insists, would not constitute ethics as a body of objective knowledge parallel to science. Indeed, the only objective ethical truth would be the general claim that a certain sort of social world is the best to live in. From this it would follow that it is best for us to have certain specific ethical beliefs (about lying, etc.); but it would not follow that these beliefs are true. We might know that such beliefs are true, but only in the nonobjective way Williams has already allowed for ethics. We would not know them, as ethical theory hopes, as conclusions from reflection on objectively known ethical principles.

7. Naturalism and Hypergoods

There is no reason to think that Taylor regards moral values as objective in the sense in which Williams says they are not. This fact alone should suggest some of the complexity of the issue of ethical objectivity. There is no disagreement because Williams understands objectivity in terms of the "absolute standpoint", corresponding to a body of knowledge to which anyone at all has access in principle. Taylor agrees that ethical values are not "absolutely" objective, but he argues against sophisticated naturalism that they must be objective in another sense.

As before, Taylor bases his case on the phenomenology of our moral experience. Reflection on this experience shows, he claims, that it makes no sense if the values guiding our behavior have no basis outside human desires, even if these are construed as desires constituted by our form of social life. Just as our ethical experience requires that the desires of individuals as individuals be answerable to strong evaluations and moral frameworks, so too does it require that the desires constitutive of social groups be answerable to transcultural hypergoods.[20]

The underlying logic of Taylor's argument is based on what he calls the "best account (BA) principle". He formulates the idea behind this principle as follows:

> How else to determine what is real or objective, or part of the furniture of things, than by seeing what properties or entities our best account of things has to invoke? . . . [In micro-physics] we have our present array of recognized entities because they are the ones invoked in what we now see as the most believable account of physical reality. . . . There is no reason to proceed differently in the domain of human affairs. . . . As a result of our discussions, reflections, arguments, challenges, and examinations, we will come to see a certain vocabulary as the most realistic and insightful for the things of this domain. What these terms pick out will be what to us is real here, and it cannot and should not be otherwise. (SS, 68–9)

Taylor notes the modern inclination to reject this sort of "moral ontology" on the grounds that its referents "wouldn't figure in an absolute account of the universe". But, he responds, this has force

> only if we have reason to believe that an absolute account, one that prescinds from anthropocentric properties, in particular from the meanings that things have for us, offers the best explanation, not only of the extra-human universe (that much seems now fairly clear), but of human life as well. And this seems not only unsupported as an assertion but highly implausible in the light of what we know both about human beings and the resources of explanations in absolute . . . terms. (SS, 69)

From this passage, it is clear that Taylor thinks values are objective in some sense other than that of Williams's absolute standpoint. Since Taylor deploys "objectivity" in opposition to ethical naturalism, this must mean that values are independent of our desires even though they are not independent of "the meanings things have for us", meanings they do not have from the absolute standpoint. Since Taylor finds this sort of objectivity in his phenomenology of moral experience, let us call it "phenomenological objectivity". But can we make sense of such objectivity? Isn't there something suspect

---

20 Here MacIntyre finds himself in fundamental disagreement with Taylor, saying that he rejects Taylor's distinction "between goods internal to practices and goods [hypergoods] which 'transcend all our practices'". See Taylor's "Justice after Virtue" and MacIntyre's "A Partial Reply to My Critics" in John Horton and Susan Mendus (eds.), *After MacIntyre: Critical Perspectives on the Work of Alasdair MacIntyre*, Notre Dame, IN: University of Notre Dame Press, 1994, 16–43 and 286–9.

about meanings that exist only "for us" and yet are supposed not to depend on our beliefs, desires, or other attitudes? What Taylor seems to have in mind is that the practices and institutions that are the subjects of moral evaluation may themselves be socially constituted and so exist only given that we have certain desires. Private property, for example, would not exist without our desires for ownership, protection against theft, and so on. Even so, given the existence of private property, practices such as distributive justice and actions such as theft might have positive or negative ethical value, regardless of whether our desires supported or opposed them. On this sort of account, there could be practices that do not exist from the absolute standpoint, since only those with desires sufficiently similar to those that constitute the practices could make any sense of them. Nevertheless, there would be ethical values associated with the practices, and these values would be objective in the sense of being independent of our desires.

Supposing that this construal of nonabsolute, phenomenological objectivity makes sense, why should we think it applies to ethical values? Here we return to Taylor's claim that we should accept whatever ontology is required to give the best account of our moral experience. According to him, our moral experience confronts us with a special class of goods "which not only are incomparably more important than others, but provide the standpoint from which these must be weighed, judged, decided about" (SS, 63). He calls these "hypergoods". In the first instance, hypergoods provide a basis for evaluating the values of a given culture. In the Christianized Roman Empire, for example, traditional Roman virtues were reassessed in terms of the new hypergood of charity, being judged, in the pseudo-Augustinian phrase, as "splendid vices". Similarly, the modern hypergood of individual rights has challenged certain values associated with the traditional hierarchical family. But there is no basis for limiting the application of hypergoods to our own culture. Since a hypergood "engenders a pitiless criticism of all those beliefs and practices within our society which fail to meet [its] standard . . . it is hard to see why this critical radicalism should suddenly fail when we get to the boundaries of our society. . . ." (SS, 67–8). In presenting us with hypergoods, therefore, our moral experience presents us with values independent not only of our individual beliefs and desires but also of the constituting beliefs of our own and others' cultures.

A first question for Taylor is why he thinks we should privilege our first-person moral experience. He might reply that, at least in moral matters, an external viewpoint is always less concrete, less fully real, than an internal one, so that, if we are interested in what is "really" happening, we need an internal account. But this is not always so. A theoretical account of my behavior, formulated in terms of, say, psychology or cultural anthropology, may be far richer and more concrete than one that employs the self-deceptive abstractions through which I consciously understand my life. Actions that I see as prompted by concerned friendship might really reflect a distasteful *Schadenfreude*. We often need to take an external view to get beyond our narrow self-understanding of our actions to see what we are "really doing".

To this, however, Taylor can respond that, despite all the complex possibilities of different perspectives, my ultimate moral orientation (framework) defines a perspective that is by definition privileged. It is, willy nilly, my perspective, the way, when the last card is played, I do see things. Attaining a reflective understanding of this perspective may require cutting through many layers of self-deception and self-misunderstanding. But an accurate grasp of this perspective cannot be gainsaid. It simply is what I believe about morality.

But even if we grant the ultimately privileged place of our moral experience over theoretical reinterpretations of it, there is still the question of whether we really require hypergoods in order to make sense of this experience. Our response to the possibility that a direct introspective account might not reveal my true moral perspective did not exclude this possibility. It merely said that reinterpretations suggested by an external psychological or anthropological account would have to be confirmed by a "deeper" reflective first-person account. Since our inherited moral language is couched in objectivist terms, it is not surprising that such terms frequently appear in spontaneous descriptions of moral experience. It does not follow that deeper levels of description would preserve this objectivity. Also, many modern people are acutely aware of the existence of alternative moral perspectives and of the plausibility of psychological and sociological accounts of the contingent origin of these perspectives. Even spontaneous self-reports of their moral viewpoints often show an unwillingness to absolutize moral claims. They say that certain actions are right or wrong, but they seem to find no sense in the idea that morality expresses anything other than the contingent attitudes of their social group. Why should we expect that their descriptions but not those given in traditional terms will turn out to be self-deceptive?

Taylor might well agree that the existence of hypergoods is not a foregone conclusion. He frequently insists on the need for careful investigation of our moral experience and criticizes ethical naturalists because they think it is obvious a priori that they can trump such experience by appeals to science. I agree that we need a close, reflective examination of the actual content of our moral experience. But I do not share Taylor's confidence that such an examination is likely to confirm unequivocally and universally the role of hypergoods. It is much more likely that many of us will come up with no firm conclusion about the applicability of our values outside their ordinary social domain. Even among those who do conclude something definite, we should expect that some will endorse hypergoods and some will not, and that, even among the former, there will be disagreement about which values are hypergoods. The result will, at best, not be the establishment of the reality of hypergoods as a firm truth but as an opinion some of us are entitled to hold on the basis of our own personal experience. It is, therefore, unlikely that we will find that hypergoods are phenomenologically objective.

But even if hypergoods were definitely established as an essential part of everyone's moral experience, it is not clear that Taylor's case against ethical naturalism would be made. Suppose that, at least when I'm engaged in practical deliberation and action, I truly experience my moral values as objective features of the world. This experience may still express only the *manner* in which I hold moral values, not what I take to be my *basis* for holding them. I may, for example, believe that the only reason I see values as objective is that I have been socially conditioned in a certain way. An objectivist manner of belief can be compatible with a naturalist understanding of the nature of belief.

Taylor's approach obscures this point because of its insistence that there is a single "best account" of our moral experience. In fact, of course, moral accounts (like scientific explanations) are context dependent. Consider, for example, the opening of William Faulkner's *The Sound and the Fury*:

> Through the fence, between the curling flower spaces, I could see them hitting. They were coming toward where the flag was and I went along the fence. Luster was hunting in the grass by the flower tree. They took the flag out, and they were hitting. Then they put the flag back and they went to the table, and he hit and the other hit.[21]

This is an account, given by the book's narrator, Benjy, a thirty-three-year-old retarded man, of a game of golf. Is it a good account? In one sense, yes; it is meticulously accurate, an exact description of the overt behavior of the golfers. On the other hand, it omits everything concerned with the meaning of the behavior from the internal viewpoint of the participants. Ordinarily, we would take this viewpoint as privileged and regard an account like Benjy's as a pathetic caricature. But there is nothing absolute about this privilege. Reading Faulkner's "tale told by an idiot", for example, we may come

---

21   *The Sound and the Fury* and *As I Lay Dying*, New York: Modern Library, 1946, 23.

to see Benjy's description as more adequate to the cosmic meaninglessness of lives "signifying nothing". Depending on context, Benjy's description may be scientifically accurate, manifestly misleading, or morally profound.

The point, of course, is that the concept of "best account" is context-dependent, varying with the purposes and viewpoint we have in giving an account. If we are interested in understanding an activity from the agent's point of view, one sort of account will be "best"; but if we are interested in any of the many external views of the activity, other sorts of account will be best. When we are engaged in certain sorts of moral evaluation and action, we may see ourselves as conforming to objective, transcultural values, the reality of which does not depend on our desires. Then an account of moral activity from this internal standpoint would have to make essential reference to hypergoods. But why should we privilege this particular standpoint?

Here the analogy with color perception may be instructive.[22] A phenomenological account of our perceptual experience and practice – parallel to Taylor's phenomenology of moral action – would decisively show that we all believe that colors are objective properties of perceived objects. In perceptual situations, we talk, think, and act this way. On the other hand, most of us also believe, from more or less popular scientific accounts, that color experiences are produced by the reflection of light from surfaces to the eye and that we see the colors we do (the visible spectrum as opposed to infrared or ultraviolet light) because of the contingent nature of our sensory physiology. Does this involve us in a contradiction? On some formulations, it would seem so. When actually perceiving a color, I believe that the color is objective; when I reflect on the causal origin of my perception of the color, I believe that it is not. Presumably, then, when I perceive a color and at the same time reflect on its causal origin, I believe that it is objective and that it is not objective. But this formulation inappropriately forces the issue. It insists that it makes sense to speak of a color as something in itself, apart from any specific context. But perhaps colors (at least as we know them) exist *only* in contexts and have different features in different contexts. In perceptual contexts, they are objective; in theoretical, explanatory contexts, they are not. Similarly, values might be objective in the context of moral experiences but not in the context of causal explanations of these experiences.

---

22 I employ this analogy only to make a single relatively narrow point. For fuller discussions of the very complex comparison of moral values to colors (and secondary qualities in general) see John McDowell, "Values and Secondary Qualities", and Bernard Williams, "Ethics and the Fabric of the World", both in Ted Honderich (ed.), *Morality and Objectivity: A Tribute to J. L. Mackie*, London: Routledge and Kegan Paul, 1985; also Colin McGinn, *The Subjective Point of view*, Oxford: Oxford University Press, 1983.

The point I am trying to make by the distinction of explanatory and practical contexts can also be made in terms of Bernard Williams's distinction of the "inside view" and the "outside view" of ethical dispositions (ELP, 50–1). His "ethical dispositions" parallel my "desires"; they "are dispositions to want certain things, to react in certain ways to other people and to their actions, to use such notions as that of obligation, to promote certain outcomes as being just, and so on". Williams notes that when, from an external stance, we ask of an ethical point of view, "'what has to exist in the world for that ethical point of view to exist?' . . . the answer can only be 'people's dispositions'." But if we look at things from an internal point of view, from the standpoint of the ethical dispositions as they determine our practical actions, "it is not true . . . that the only things of value are people's dispositions". From this standpoint, what have value are such things as "other people's welfare" and "the requirements of justice". We take the internal point of view when we are actually engaged in the business of ethical reflection leading up to a decision. Taylor is assuming this point of view when he insists that our moral experience requires the objective reality of values. As Williams puts it, "in thinking about ethical and other goods, the agent thinks from a point of view that already places those goods, in general terms, in relation to one another and gives a special significance to ethical goods". But this does not mean that the existence of ethical values is derived from anything other than ethical dispositions (desires). From an external viewpoint, the agent's internal acceptance of the objectivity of ethical values merely reflects the fact that the agent is "someone in whom the ethical dispositions he has acquired lie deeper than other wants and preferences" (ELP, 51).

If, then, values were phenomenologically objective, this would restrict but not simply eliminate the validity of ethical naturalism. We would still need to allow a context in which naturalism was true, just as we would admit a context in which values are objective. But, in any case, as I have argued, there is no reason to agree that values are phenomenologically objective.

What, finally, should we say about the objectivity of ethical values? If we follow Williams in characterizing objectivity in terms of validity from the absolute standpoint, then there is no basis for saying that values are objective. Even Taylor agrees that "an essential condition of the existence of [moral] properties is that there are human beings in the world, with a certain form of life, and kinds of awareness, and certain patterns of caring" (SS, 68). In some sense, values need exist only "for us", not absolutely. But is it possible to understand objectivity more broadly? In any form, the notion always connotes some sort of independence from the subject; the objective is what is true regardless of what anyone may think, what is "there in any case". But couldn't something possess this independence without its truth being accessible in principle to any possible knower? Taylor says yes, and proposes in particular that, although ethical values may exist only in a human world, within this world they are valid regardless of our desires. This phenomenological sense of objectivity is similar to Williams's case of ethical knowledge within a hypertraditional society. The values of such a society would be encountered by its members as givens independent of any desires, and the only reason Williams does not call them objective is that he reserves the term for absolute truths. The difference, however, is that Taylor thinks this sort of "objective" ethical knowledge exists not only in the hypertraditional case but also in our world of critical moral reflection and awareness of alternative values.

Here, I have argued, Taylor is overoptimistic. We should not expect reflective scrutiny of each individual's moral experience to yield objective values; and there is even less reason to think that such values would be found universally. So I see no grounds for accepting the phenomenological objectivity of values. There may, however, be room for a still weaker sense of moral objectivity. It is possible that certain truths are perspectival in the sense that they are not independent of the mental standpoint (cognitive and/or emotive) from which we approach reality. But they are true no matter what *given* the standpoint. We can then speak of something being "true from a standpoint" other than the absolute standpoint, and the question is whether there can be any objectivity for such truths.

This question can be formulated in terms of the objectivity of the standpoint from which certain truths are perceived. Can a standpoint be said to have "objective validity" even if it is not the absolute standpoint? As our discussion of literary "visions" in Section 4 showed, the answer is yes. Homer, Dante, Dostoyevsky, and Proust all offer perspectives that have a "certain validity" that no one can safely ignore. None of them tell us the whole story about human life, and none of their "insights" can stand alone as the simple truth. Each perspective needs to be somehow complemented by others. (A parallel claim holds for interpretations of literary works.)

Similarly, there may be a variety of theoretical standpoints other than the absolute that have objective validity. I find Freudian psychoanalysis a good example. (Those who think I am egregiously over- or underrating psychoanalysis should be able to find examples more congenial to them.) As I see it, this is a theory that has no sustainable claim to absolute validity. There is simply not adequate evidence to support its claims about the nature of unconscious processes. Nonetheless, I do not place it on the same level as, say, the theory of the humors or astrological views of personality. I want to say that, although I don't accept it, "it has a certain validity" that is independent of what I or anyone else thinks. But what can this mean? At least two things are involved. First, although psychoanalysis is not generally valid as an account of the human psyche, there are some cases and situations for which it does fit accurately. There are certain slips of the tongue, certain neuroses for which it is a splendid account. (If all cases were like these, the theory would be absolutely true.) Second, even for cases where the theory doesn't work very well, there is often something in its perspective that is worth taking account of. It's a flawed and limited but still useful instrument (or grid) for studying the psyche.

In these aesthetic and theoretical examples, what we have are objectively valid although not absolute perspectives. What is true from such perspectives we can call "perspectivally objective". Different people will be more at home, cognitively and affectively, at one standpoint as opposed to others, but no one can rightly deny that there is something to be learned from at least some other perspectives, that they have validity even for those who don't occupy them (and are in this sense objective).

We might be tempted to "reduce" perspectival objectivity by trying to separate out, in each perspective, what is absolutely valid and what is absolutely wrong (or at least unjustified). Then it would be the former alone that really constituted the validity of the perspective. The trouble, however, is that the separation cannot always be so neatly effected. As we have seen, Taylor himself points out that the truth available from a perspective may not be detachable from the perspective as a whole (SS, 492).

Some ethical values very likely have perspectival objectivity. But such objectivity does not require that these values are ultimately rooted in something other than our beliefs and desires. My deepest beliefs and desires are, as Taylor would surely agree, not something that I can ever fully articulate. The claim that an ethical view that I do not explicitly hold has "some validity" for me may simply mean that taking up the view will allow me to articulate further the sense of my deepest beliefs and desires. Perspectival objectivity does not exclude ethical naturalism.

Ethical naturalism holds that morality makes sense even if it is grounded in nothing more than human desires. Against this claim, Taylor puts forward what he says are three features of our moral experience that cannot be understood solely in terms of our desires: strong evaluations, moral frameworks, and hypergoods. I have argued that we can understand strong evaluations and moral frameworks in terms of our desires and that there is no reason to think that hypergoods are essential for understanding our moral experience. With regard to objectivity, Taylor and I both agree that morality does not require the absolute objectivity of values. He holds, however, that values (specifically, hypergoods) are phenomenologically objective. I maintain that there are no good reasons for claiming that values are phenomenologically objective, but I do allow that values may be perspectivally objective.

I have been arguing that entirely naturalist accounts of values are consistent with a proper understanding of our ethical lives. But often the critique of naturalism is rather that it undermines our motivation for living an ethical life. Even if we need nothing more than our desires to understand morality, we cannot, it is said, be moral if we think (even correctly) that there is nothing to morality but our desires. The belief that my moral commitments come entirely from myself will sap their force. I have already argued (in Part I, Section 7) that this is simply not the case. But perhaps I can drive the point home in this new context by outlining what I see as our likely responses to encounters with those who reject our deepest moral convictions.

Ordinarily, our assumption is that apparent rejections of our ethical principles reflect insufficient understanding, information, or emotional development. We accordingly respond to, say, racists by explaining just what their view involves, showing how it is in tension with other views they hold, making them better acquainted with the achievements of other races, and so forth. Sometimes our persuasive efforts succeed. When they do not, we typically have reason to think that our opponents are mentally confused, incorrigibly ignorant, or just morally corrupt. On other occasions, we may discover that we have misunderstood our opponents' views and that the disagreement is not as deep as we thought. The unity of the human genome and the broadly similar environments in which all humans have to survive generally ensure that moral disagreements do not go all the way down to our most fundamental, undiscussable desires.

In the preceding sorts of cases, the reactions of the naturalist will be exactly the same as those of believers in the universal validity of hypergoods. But suppose we do encounter someone with whom our moral disagreement does go all the way to the bottom (perhaps one of Harman's space aliens or Hare's moral fanatic). Believers in universal validity may well keep arguing with the alien or the fanatic, though there will be only a very limited range of Kantian arguments available and scant prospect of dialectical success. But, as naturalists, we have to acknowledge the possibility that the viewpoints are ultimately incommensurable. Such a possibility confronts us with the objective "groundlessness" of our deepest ethical commitments. But, since we have almost certainly not been led to these commitments by a process of objective reason-giving, why should this make any difference? The complex causal mechanisms of biological inclination and social conditioning that underlie ethical commitment will not cease to operate for lack of an argument. We will, therefore, almost certainly remain faithful to our own moral position and either ignore the aliens and the fanatic or, if things get too threatening, employ force against them.[23]

Perhaps the critics' point is not that naturalism literally undermines our deepest moral commitments but that it provides an all too ready excuse for ignoring moral demands. Knowledgeable liars and adulterers can evoke cultures that smile on their vices and note that we can't prove our standards superior. But we have never had any problem finding rationalizations for our sins, and this highly intellectualized addition adds a quite small weight to an already heavy pan.

There is, however, one final way that Taylor in particular might argue that naturalism is motivationally inadequate in our ethical lives. He has maintained that the strong evaluations characteristic of ethical life require "articulation" and "depth", that is, an ability to "characterize one desire or inclination as worthier, or nobler, or more integrated . . . in terms of the kind of quality of life which it expresses and sustains".[24] We may, like Owen Flanagan, suspect that Taylor here requires too much reflexivity as a necessary condition of ethical life.[25] It is nonetheless plausible that, beyond a certain cultural and intellectual level, moral evaluation does require a standpoint that provides a sufficiently rich articulation of the meaning of our ethical agency. Moral life requires not just a series of judgments that "deep down" we prefer certain alternatives. It also requires a language that can situate our judgments in the context of a wider moral vision of the world and our place in it that we find plausible and inspiring. Traditional religious ontologies, as well as secular philosophical accounts such as those of Kant and Hegel, provide the needed vision. Naturalism, it might be claimed, does not.

But such a claim ignores the distinctive moral force that naturalism has developed in both its ancient and modern forms. Put simply, naturalism offers the ethical ideal of living honestly according to principles that, though deeply imprinted on us, require no sustenance from the wider cosmos. This is the ideal that Bernard Williams has found, among the ancients, in Thucydides and Sophocles in opposition to Plato, Aristotle, and their modern suc-

---

23 To adapt Williams's terminology, "confidence" (as a social psychological reality) does not require (epistemic) "certainty." Cf. ELP, 169–71.

24 "What Is Human Agency?" in *Human Agency and Language: Philosophical Papers I*, Cambridge: Cambridge University Press, 1985, 25.

25 Owen Flanagan, *Self Expressions: Mind, Morals, and the Meaning of Life*, Oxford: Oxford University Press, 1996, chapter 9.

cessors. The latter, including Taylor, believe "that somehow or other, in this life or the next, morally if not materially, as individuals or as an historical collective, we shall be safe; or, if not safe, at least reassured that at some level of the world's constitution there is something to be discovered that makes ultimate sense of our concerns". In contrast, the ethical naturalist stands with Sophocles and Thucydides in representing "human beings as dealing sensibly, foolishly, sometimes catastrophically, sometimes nobly, with a world that is only partially intelligible to human agency and in itself is not necessarily well adjusted to ethical aspirations".[26] There is starkness in this naturalist vision, but those who have felt its force in the great tragic formulations of Sophocles or Nietzsche will not deny the depth of its moral power. Taylor himself has, as we saw, well expressed the moral force of naturalism in his characterization of the "neo-Lucretian" standpoint (SS, 347).[27]

There may well be those who do not find naturalism, even in its most eloquent and attractive forms, adequate to their own moral needs and projects. The point is not that such people have no right to conceive of their ethical agency in terms of a nonnaturalist ontology. It is rather that there is no general, publicly compelling case to be made for the ethical necessity of any such ontology. Such ontologies belong in Rorty's private sphere and should not be introduced as requirements on the intelligibility or viability of our public morality or even of every private morality.

I conclude, then, that ethical naturalism, at least in the form maintained by pragmatic liberalism, is not the moral threat Taylor takes it to be. It is, however, worth emphasizing once more that the naturalism I have been defending concerns only the necessary basis for our ethical lives. The claim is just that nothing beyond the natural is required to make sense of ethics. The question remains whether there might be other adequate grounds for accepting entities outside the natural order (e.g., God). Also, as noted just above and in our discussion of MacIntyre, the private spheres of self-creation may well involve commitments to (for example) religious traditions that require a nonnaturalist ontology. Accordingly, the issue of ethical naturalism is, in important ways, independent of the issue of metaphysical naturalism. Of course, those who reject ethical naturalism thereby accept realities or truths beyond the natural order and so reject metaphysical naturalism (the

---

26 *Shame and Necessity*, Berkeley: University of California Press, 1993, 163–4.

27 Rorty points to such a vision when he says that "what matters is our loyalty to other human beings clinging together against the dark" ("Pragmatism, Relativism, Irrationalism", CP, 166). For a fuller sense of the moral force of Rorty's version of naturalism, see his "Trotsky and the Wild Orchids" in Mark Edmundson (ed.), *Wild Orchids and Trotsky*, New York: Penguin, 1993, 29–50.

denial that there are any such realities or truths). But proponents of ethical naturalism are not thereby committed to metaphysical naturalism. Their claim is merely that ethical commitments are not undermined if there is nothing beyond the naturalist ontology. An ethical naturalist may well have other reasons for accepting any of a variety of nonnatural entities, from Platonic Forms to the Christian God.[28]

Rorty has combined his ethical naturalism with an insouciant atheism that does not hesitate to hope for a culture with "no trace of divinity" ("The Contingency of Community", CIS, 45). As this phrase suggests, his atheism goes well beyond the denial of standard conceptions of a transcendent cause of the universe. It denies anything that might take on the role of an absolute and urges us "to the point where we no longer worship *anything*, where we treat *nothing* as a quasi-divinity, where we treat everything – our language, our conscience, our community – as a product of time and chance" ("The Contingency of Language", CIS, 22). But whatever the basis for this atheism – and Rorty certainly makes no case for it – it is not required by the ethical naturalism that I have been defending against Taylor. My case against Taylor cuts off one route to theism, but it by no means requires atheism. Indeed, the confidence with which Rorty rejects any vestige of the divine is hardly consistent with pragmatic liberalism's distrust of grand philosophical claims.[29] We simply do not know enough to reject religious claims root and branch. We owe religion at least the respect due a profound possibility that we cannot exclude.[30]

Taylor's superb discussion of modernity has suggested significant improvements in our formulation of pragmatic liberalism. His discussion of the affirmation of everyday life opened the way to a more subtle and historically resonant formulation of our pragmatic epistemology. His treatment of the Romantic movement showed the need for a naturalist account of evil and deepened our understanding of the private sphere of ethical self-creation.

28 Taylor hints at an ethical case for theism, suggesting that it is required for a full assertion of human worth – "a divine affirmation of the human, more total than humans can ever attain unaided" (SS, 521). But, as we have seen, he does not develop the hints and admits that he has no worked-out arguments for his position.

29 In a recent paper Rorty offers his sketch of a "pragmatist philosophy of religion that, without renouncing his naturalism, does move along the lines of Dewey's more positive view of religion. See "Pragmatism as Romantic Polytheism" in Morris Dickstein (ed.), *The New Pragmatism*, Durham, NC: Duke University Press, 1998.

30 For a discussion of the rationality of religious commitments, see my *Religious Belief and Religious Skepticism*, Notre Dame, IN: University of Notre Dame Press, 1982.

But his central challenge to pragmatic liberalism, the claim that our moral experience requires an irreducibility of values to human desires inconsistent with ethical naturalism, is not ultimately convincing. It has, however, led us to a much more careful understanding of the status of moral values, one that allows us to recognize them as objective in an attenuated sense.

PRAGMATIC LIBERALISM

CONCLUDING REFLECTIONS

The preceding parts have developed pragmatic liberalism through a series of variations on themes from Rorty, MacIntyre, and Taylor. By way of conclusion, I offer a recapitulation of the pragmatic liberal position and a coda on its metaphilosophical implications.

1. Recapitulation

Pragmatic liberalism is my response to the problem of modernity. The position arises from a critique of classical modern claims to ground knowledge in a body of distinctive fundamental knowledge, whether epistemological or ethical. The pragmatic liberal regards both knowing and doing as nothing more than human social practices, governed by norms derived entirely from the deep desires that constitute individuals as members of cognitive and moral communities. This position rejects the project of the philosophical Enlightenment in favor of the affirmation of ordinary life characteristic of the humanistic Enlightenment. The Enlightenment ideal of autonomy is ensured by situating all norms entirely within human communities. Critics may urge that pragmatic liberalism nonetheless abandons the Enlightenment commitment to reason. But this is so only with respect to a philosophical reason claiming a privileged perspective on reality. There is a full endorsement of our ordinary modes of knowledge and of the truths, both humdrum and scientific, that they yield. With regard to such knowledge, all that is rejected are incoherent philosophical theories of justification and truth. Pragmatic liberalism allows but does not require any of a range of views on the objectivity of values; my own view is that there is no basis for asserting the absolute or phenomenological objectivity of values but that some values may well be perspectivally objective. In any case, pragmatic liberalism remains ethically naturalistic by claiming that our moral lives require grounding in nothing more than our beliefs and desires.

Pragmatic liberalism is distinctively liberal in its affirmation of the basic Enlightenment values of human freedom and natural happiness. But, in contrast to some other Enlightenment views, there is no categorical rejection of tradition and no facile optimism oblivious to the darker aspects of human existence. Pragmatic liberalism, with its post-Hegelian recognition of historicity, accepts the inevitability and the value of traditions without giving absolute privilege to any one of them. Further, it recognizes the moral ambivalence of human existence and is open to a variety of sophisticated naturalistic responses to evil. The position's liberalism is also distinguished from some other contemporary formulations by its complete neutrality (up to interference with others' freedom) regarding private modes of self-creation. There is, in particular, no preference for the more aesthetically original or interesting forms of private existence and no disdain for lives of dull integrity. Finally, pragmatic liberalism is open to religion, not only for those who find it an essential element of their private self-creation but also generally, as an ineliminable possibility of our mysterious existence.

A fuller formulation of the distinctive claims of pragmatic liberalism can profitably begin with its historical understanding of modernity as deriving from the seventeenth-century scientific revolution. Before the seventeenth century, we regarded the world as structured by forms (Platonic or Aristotelian) that provided the fundamental intelligibility and value of things. Thus, forms independent of human concerns or interests determined both natures and norms. Corresponding to these ontological structures were special cognitive endowments of human beings that enabled us to attain insight into the forms (and thus the natures and norms they determined), for example, Platonic noesis and Aristotelian abstraction.

By the seventeenth century, we realized that the natural world was not adequately knowable through philosophical insight. The alternative method of testing hypotheses empirically has offered a very different picture of nature and one that is far better justified. The key point is this: the ability (properly understood) of an account to predict new and even surprising phenomena is a decisive test of its truth. The results of empirical science are justified in precisely this way – indeed, spectacularly so. These results reveal a world very different from that of the ancient forms.

It does not follow that the ontology of forms is false. Modern science may, as scholastics have argued for the last four centuries, simply show that there is a dimension of nature susceptible to quantitative and empirical scrutiny. This dimension need not exhaust the truth about nature and may (if traditional accounts are correct) depend on the deeper truths of the ontology of forms (properly modified to be consistent with the new empirical truths).

The scientific challenge to premodern thought was more epistemological than metaphysical and can be best formulated in terms of the notion of "intuition". On the ancient account, intuition meant a special cognitive ability that provided privileged access to the forms. The triumphs of modern science showed that, first, there was another, even stronger, method of knowing the world; second, this new method contradicted the results of intuition on some key points. This supported the conclusion that "intuition", at least regarding nature, could not be simply assumed to be a privileged source of truth rather than merely a reflection of our contingent peculiarities as cognizers (or even, perhaps, of deep-rooted ideological prejudices). Thus, "intuition" became "intuitions" (in Williams's phrase[1]) – mere preliminary suggestions of how things seem to us, prior to rigorous investigation.

Although the failure of "intuition" was obvious only for nature and not for norms, the epistemic challenge plausibly extended to our intuitions about values. These were even more susceptible to ideological distortion, a possibility that had to be taken all the more seriously as we became more impressed with the different moral intuitions of different cultures.

So, in sum, the success of modern science did not, as has often been claimed, falsify the ontology of forms. But it did undermine the epistemic authority of the intuitions on which it was based. It was wrong to conclude that the traditional picture was false or that there was nothing to the world except what could be known by science. But it was fair to suspect that we had no reliable way of knowing aspects of the world that might be beyond the scope of the empirical methods of science. The victim of the scientific revolution was traditional philosophical knowledge.

Given this, it becomes plausible to read at least one strand of the history of modern philosophy as an effort to achieve the results of ancient philosophizing by new means. The idea was that we could give up the ancient intuitions and still find a way of supporting the standard conclusions about a

1   ELP, 93–4.

world of natures and norms that had characterized ancient thought. The fundamental step in this enterprise was the move inward. This meant rejecting intuitions of cosmic order in favor of immediate givens of consciousness that were seen as implicit in even the rigorous methodology of natural science, which thus would itself be grounded by the new philosophical project. With this, there began a new construal of philosophy (and hence of reason) as a matter not of intuitive insight but of careful analysis (of the immediate givens) and rigorous argument (to traditional conclusions from the immediate givens). With this move, reason becomes, as for Descartes and Locke, no longer the vehicle of direct illumination (from which further conclusions might, of course, be logically inferred), but rather a procedural instrument for gradually, methodically discovering the truth. Where the failure of ancient philosophy was the failure of philosophical intuition, the failure of this modern project was the failure of philosophical argument.

As I use the term, "pragmatism" refers primarily to the view that, first, philosophy, in both its intuitive and argumentative forms, has failed and that, second, this failure does not, contrary to certain forms of skepticism, call into question the fundamental Humean truths implicit in the very conduct of human life. So understood, pragmatism is a metaphilosophical view, based on a reading of the history of Western philosophy (not, incoherently, on a philosophical account of human cognition). Rorty defends pragmatism in this sense through his *Geistesgeschichte* in PMN. Although agreeing with his final conclusion, I remain uneasy with two aspects of his case for it. First, he pays only passing attention to the premodern philosophy of forms and, as a result, uncritically accepts the standard metaphysical naturalism of the proponents of science who think that modern science simply refuted the ontology of forms and proved that the world contains nothing beyond what is included in scientific descriptions of it. My own position, based, I maintain, on a better reading of the modern scientific case against Aristotelianism, remains agnostic on this issue, allowing that science has not shown its own account of reality to be complete. Second, Rorty's negative conclusion regarding modern philosophy assumes that the entire enterprise is based on an indefensible representationalism. Although representationalism is one strand in the modern project, there are other ways of trying to carry out the project (e.g., Reid's commonsense realism, various contemporary nonfoundationalist approaches to epistemology). Consequently, pragmatic metaphilosophy needs the support of a specific and continuing examination of the arguments of modern and contemporary philosophers. A generic rejection of representationalism is not sufficient.

My reservations about Rorty's reading of the history of modern philosophy can also be put in terms of the rejection of foundationalism. Foundationalism is indeed to be rejected out of hand when it maintains that substantive truths about God, values, human nature, and the like can be derived from premises ("self-evident" or otherwise privileged) known by special philosophical insight. We have good reason to think that there are no such premises available. But from this it does not follow that there are no good arguments (deductive or inductive) from humdrum truths about the world and ourselves to substantive philosophical conclusions. To reject, as I think we should, this sort of foundationalism – where the foundations are not special philosophical intuitions but indisputable humdrum truths – requires specific critical scrutiny of the arguments that philosophers have put forward.

Pragmatism is the denial not only of philosophical foundations for humdrum beliefs but also of the need for such foundations. Here the principle is the Humean one that, at least in epistemic matters, necessity provides its own right: there is no need to justify what we cannot but believe. But what of beliefs we find ourselves committed to that go beyond the humdrum inevitabilities but cannot be justified by valid arguments from humdrum premises, as scientific beliefs often can? Some of the beliefs in this epistemic middle range are just errors or illusions and are shown to be so by evidence and arguments to which we have access. Such beliefs we ought to give up, though we often maintain them out of emotional or cognitive defects such as prejudice or stupidity. But in other cases, we hold middle-range beliefs to which, even after appropriate reflection and discussion, we find no compelling objection, though likewise no compelling support. Here most of us will find many of our ethical, political, and religious beliefs. (These may include not only higher-level commitments of principle but also low-level, quite mundane beliefs such as the desirability of going to a certain restaurant or having a given casual conversation.)

The "liberalism" of pragmatic liberalism can be understood as a position regarding beliefs of this sort. It has two aspects, one epistemic, the other moral/political. Epistemically, liberalism maintains that everyone has a right to such beliefs. Ethically and politically, it maintains that everyone has a right to act on such beliefs, subject to the key constraint that their action not interfere with others' rights to corresponding action.

So understood, liberalism is an interpretation of and a response to the revolution in cognitive authority that goes by the name of "modernity". The first stage of this revolution established the fundamental rejection of rationally arbitrary external authorities over human beings – what I called in my introduction the "minimal commitment to modernity" that virtually all

of us now share. (Even those, like MacIntyre, who argue for a return to traditional authorities, do so by alleging that such a return is the rational thing
to do. They do not merely summon us to obedience.) The second stage, which
we have just been discussing, was the rejection of ancient philosophical authorities in favor of modern science. The third stage, which I am urging (and
which seems implicitly accepted by most people outside the community of
professional philosophers), is the rejection of modern philosophical efforts
to replace the cognitive authority of ancient philosophy. With these three
degrees of modernity, we are left with no generally accepted cognitive authority for guiding our lives except that of modern science (and even here,
I would argue, there are severe limitations once we move beyond the core
natural sciences). Liberalism, as I am understanding it here, is the view that,
given the modern rejection of cognitive authority for most of the beliefs that
underlie our ethical, political, and religious lives, we should neither suc-
cumb to skepticism nor revert to dogmatism. Rather, we should acknowledge the right of individuals to ungrounded beliefs, provided their exercise
of them is combined with a tolerance for the conflicting beliefs and behavior of others.

For pragmatic liberalism, the human noetic structure has a broadly foundationalist form. All knowledge and discussion must begin from beliefs that
are themselves unjustified, although we are entitled to hold them. These include, first, the Humean beliefs (or, we might say, primary basic beliefs) without which human life is simply impossible (and which, consequently, we all
share) and, second, beliefs (secondary basic beliefs) that we need not but
do happen to hold, which are neither justified nor refuted by any considerations to which we have access. We are entitled to hold both our primary and
secondary basic beliefs – they are, as Plantinga says, properly basic beliefs –
as well as any beliefs that we see as following (deductively or inductively) from
these beliefs.[2] Pragmatic liberalism is self-referentially coherent in the sense
that it can consistently categorize its own assertions in terms of its account
of our noetic structure. Specifically, any of its key claims that go beyond humdrum truths and inferences from them it presents simply as properly basic
secondary beliefs (or inferences from them).

An important limitation of properly basic secondary beliefs is that we are
in no position to make a cogent case for them to those who have contrary
properly basic secondary beliefs. Liberalism has a privileged position as a

---

2   See Alvin Plantinga, "Reason and Belief in God", in A. Plantinga and N. Wolterstorff (eds.),
    Faith and Rationality: Reason and Belief in God, Notre Dame, IN: University of Notre Dame
    Press, 1983.

secondary basic ethical belief in our culture simply because almost everyone accepts its fundamental principle of freedom for all up to interference with the freedom of others. But hardly any of us are content to live our lives solely on the basis of this principle of liberalism. Most of us seek a human good that is more substantive (and restrictive) than mere liberal freedom. Given a society such as ours, in which there is both general agreement on the value of liberal freedom and widespread disagreement about more substantive conceptions of the human good, we are led naturally to distinguish between ethical issues that can be resolved solely by appeal to the liberal values accepted throughout our society (the public sphere) and those that can be resolved only by appeal to substantive values that are accepted only locally (the private sphere).

Liberalism is easily identified with a view that, first, rigorously subordinates private values to public ones and, second, insists on the need for a wide diversity of privates values in a society. (As we have seen, Rorty's liberal ironism is a good example.) It is important to see that neither of these claims follows simply from an acceptance of the liberal commitment to freedom. There are, for example, those (particularly among traditionally religious people) who accept the liberal commitment, but merely as the best means in our pluralistic society of preserving their distinctly nonliberal conceptions of the human good. Given a majority endorsing their conception, they would find it entirely appropriate to reject liberalism and impose this conception on society as a whole. The mere acceptance of liberalism is consistent with a subordination of it, in principle, to one's private values. Although I have no sympathy with this version of liberalism, there is a related position that I do endorse and that is implicit in the practice of all liberal states. This is the acceptance of what I have called secondary public goods, beyond the primary public good of freedom, that are properly supported by the state. To this extent, I allow for public support for what would otherwise be entirely private goods and do not entirely subordinate private to public goods.

Nor does liberalism of itself commit us to the value of a diversity of private goods. Rorty and many other contemporary liberals are so committed. But that is just *their* private conception of the substantive human good. Others who just as fully endorse the public values of liberalism (and even endorse them in the strong way that makes them dominant in principle over all private goods) may accept a much more restricted conception of the substantive human good. They may, for example, believe that human beings are best fulfilled by the scrupulous observance of particular religious rituals and ethical codes. Their view, which they might try to implement by all persuasive means at their disposal, might be that society would be far better off if everyone accepted their religion and there was no significant diversity of personal visions of the good. So long as they think it inappropriate to impose their view on others (even if it were shared by the large majority), they accept the fundamental liberal commitment.

Understood in this broader way, liberalism no longer appears as the simple rejection of tradition. As we have already seen, even a Rortyan liberal, who sees the human good as essentially diverse, can appreciate a tradition and even engage with it from "a certain distance". Likewise – and this comes closer to my own preference – individuals can define themselves by playing off several traditions with which they have close connections, without a full commitment to any one of them and without a commitment to the value of maximal diversity. But liberalism is also consistent with a full-hearted commitment to a tradition defined by a substantive and exclusive conception of the human good. Given all these possibilities, it should be no surprise that in a liberal society, traditions may still be the primary instruments for the preservation and transmission of private goods. Private goods need not be individualistic or antitraditional.

Nor should we think that traditions always represent premodern (generally religious) conceptions of the human good. Our reading of Taylor has shown, contrary to MacIntyre, how modernity has developed its own traditions, based, for example, on naturalistic conceptions of human good (and evil) that go far beyond the minimal conception of the self that suffices as a source of the liberal public good of freedom. We have also noted the connection of these traditions with the great naturalistic thinkers of antiquity.

Still, the most venerable, most structured, and most influential traditions in the modern world remain those associated with the great religions. Pragmatic liberalism's acceptance of traditions as the primary vehicle of private goods implies acceptance of a legitimate role for traditional religions. But the role has its limits and reflects a characteristically modern circumscribing of religion's significance. Since issues about the status of religion in modern societies have frequently surfaced in our discussions, it may be helpful to offer some final reflections on the pragmatic liberalism view of religion.

The most obvious point is that, since the beliefs and values of specific religions are not generally accepted, they do not enter into our conception of the public good. From the viewpoint of society as a whole, religious beliefs have standing simply as the opinions of a certain subset of the citizenry, with no particular claim on the general allegiance (in contrast, for example, with the beliefs of the scientific community). For the nonbelieving pragmatic liberal, there is little more to be said about religious beliefs. But what about pragmatic liberals who also have religious convictions? In principle, their pragmatic liberalism need not affect either the content or the manner of their belief (short of any inclinations they may have to impose those beliefs forcibly on others). In fact, however, the pragmatic liberal view is likely to make a major difference. On this view, religious convictions are, in the best case, secondary properly basic beliefs. Epistemically, I am entitled but not required to hold them; there are many people who hold, and are entitled to hold, contrary beliefs. Thinking of religious beliefs this way need not affect the strength of my religious faith, but for many it is very likely to do so. This will be particularly so for believers who come to take seriously the question of whether they must retain their faith. Once this question is raised in a fundamental way – as it is likely to be in a pluralistic society – a pragmatic liberal view of religion leaves little room for response. The stability of faith seems to depend almost entirely on the individual's will to believe.

There is also the issue of just how far the proper basicality of religious belief is likely to extend. We can readily make sense of someone's accepting God's existence, goodness, and power as properly basic beliefs or holding fundamental religious ethical principles in this way. But such epistemic status becomes increasingly unlikely for beliefs of greater specificity and complexity. It is possible, but not very likely, that people "just see" in the way required for a properly basic belief that there are three persons in God, that the Spirit proceeds from both the Father and the Son, that Christ is really present in the Eucharist. Believers will, of course, point out that all they require is a properly basic belief in some religious authority, which in turn justifies the beliefs promulgated by the authority. But, first of all, it is hard to see how we can just directly recognize the authority of some book, individual, or person. It seems much more likely, at least once we reach a certain level of reflection, that the authority is inferred from our experiences of the authority's reliability.

It is even harder to imagine having properly basic belief in the precise nature and extent of the authority's scope. Is the Bible authoritative in every sentence or just as a general guide? On scientific as well as moral subjects? Are the direct sayings of Christ more authoritative than other passages? Do the Old and New Testaments have equal authority? Finally, even given the authority of a source and a delineation of its scope, anything beyond the most generic religious belief requires serious interpretation of the meaning of the authoritative claims. Does the authority of the Council's pronouncements on the Eucharist extend to the hylomorphic theory implicit in its formulation? Is the Prophet's injunction to wage war for God to be taken literally or metaphorically? Any religion that is more than a bare theism plus ethical platitudes is going to require quite detailed interpretation of its

authoritative revelation. It is scarcely plausible that the principles and applications of such interpretation are held as properly basic beliefs. In sum,
although the pragmatic liberal view does not in principle exclude any sort
of religious belief, it is likely, in practice, to limit significantly the strength
and richness of that belief. This, of course, is precisely what we find among
most modern religious believers.

We have been discussing the pragmatic epistemology and the liberal ethics
at the core of pragmatic liberalism. But the position also involves commitments to realism and naturalism. The realism is, first of all, an acceptance
of the humdrum truths of common sense (we might rather say, of sanity)
that express the reality of our world and our everyday knowledge of it. I have
argued that such realism is essential to avoid incoherence but insufficient
to support any deeper philosophical theories about truth or reality. On my
reading (particularly of Rorty and his critics), contemporary debates about
realism have vacillated between self-refuting retreats from humdrum realism for the sake of avoiding theoretical excesses and efforts to parlay humdrum realism into a theoretical structure. Critics of metaphysical realism
rightly attack its representationalist assumptions but wrongly think that their
critique requires an idealistic rejection of mind-independent realities. Defenders rightly assert the humdrum truth of realism but falsely conclude that
this establishes full-blooded metaphysical realism with its representationalist presuppositions. Both sides go wrong by insisting on a substantive philosophical account. I have suggested that we can firmly establish ourselves
simply within the limits of humdrum realism, lapsing neither into incoherently skeptical antirealism nor into gratuitous theoretical explanations. Nature endows us with just enough epistemology and metaphysics, and we go
badly wrong when we seek either more or less than this endowment.

There is, however, one (nonphilosophical) direction in which pragmatic
liberalism supports the extension of humdrum realism – that of scientific
realism. Pragmatic liberalism sees scientific knowledge as simply the outcome of ordinary methods of knowing (from experience and reasoning) deployed with extraordinary rigor and accuracy. We thus have the same kinds
of reasons for believing that the earth has a core or that stars are far-distant
gaseous masses as we have for believing that a rabbit has eaten our garden
plants or that a car needs a valve job. The issue of the status of unobservable
entities postulated by scientific theories is another matter, although my own
view is that, at least for many standard cases, there is good reason to extend
realism to them also.

The arguments that establish the reality of scientific entities are scientific,
not philosophical. At most, the philosopher is needed to point out, in re-

sponse to antirealistic philosophical attacks, that the logic of these arguments is parallel to that of entirely unproblematic humdrum inferences. Further, the arguments in question are all ultimately based on the predictive fruitfulness of scientific accounts. It is overwhelming evidence that something is involved in the causal production of what we observe that settles the case for its existence; and causal effect is established only by predictive success. (It follows that our privileging of scientific knowledge should include most of the natural sciences but very little of what are called the "social sciences".)

We begin, then, with an inevitable humdrum realism about the world in which we find ourselves, and consistency requires extending this realistic attitude to certain results of science. But none of this commits us to any philosophical theory about the nature of reality or of knowledge. In particular, it does not commit us to metaphysical realism.

This combination of scientific realism and a refusal of metaphysical realism might suggest that pragmatic liberalism will be committed to metaphysical naturalism – the claim that there are no realities beyond those discovered by our ordinary sense experience and its extensions by scientific instruments and reasoning. But such a commitment could be based only on a philosophical argument that no such realities are possible; and this is just the sort of argument our pragmatic metaphilosophy calls into question. Whatever else philosophy may be able to accomplish, we have no reason to think that it offers special access to information about the ontology of the world. This, as we have seen, was the import of the scientific revolution. But neither should we conclude anything from the failure of empirical methods to discover entities beyond the physical domain. Pragmatic liberalism remains resolutely uncommitted about both sides of traditional metaphysical disputes.

Their metaphilosophical attitude makes pragmatic liberals both epistemological and ethical naturalists. In both cases, however, the naturalism is merely a denial of the need for a special ontology to support norms. Pragmatic liberalism does not claim, for example, that mental representations and objective values do not exist. Its claim is merely that the truth and justifiability of our epistemic and moral standards (hence the viability of our cognitive and ethical lives) do not require the existence of any entities beyond the natural world of humdrum and scientific realism. There may be such entities; and truths about them, should we know them, might provide a justification of our norms. But the intelligibility and propriety of our normative commitments do not depend on any such entities or any such justifications. Norms remain stable in a world of nothing but naturalistic facts. Pragmatic liberalism's metaphysical epoche does not of itself make moot the question of the objectivity of norms. A claim may not be objective in the sense of being about an irreducible, independently existing object and still be objective in the sense of being a truth required in any inquirer's adequate account of the universe (what Williams calls an account from the "absolute standpoint"). There is also the possibility of what I have called "phenomenological objectivity". I have, however, maintained that ethical claims are not objective in either of these senses (although they may be objective in a perspectival sense) and that this does not undermine their normative status.

The realism and naturalism of pragmatic liberalism express the special role that modernity has always accorded natural science. The characteristic problem of modernity has been to construct a worldview that accords science primary cognitive authority without making unintelligible or trivial the normative core of human existence. Very roughly, pragmatic liberalism maintains the primacy of science by asserting humdrum and scientific as well as epistemic and ethical naturalism. It maintains the normative core by rejecting reductive forms of naturalism and by denying that values require an objectivity that nonreductive naturalism cannot provide.

My disagreements with Rorty and Taylor are primarily over issues of realism and naturalism. I disagree with Taylor primarily in accepting the ethical naturalism he so strongly opposes, while my disagreement with Rorty is primarily over his rejection of scientific realism and over the metaphysical naturalism implicit in his atheism. For me, pragmatism is a matter of maximizing both naturalism and realism without succumbing to dubious metaphysical assertions or denials. Thus, pragmatic liberalism is naturalistic but short of metaphysical naturalism and realistic but short of metaphysical realism. In both cases, pragmatism means accepting only the metaphysics that we need to make sense of our ethical commitment to liberalism. My disagreement with MacIntyre cuts deeper, since he rejects the ethical liberalism at the core of my position. But I find much of MacIntyre's position congenial because, as I have argued, it provides pragmatic liberalism with an invaluable articulation of the social and historical dimensions of human life.

I have presented pragmatic liberalism as a defense of modernity, that is, of Enlightenment reason. This defense, however, requires some precision in defining just what we mean by "Enlightenment" (and, correspondingly, by "modernity"). We have had, first, to distinguish the philosophical from the humanistic Enlightenment. The humanistic Enlightenment rejected the traditional external authorities of king and priest and maintained that humans should themselves be the ultimate judges of how they should live. Such a view gives priority to reason, but only in the indeterminate sense of whatever it is that enables us to be our own guides. The philosophical Enlightenment goes further, offering a specific and, as it turns out, very flawed conception of reason as a set of philosophical procedures for constructing the truth of both the natural and the ethical worlds from primitive given elements (Cartesian perceptions, Lockean sensations, etc.). Whereas the humanistic Enlightenment eschews the philosophical theorizing of knowledge and the world, the philosophical Enlightenment requires such theorizing as the necessary ground for any certainty. The epistemic naturalism and humdrum realism of pragmatic liberalism express my choice of the humanistic over the philosophical Enlightenment.

While the virtue of the humanistic Enlightenment is to resist excessive philosophical theorizing, its distinctive temptation is to embrace a naively commonsense ethical optimism. This is the foolish faith that, once we eliminate external authorities, human nature will readily and steadily progress along the path to final happiness. Such faith was rightly derided in the nineteenth century by the Romantics and others, and has become embarrassingly absurd before the unprecedented atrocities of the twentieth century. It is, however, a mistake to read all major modern critics of the more optimistic eighteenth-century thinkers as simply rejecting the Enlightenment. Many critics, from Rousseau through Foucault, have in fact maintained the core Enlightenment view: an assertion of the autonomy and integrity of human life in its own terms against the pretensions of external traditional authorities. Their critiques concern the moral complexity and ambivalence of the human existence that they nonetheless ultimately endorse as the ultimate source of all our values.

These critiques of Enlightenment optimism begin with Rousseau and the Diderot of *Le Neveu de Rameau,* continue through Schopenhauer and Nietzsche, and reach a peak of suspicion with Freud and Foucault. They have excavated the internal fault lines of human freedom, developing naturalized doctrines of original sin and presenting our fulfillment as requiring struggle against both external and internal destructive forces. But all these critics have ultimately offered means for winning the struggle, whether through harmony with nature, analytic insight, or an aesthetics of finite existence. They reject the naive optimism of the "first-born" Enlightenment; but, after passing through the purgatory of this rejection, they reassert the validity of human existence in its own terms. They are the heralds of a "twice-born" Enlightenment.

Once we understand modernity as an expression of a twice-born humanistic Enlightenment, there is no room left for a postmodern rejection of the Enlightenment that does not collapse into either a reactionary return to tradition or an incoherent skepticism. Postmodernism often uses a rhetoric of radical skepticism, suggesting that "truth", "reality", and "knowledge" are empty terms deployed only to disguise the thrusts of power. There is often point to the rhetoric when it is directed locally, toward undermining the pretensions of specific social or theoretical structures. But this sort of deconstruction is entirely consistent with the twice-born humanistic Enlightenment I have been defending. Postmodernism separates itself from this Enlightenment only when it makes its attacks global, purporting to deconstruct our humdrum world and knowledge. But then it explodes into a self-referential inconsistency that is incapable of articulating its own content.

The postmodern is an impulse of modernity itself. The Enlightenment drive is for critique; and this, as Horkheimer and Adorno have above all emphasized, must eventually mean self-critique. But self-critique has sense only when it remains local. We can reasonably question any specific conception or deployment of reason, but this will always have to be on the basis of some (unquestioned) broader conception or deployment of reason. More precisely, the very project of critique is rooted in the precritical stance defined by what I have called humdrum truths about the world and our knowledge of it. Implicitly, since Descartes, and explicitly, since Kant, modern thought has understood philosophy as the instrument of fundamental critique. But modernity has tended to forget that the project of living precedes the project of philosophy. As Bernard Williams puts it, "philosophy is related to the world not as theory to practice but as a part to the whole".[3] Postmodernism is simply modernity forgetting this truth.

But just as rational critique can forget its humdrum limits, so too can opposition to legitimate critique mistake itself for antiskeptical common sense. Like contending theologians denouncing one another as atheists, we readily see critiques of our specific conceptions and deployments of reason as assaults on reason itself. It is all too easy to reject Derridian critiques of logocentrism or feminist defenses of standpoint theory as simple irrationalism. Such facile dismissals typically ignore coherent challenges to particular formulations to which there are alternatives. Contemporary debates over postmodernism fall into a fruitless dialectic of dogmatism and skepticism when they are taken as being about the viability of the very project of Enlightenment critique. But they can be of the greatest importance when understood as self-critical instances of this project.

---

3   "La modernité et l'échec de la morale", in M. Canto-Sperber (ed.), *La philosophie morale britannique*, Paris: Presses Univeritaires de France, 1994, 132. My translation.

2. Metaphilosophical Coda

Pragmatic liberalism is built on a critique of the philosophical enterprise, although it is itself obviously in some sense a philosophical position. This makes inevitable questions about pragmatic liberalism's ultimate view of philosophy and of its own philosophical status. Since my discussions have been in the mode of analytic philosophy, expanded by the historical and cultural sensibilities characteristic of Rorty, MacIntyre, and Taylor, I will focus on it, though with some brief references to continental approaches.

Current analytic philosophy is the methodological residue of logical positivism and ordinary language analysis. The latter two movements were marked by distinctive views on first-order philosophical issues, such as the positivists' verification principle and the ordinary-language idea of meaning as use. Since about the mid-1950s, Anglo-American philosophy has seen critiques of every major positivist and ordinary-language doctrine and the flourishing of all manner of philosophical views. Perhaps most strikingly, where Anglo-American philosophy had been resolutely antimetaphysical, philosophical positions of the greatest metaphysical extravagance now are advocated in the strongest bastions of analytic philosophy. Nor are analytic philosophers now typically reductionists, emotivists, or foundationalists. This has led some to think that analytic philosophy is now nothing more than a method or, as Bernard Williams puts it, a style of thinking, one that places a particular emphasis on clarity of understanding and rigor of argument.[4]

Critiques of modernity, however, suggest that the very project of analytic philosophy involves substantive and questionable philosophical assumptions. To see the precise sense in which this might be the case, let us return to some reflections on the historical genealogy of the project of analytic philosophy. Here it will be helpful to start with some recent work by Thomas Cole, a classicist who has challenged the standard idea that philosophy first emerged as the foil and opponent of an entrenched rhetorical tradition.[5] This idea has reached most of us philosophers in the form of the myth of Plato's bitter fight, in the name of responsible reasoned argument, against the rhetorical perversions of the sophists. But, according to Cole, Plato (along with Aristotle)

---

4 Williams characterizes the analytic "style" as follows: "What distinguishes analytical philosophy from other contemporary philosophy (though not from much philosophy of other times) is a certain way of going on, which involves argument, distinctions, and, so far as it remembers to try to achieve it and succeeds, moderately plain speech" (ELP, xiii).

5 Thomas Cole, *The Origins of Rhetoric in Ancient Greece,* Baltimore: Johns Hopkins University Press, 1991. I am more concerned with Cole's helpful formulation of the rhetoric–philosophy distinction than with his controversial claim that the distinction was invented by Plato and Aristotle.

is the inventor of both philosophy and rhetoric, the two being aspects of the same project. The invention is based on a new dichotomy: between a core of unadorned content and the variety of ways in which that content can be expressed. The content is formulated by the dialectical (e.g., argumentative) methods of philosophy, aimed at the *telos* of truth; the mode of expression is the concern of rhetoric, aimed at persuasion. Essential to Cole's position is the thesis that prior to Plato the content–expression distinction has no deep and comprehensive purchase (although, of course, there are lots of partial formulations and anticipations).[6]

In what sense is Greek literature before Plato free of the content–expression distinction (i.e., in what sense is it "arhetorical")? According to Cole, it is "full of eloquence and argument but usually posited on the assumption of an essentially transparent verbal medium that neither impedes nor facilitates the transmission of information, emotion, and ideas".[7] When the medium is "transparent", there is no role for the rhetorician's project of "controlling" it, of reducing its impediments or enhancing its facility. The idea is that, if there is no significant resistance of medium to message, that must be because there is no effective distinction between the two. This is not the McLuhanesque reduction of message to medium, but rather lack of effect of medium on message. The rhetorician's project emerges once two conditions are satisfied: "audiences and composers had to acquire the habit of abstracting essential messages from verbal contexts" and there had to develop a "'written' eloquence" that could be a basis for rhetorical analysis.[8]

Philosophy, in turn, is the enterprise of constructing the pure core discourse by eliminating all inessentials and ambiguities, an enterprise that is at least a close ancestor of analytic philosophy. To this we must add, here going beyond Cole, the key epistemological assumption that the attainment of analytic clarity – the isolation of the pure core of meaning – will produce direct insight into the truth value of a core formulation. This is the realm of Platonic vision, Aristotelian self-evidence, Cartesian clear and distinct perception, Husserlian intuition, positivist sense data. Cole is less interested in this philosophical project than in the rhetorical project of creating a theory and art of the expression of core truths. My emphasis is, of course, the reverse.

We can think of Cole's account as pointing toward a Foucaultian genealogy of philosophy: an account of its origin as a contingent turn of history

---

6 Cole, influenced here by Eric Havelock, connects the emergence of the distinction to the transition from oral to written culture.
7 Cole, *The Origins of Rhetoric*, x.
8 Ibid.

rather than as a necessary emergence of essential structures. The genealogy begins with the Greek revolution of the sixth to fifth centuries B.C. In this period, rhetoric replaced poetry and eloquence (spontaneously inspired by the Muse), philosophy replaced mythology, science magic, politics ancestral law. The heart of the revolution was, in each case, a fundamental change in the conception of "getting it right". For mythology, magic, and politics, getting it right is a matter of following given procedures: to express the truth about human life, we tell the stories as they have been received; to cope with nature, we perform the ordained rituals; to run the city, we follow the laws of the ancestors. In each case, the truth is given from outside, and we need only reproduce it. The new idea is that the truth is not already there in an unquestionable form; it needs to be discovered and justified. From this follows the basic dichotomy between content and expression. Under the old regime, the truth came from outside in a way that possessed its own authority. There was no need to lead ourselves or others to an acceptance of it. But now there is no pregiven authoritative truth. Truth is, rather, ours to discover *and* to perceive as truth. The duality of this formulation is no accident: it is now necessary to distinguish the question of what is said (assertion) from the question of whether or not it is true (justification). Previously, simply knowing that certain things were said – in standard circumstances – was enough to know that they were true. The pronouncement of the father, the king, the priest, the poet was sufficient. Now there is first the bare content of an assertion, then the proper (dialectical) justification that establishes it as a truth, then the rhetorical techniques for convincing others of it.

Michel Foucault also evokes this transition in his Inaugural Lecture at the Collège de France. Prior to Plato, he says, true discourse "was pronounced by men who spoke as of right, according to ritual"; the "highest truth. . . resided in what discourse *was*, . . . in what it *did*". After Plato, the truth of a discourse depended entirely on what it *said*, on "its meaning, its form, its object and its relation to what it referred to". As a result, the evaluation of discourse as true or false depended not on the authority of its source ("true discourse . . . had ceased to be discourse linked to the exercise of power") but on the possibility of its being dialectically justified. But Foucault has not quite reached Cole's position, since he still sees this reconception of truth as a challenge to a preexisting rhetorical tradition, concluding "and so the Sophists were routed" rather than "and so the Sophists were possible".[9]

The history of Western philosophy, like that of Western science and

9 "Discourse on Language", in *The Archaeology of Knowledge*, tr. A. Sheridan, New York: Pantheon, 1972, 218.

politics, is the history of efforts to achieve justified assertions of truth in each domain. Of course, the prerevolutionary authorities never disappeared. Or, if they did, they reappeared transformed and often more subtle and stronger than ever. So the history of Western thought is also the history of the interaction (and even intertwining) of the two attitudes toward truth – the authoritative and the philosophical, let us say. There is, however, a crucial third dimension. This is the gradual emergence of a radical questioning of the philosophical project (or the project of rationality) that, at the same time, was not a reversion to the authoritative standpoint. This third dimension no doubt has quite distant antecedents, but, at least in philosophy proper, it doesn't become prominent until the nineteenth century.

At that time, the idea began stirring that the core presupposed by the philosophical enterprise might not exist, even as a remote ideal of aspiration. Such thoughts were primarily occasioned by reflections on the two endpoints of the philosophical enterprise. Nietzsche, reading Plato, concluded that Plato had not discovered the core, but merely invented it for entirely contingent (and ultimately unsavory) purposes. Kierkegaard, reading Hegel, concluded that the ultimate effort to articulate and appropriate the core through historical and logical analysis ended in incoherence.

As we have seen, it is possible to reach the same conclusion through reflection, à la Rorty, on the recent history of analytic philosophy. Moreover, Rorty's account converges in this respect with the contemporary continental philosophy that triumphed in the 1970s and 1980s in the work of the late Heidegger, Foucault, Derrida, and Deleuze. This philosophy was the full bloom of the rejection of the Platonic tradition germinated by Kierkegaard and Nietzsche: a rejection of the core of rhetorically unadorned truth, the search for which had sustained the philosophical project, and hence a rejection of the fundamental distinction of philosophy and rhetoric. By contrast, analytic philosophy is what remains faithful to the Platonic project of discovering the core of unadorned truth.

It might well seem that, given this account, pragmatic liberalism should simply reject analytic philosophy and make common cause with recent continental thought. But such a move would be precipitous. We need to note, first of all, the persuasive case that it has been precisely recent analytic philosophers (Wittgenstein, Quine, Sellars, Davidson, Putnam) who have undermined the core that grounded analytic philosophy. We also need to note that the upshot of these critiques has not been the elimination of analytic philosophy. On the contrary, they have engendered a new generation of more sophisticated and more powerful analytic philosophy. What's going on here? We should distinguish two aspects of the traditional philosophical enterprise: the isolation of a purified core of meaning (analysis) and the direct insight into the truth about that core. As I noted earlier, the traditional assumption was that the two were inextricably tied. Analytic clarification was thought to be inevitably accompanied by justificatory insight. The critical work of Rorty's favorite analytic philosophers has not eliminated the "arhetorical core" as an object of philosophical analysis, but it has broken the tie between such analysis and the attainment of deep philosophical truth. In the wake of Sellars, Quine, and company, the project of philosophical analysis remains viable, but there is no longer any reason to think that it will result in the epistemic payoff (philosophical truth) it is supposed to provide. Analytic critics of Rorty are appropriately disdainful of his suggestion that analytic philosophy is (or should be) moribund, but they are also inappropriately unembarrassed by the implicit disconnection of such philosophy from the high Platonic and Aristotelian ideal.

To get a sharper view of these issues, let us briefly look at them through the lens of an important and typical instance of analytic epistemology. Alvin Goldman opens his classic article "What Is Justified Belief?" with the following metaphilosophical declaration:

> The aim of this paper is to sketch a theory of justified belief. What I have in mind is an explanatory theory, one that explains in a general way why certain beliefs are counted as justified and others as unjustified. Unlike some traditional approaches, I do not try to prescribe standards for justification that differ from, or improve upon, our ordinary standards. I merely try to explicate the ordinary standards, which are, I believe, quite different from those of many classical, e.g., "Cartesian," accounts.[10]

This statement suggests that we need to distinguish two projects: (1) that of explicating what, in fact, are the norms that govern our social practice of justification and (2) that of determining, via special philosophical techniques, what should be the norms of justification. Goldman explicitly says he is doing (1) but not (2). What, then, about the pragmatic liberal discussion of justification, based on Rorty's critique of epistemology, that we developed in Part I? It is clearly not an instance of (2), since its entire thrust is to convince us of the vanity of such an enterprise. But neither is it an instance of (1). We can readily think it is, and then conclude that it offers an outrageously wrong account of what we mean by justification. As critics rightly point out, our practice of justification does not say that we should

---

10 In George Pappas (ed.), *Justification and Knowledge*, Dordrecht, the Netherlands: Reidel, 1979, 1.

believe what everyone else agrees is true or accept conclusions that are rhetorically persuasive but not logically sound. Rather, our practice gives a central role to evidential support, rigorous argument, objectively reliable faculties, and other factors that are not a matter of group consensus. But in fact, our pragmatic approach to justification is concerned not with what the norms that govern our practice of justification are but rather with their basis. The suggestion is that, ultimately, we have no alternative but to accept our norms simply as ours, with no need for a justification of them via some foundational philosophical analysis or argument.

But then the question arises of how relevant the pragmatic "critique of epistemology" is to the actual practice of contemporary epistemologists such as Goldman. They do not present their philosophical analyses (or "theories") as privileged foundations of the norms of our practice of justification. Is there anything, then, that pragmatic liberals should find wrong (misguided, uninteresting, confused) in the project these epistemologists do have: to formulate and clarify the norms that we do de facto employ? I think that, contrary to at least the tone of many of Rorty's comments, we ought to agree that the project is not flawed in principle, as, for example, the classical foundationalist project is. Indeed, we should applaud the basic presupposition that there is no place for a philosophical grounding of knowledge in the classical modern mode, since this is precisely a central thesis of pragmatic liberal metaphilosophy. Nonetheless, there is room for several pragmatic reservations about contemporary epistemology. First, there is a tendency in some quarters to forget that the results of explications such as Goldman's do not have the normative, foundational status claimed by classical epistemology. Despite the explicit disclaimers, it is easy to interpret our analyses as laying bare the true essence of truth, knowledge, and so on. Second, as Charles Taylor and Thomas Kuhn, among others, have persuasively argued, the norms of a social practice can never be made entirely explicit; there will always be a residual level of implicit know-how or judgment that will elude our explications. The precise definitions of analytic epistemology often forget or even explicitly deny this. Third, although there is surely a need for explicit reflection on our norms, there is no reason to think (and some reason not to think) that the abstract generality of philosophical analysis is the best (or even always a positive) way of carrying out such reflection. The more local, contentful reflections of those involved in specific cognitive enterprises may be far more acute and relevant. Finally, there is an inherent tendency toward conservatism in the effort to understand our norms. Sometimes the point should be to change them, and philosophical analysis often has little to contribute here.

Nonetheless, as the preceding discussion of justification illustrates, pragmatic liberalism can and should accept Rortyan critiques of analytic philosophy and still retain it as an essential intellectual resource. We can include nonfoundational epistemology (and other parallel projects of analytic philosophy in, for example, metaphysics, philosophy of mind, and ethics) as instances of legitimate philosophizing. This allows us to make something more of analytic philosophy than a mere style of thought and expression. Analytic philosophy also has a distinctive subject matter: the explication of the fundamental concepts and norms underlying our cognitive and evaluative practices. But, contrary to the aspirations of classical modern philosophy, there is no presumption that philosophical analysis in this sense reveals fundamental, foundational truths; it simply makes relatively explicit the de facto norms that govern the practices of our epistemic, moral, and aesthetic communities.

The advantage of this construal of analytic philosophy becomes particularly clear if we reflect once more on the status of philosophical intuitions. The traditional ideal, from Platonic noesis through Cartesian clear and distinct perception to positivist sense-data reports, has been to ground the core philosophical truths in some sort of self-justifying intuitive insight. Much of our contemporary lack of philosophical confidence is the ultimate outcome of the scientific revolution, from which we learned that our intuitions about nature (allegedly insights into the essences of things) often told us more about ourselves than about the world and that genuine access to the natural world required methical empirical testing that frequently refuted our "insights". The subsequent history of philosophy was a matter of our coming to see, both historically and analytically, that intuitions about the non-empirical realm (introspection, conceptual analysis, etc.) were similarly questionable. Analytic philosophy had begun with a rejection of intuition in the sense of special intellectual insights into reality. The positivists spoke not of intuitions but of analytic truths about meanings or the incorrigible givens of sense experience. But, in the wake of devastating critiques of analyticity and of the myth of the given, analytic philosophers have begun to speak once again of intuitions, now meaning simply the "spade-turning" beliefs they find themselves forced to take as basic in their search for philosophical truth. This is apparent in the widespread acceptance of "reflective equilibrium" (explicitly formulated by Goodman and Rawls) as the method of analytic philosophy. This method simply codifies the fact that we have no alternative to beginning with our own de facto intuitions, even though they have no certification beyond our inability to get past them.[11]

---

11 Saul Kripke holds an even stronger view: "Some philosophers think that something's having intuitive content is very inconclusive evidence in favor of it. I think it is very heavy

Despite their admittedly questionable status, intuitions still have a fundamental place in philosophy – indeed, in any effort to understand ourselves and our world. They represent the inevitable starting point of any intellectual inquiry. Analytic philosophy, now construed as the effort to attain maximum clarity regarding the content and basis of our intuitions, is essential not as a final determinant of truth but as a preliminary grasp of the precise nature of our starting point.[12] Pragmatic liberalism insists on this essential role for analytic philosophy, while at the same time maintaining that our intuitions require not only analytic clarification but also evaluation in light of the historical processes that have produced them.

This last point can perhaps be made most effectively in terms of the "problems" that define the contemporary analytic project. Analytic philosophers accept as given a set of canonical philosophical problems (mind–body, free will–determinism, the existence of God, the nature of moral judgments), which they set out to solve (or dissolve) through a combination of conceptual analysis and logical argument. Pragmatic liberalism interrupts this project before it begins by suggesting that there may be nothing at all privileged about the problems on which analytic philosophers focus, that they may be just the residue of contingent turns of past thought. More specifically, it suggests that the problems pose themselves only because we have unwittingly accepted assumptions (e.g., a certain picture of the mind, a conception of freedom, norms of rational acceptability) that are by no means inevitable but merely reflect a heritage from our philosophical past. Analytic philosophers may suggest that any questionable assumptions present at the beginning of their discussions will be unearthed in the process of analysis and argument. But pragmatic liberalism maintains that, without explicit reflection on historical origins, many assumptions are likely to go unnoticed. Moreover, even if unearthed by other means, many assumptions will still appear inevitable unless compared to alternatives provided by a historical sensibility.[13]

---

evidence in favor of anything, myself. I really don't know, in a way, what more conclusive evidence one can have about anything, ultimately speaking" (*Naming and Necessity*, Cambridge, MA: Harvard University Press, 1972, 42).

12 The dangers of clarity are well expressed by Proust's comment on his fictional author Bergotte: "his ideas seemed as often as not to be confused, for each of us sees clarity only in those ideas which have the same degree of confusion as his own" (*Within a Budding Grove*, tr. C. K. Scott Moncrieff, T, Kilmartin, and D. J. Enright, New York: Modern Library, 1992, 171). But, while clarity may not at all signal the truth, it is always necessary to show just where we may be going wrong. In the same vein, as Charles Larmore points out, without clarity, we close our ideas off from the criticism of others. See his excellent discussion of clarity in *The Morals of Modernity*, Cambridge: Cambridge University Press, 1996, 14–16.

13 Rorty, MacIntyre, and Taylor have all developed cases for the need for historical reflection in philosophy. See their essays in R. Rorty, J. B. Schneewind, and Quentin Skinner (eds.),

In light of this historical sensibility, pragmatic liberalism offers a new conception of philosophical problems. According to this conception, (1) problems vary from period to period in the history of thought; (2) there is no privileged position for the problems and solutions central for contemporary philosophical inquiry; and (3) an understanding of the nature and significance of contemporary problems requires appreciating their historical origin. Contemporary analytic philosophers typically take a Whiggish and heuristic view of the philosophical past. As Whigs, they either deny that philosophical problems have changed over time and prefer contemporary solutions, or, at least, they maintain that contemporary problematics have superseded the halting formulations and pseudoproblems of the past. In either case, there is no genuine need for reflection on the history of philosophy. Studying the past may sometimes suggest something worthwhile to our philosophical reflections, but there is no special need for successful philosophical thought to be based on an understanding of the history of philosophy.[14] Pragmatic liberalism recommends a history of philosophy that is neither Whiggish nor merely heuristic.

Although pragmatic liberalism offers serious critiques of the intuitions at the root of philosophical analysis, its own projects (for example, the argumentation of this book) are impossible without such analysis as an ongoing enterprise. Limited or misleading as they may be, our intuitions remain an inevitable starting point for any intellectual inquiry. Accordingly, historicist critiques cannot aim at eliminating intuitions, only at correcting them. Since the process of correction requires the best possible understanding of the intuitions to be corrected, pragmatic liberalism requires their detailed articulation through analysis and argument. This was apparent, for example, in my critique of representationalism and in my defense of ethical naturalism. From the pragmatic liberal perspective, all inquiry requires a continuing process of philosophical analysis; but this process must itself be continuously monitored and evaluated by historical reflection. Philosophical achievement is the product of an enterprise defined by these two irreducible and ineliminable moments.[15]

Philosophy in History, Cambridge: Cambridge University Press, 1984. Rorty's essay, "The Historiography of Philosophy: Four Genres", is reprinted in TP, 247–73.

14 A currently less popular antihistoricist view is philosophical nostalgia (particularly associated with neo-Scholasticism). This denies (1) and accepts (2); but it accepts (2) only because it holds that all major problems have already been solved – or, at least, that a framework for the solution has been provided – by some great philosopher of the past.

15 We should, indeed, notice that we have arrived at this characterization by just such a historical reflection on the development of analytic philosophizing. Also, these two moments do not exhaust the philosophical enterprise, since it also includes the more creative efforts of continental philosophy, discussed briefly later.

Pragmatic liberalism, then, by no means rejects the standard projects of analytic philosophy. It recognizes their legitimacy and, indeed, their essential place in the overall enterprise of human knowing. But, at the same time, it insists that ahistorical analysis must be complemented by historical reflection on the significance of analytic results. Ordinarily, we can distinguish a discipline from the history of the discipline. But philosophy, from the pragmatic liberal standpoint, must include its own history. This makes particularly apparent the Hegelian strand of pragmatic liberalism.

But pragmatic liberalism's endorsement of analytic philosophy requires detaching its clarificatory function from grandiose traditional projects of providing rigorous philosophical answers to deep questions about human existence. Such projects, often seen as originating with Plato, are misguided efforts to find a truth that goes beyond the contingent consensus of the intellectual conversations to which our history has led us. Not that pragmatic liberalism has no views on the great Platonic question of how we should live. It is quite convinced that we should live in accord with the democratic liberalism that has built and informed the North Atlantic nation-states of the twentieth century, that is, lead a life of individual self-creation amid a social atmosphere of equality, justice, and toleration. But it sees as wrongheaded any effort to ground this ethical view in fundamental truths about human nature and its place in the cosmic scheme, and it rejects any suggestion that the lack of such a grounding would or should weaken our ethical commitment to our ideals. Pragmatic liberalism can (and should) endorse and encourage analytic philosophy, as long as it does not claim any privileged access to truth and is willing to take its place with everyone else at the conversational Round Table. Once we have demystified the pretensions of philosophical privilege, we can recognize the distinctive though not dominating contribution of analytic philosophy to our continuing conversation.

Rorty has recognized the enduring role of analytic philosophy in his distinction between systematic and edifying philosophizing. The former is (or at least aspires to be) normal philosophical discourse, progressively solving problems by shared, neutral criteria. Analytic philosophy is clearly a primary contemporary instance of systematic philosophy.[16] In fact, we would be better off simply referring to this sort of philosophy as "analytic philosophy". So understood, analytic philosophy would include some major strands of what has come to be called "continental philosophy", for example, much of

---

16   This fact should make it clear that Rorty is not using "systematic philosophy" in its ordinary sense of a unified account of all reality. In his sense, a systematic philosopher need not have a philosophical "system".

the classical phenomenology of Husserl, Sartre, and Merleau-Ponty. We need only distinguish several varieties of analysis, including formal, conceptual, and phenomenological. Analytic philosophy would also include much of the philosophical work of Jürgen Habermas. I suggest that such a terminological change would be more of an advance than an oddity.

Rorty's edifying philosophy renounces the goal of normality and devotes itself to developing radical alternatives to contemporary normality. It has been the gadfly stinging systematic philosophy from Diogenes, through Kierkegaard and Nietzsche, to Foucault and Derrida. Although Rorty typically casts a cold eye on the alleged achievements of systematic philosophy and finds his heroes among those pursuing the edifying path, he does admit that there could be no edifying philosophy without systematic philosophy (and hence no philosophy at all, since these are the only two types): "abnormal . . . discourse is always parasitic upon normal discourse, . . . edification always employs materials provided by the culture of the day" (PMN, 365–6).

In *Philosophy and the Mirror of Nature*, the primary reason for his aversion to systematic philosophy is that it seeks (and often claims to attain) truth. By favorable contrast, "edifying philosophy aims at continuing a conversation rather than at discovering truth" (PMN, 373). Indeed, "edifying philosophers can never end philosophy, but they can help prevent it from attaining the secure path of a science" (PMN, 372). Such claims make sense in the light of Rorty's early eschewal of truth and objectivity. But they lose their force once we realize that Rorty has no grounds for rejecting truth and objectivity as such, just representationalist theories about them. We would have to reject systematic philosophy – and therefore analytic philosophy – if its historical association with representationalism and hence epistemology in the classical modern sense were inevitable. But, as Rorty admits, it is at least possible that "a new form of systematic philosophy will be found which has nothing whatever to do with epistemology" (394).[17] Moreover, as I have

---

17 Nonetheless, Rorty has sometimes rejected new approaches to systematic philosophy out of hand. Consider, for example, his reaction in *Philosophy and the Mirror of Nature* to Habermas's effort to develop a new sort of "transcendental philosophy", one that is not based on representationalist conceptions such as a correspondence theory of truth. There are many reasons to be critical of this project as Habermas carries it out, but Rorty is not here interested in the details. He simply rejects the very idea of what Habermas is trying to do. "We should not try to have a successor subject to epistemology, but rather try to free ourselves from the notion that philosophy must center around the discovery of a permanent framework for inquiry" (380). And again: "There is no point in trying to find a general synoptic way of 'analyzing' the [quoting Habermas] 'functions knowledge has in universal contexts of practical life'" (381). But, unless Habermas is somehow slipping back into the mistakes of representationalism (and Rorty makes no effort to show any such thing),

been emphasizing, there has been significant recent analytic work that has learned the lessons of Quine, Sellars, and Davidson and avoided the pitfalls of representationalism.[18]

Edifying philosophy is today primarily the province of continental thinkers, who are concerned more with creating new languages for describing the human condition than with offering (analytic) explications of the entrenched languages. Here I have in mind not the entire sweep of European philosophy during the twentieth century but only the radical form it eventually took in the late Heidegger and the French poststructuralists. Had this radical turn not occurred, the earlier continental–analytic division between positivism and classical phenomenology might well have been bridged once positivists broadened their notion of experience and structuralism moved phenomenologists away from literary existentialism. (This, of course, supports my earlier suggestion that we redescribe these parts of continental philosophy as analytic.) The continental–analytic split became definitive only with the outright rejection by the poststructuralists of elucidation of the core in favor of the creation of new vocabularies. This rejection constitutes an unbridgeable gap between contemporary continental and analytic philosophizing.

Continental creativity is an essential counterpart to analytic philosophy. Whereas the baseline of analytic philosophy is the commonsense intuitions it subjects to conceptual scrutiny, the edifying project of continental philosophy looks for ways to move us beyond or beneath common sense.[19] Continental creativity is based on a rejection of the analytic idea of philosophy as the discovery, elucidation, and justification of a core of fundamental

---

why should we reject his project? We may well be skeptical of its ultimate success, although we surely have no decisive evidence that it must fail, but there is reason to expect that it will increase our understanding of our current intuitions concerning knowledge. Rorty seems to have nothing against Habermas's project beyond his own disdain for systematic philosophy; and this disdain seems inconsistent with his insistence on the value of edifying philosophy, which, as we have seen, can exist only as a reaction to systematic philosophy. Subsequently, however, Rorty treats Habermas much more sympathetically. See, for example, his "Habermas, Derrida, and the Functions of Philosophy", *Revue Internationale de Philosophie*, 1995, 437–60 (TP, 307–26; see also the comment on TP, 12).

18   For an excellent recent example – and in the grand, systematic style – see Robert Brandom, *Making It Explicit*, Cambridge, MA: Harvard University Press, 1994.

19   Compare: "The main concern of philosophy is to question and understand very common ideas that all of us use everyday without thinking about them" (Thomas Nagel, *What Does It All Mean? A Very Short Introduction to Philosophy*, Oxford: Oxford University Press, 1987, 5) and "Philosophy is the art of forming, inventing, and fabricating concepts" (Gilles Deleuze and Félix Guattari, *What Is Philosophy?*, tr. G. Burchell and H. Tomlinson, London: Verso, 1994, 2).

truth.[20] As a result, continental philosophy is typically sexier than analytic philosophy, promising the excitement of novelty and iconoclasm. This very feature is also responsible for the continentalists' characteristic weakness of pretentious obscurity. When the effort to move creatively beyond old categories fails, as it often does, the result may well be little more than self-important gibberish or, marginally better, an excruciating restatement of the obvious. Correspondingly, analytic philosophy's characteristic faults are the plodding clarity and misplaced rigor of someone who, in a glorious meadow that calls for exuberant roaming, crawls along as through a minefield. There is, of course, also a distinctive sort of novelty and creativity in the analytic domain. Granted that the analyst by definition begins from a framework defined by some "obvious" intuitive givens, it is also true that, upon analysis, such givens may conflict with one another and require, for the sake of consistency, strikingly counterintuitive adjustments. (Thus Kripke is led to bizarre views on the existence of unicorns and David Lewis to amazing claims about possible worlds.) Analytic philosophy has its own form of creativity, even though it will always be less radical than that of continental thought.

Reflection on the preceding survey of the philosophical domain should make us increasingly dissatisfied with the awkward and oversimplified dichotomy of analytic and continental philosophy.[21] I propose that we can speak more fruitfully of three major philosophical approaches: conceptual analysis, historical critique, and creative redescription. Conceptual analysis includes not only the twentieth-century Anglo-American tradition (analytic philosophy in the standard sense) but also much of earlier philosophy from

---

20 Of course, my comments here provide only an absurdly overgeneralized account of recent continental philosophy. I think it is true of major figures such as Heidegger, Derrida, and Foucault, but it is hardly a complete characterization of their fundamental projects. In each case, my general account would have to be supplemented with the use the individual philosopher makes of his conceptual creations. In the case of Heidegger, for example, the goal seems to be to wean us away from the old categories of philosophical thought, with the hope that this will prepare us for some as yet unconceived new way of thinking. For Derrida, the point seems rather to be the continual undermining of traditional categories to which, however, we have no hope of alternatives but can only keep playing against one another. Foucault, in quite a different vein, subordinates his creative philosophical constructions to specific enterprises of human liberation. There are, moreover, moments when all three of these philosophers appear to slip back into the old Platonic project. There is Heidegger's taking on the role of the vehicle of Being's speech, Derrida's hypostatization of *différance,* and Foucault's privileging of the vision of the mad. But in all such cases, critics rightly see such tendencies as relapses, inconsistent with the primary thrust of the philosopher's anti-Platonic thought.

21 Simon Critchley offers an excellent discussion of this distinction in "What Is Continental Philosophy?", *International Journal of Philosophical Studies* 5 (1997), 347–67.

Plato through Kant. It also includes much of the work of twentieth-century European figures such as Husserl and Habermas. As mentioned earlier, this last inclusion makes perfect sense once we exclude positivist scientism and verificationism from our definition of philosophical analysis and do not insist on linguistic or logically formal analysis as the only ways to explicate our basic intuitions.

Historical critique is the effort to understand the limits of conceptual analysis by historically situating the contemporary intuitions that form the starting points of such analysis. Much of the work of Rorty, MacIntyre, and Taylor belongs in this category, but it also includes Michel Foucault's archaeological and genealogical projects, as well as the historical studies of philosophers such as Heidegger and Derrida. Some work by historians of philosophy that is too often categorized as "merely historical" is also historical critique, in function even if not in intent. Its reconstruction of a lost or neglected mode of thought may by that very fact implicitly suggest alternatives to our contemporary conceptions. (There is also a tradition, paradigmatically represented by Strawson's book on Kant, of using historical discussions as vehicles of conceptual analysis.)

Creative redescription (which pretty well corresponds to Rorty's edifying philosophy) replaces the project of understanding our concepts with the project of changing them and is distinguished by the creation of new and (at first) highly counterintuitive vocabularies. Sometimes, as in the counter-philosophical ironies of Kierkegaard, Nietzsche, and Derrida, novelty is deliberately courted as a means of undermining entrenched modes of thought. In other cases (Hegel, Heidegger), it is rather the product of an effort to formulate the sort of deep philosophical truth about which pragmatic liberalism is skeptical. The category of creative redescription allows us to appreciate in our own terms such major philosophical creations even when we deny them the status to which they aspired.

We see then that pragmatic liberalism supports the viability of a variety of distinctively philosophical projects. But we may still be uneasy about the overall cultural significance of such projects, given that we have renounced the traditional philosophical goal of rationally established fundamental truths about what the world is like and how we ought to live. What significance remains for a philosophy that has abandoned so much of its heritage?

We can begin a response by noticing that a successful piece of philosophizing can "make intellectual room" for important claims that we might otherwise reject out of hand or not even think of. Much of the best contemporary analytic philosophy does this. Kripke, Rawls, and Plantinga, for example, have injected new life into traditional views in metaphysics, ethics, and religion that many had thought decrepit. Not, of course, that Kripke has proven the truth of his metaphysical essentialism or that Rawls or Plantinga has done the same for liberalism or theism. But their clarifications, refutations, and new formulations have at least made their positions viable options on the contemporary intellectual scene: views that opponents need to take seriously and that proponents can espouse (as, in our earlier terminology, secondary basic beliefs) without intellectual irresponsibility.

We may, however, still wonder about the significance of such achievements, which appear meager in comparison with the traditional claims of philosophy. If we can't actually answer the big questions, what is the value in making intellectual room for what, after all, remains just one of many viable responses? Here we may turn to the common claim that, even if philosophy cannot decisively answer its fundamental questions, it can still help us to a deeper understanding of these questions. One way it might do this is by showing that certain answers (or, better, certain formulations of answers) are not correct. Thus, Thomas Nagel has suggested that the reason "we study the works of philosophers like Plato and Berkeley, whose views are accepted by no one", is to maintain "a strong grasp of the problem" by understanding the failures of attempts to solve it. But we need to be careful in speaking of the refutation of philosophical views. It is very important to distinguish between the *theory* that provides a specific, detailed formulation of a philosophical position such as Platonic realism or Berkeleyan idealism and the general *picture* of reality that such formulations are trying to articulate.[22] Philosophers are often able to refute a particular theoretical formulation (the dualism of Descartes's *Meditations,* the phenomenalism of Ayer's *Language, Truth, and Logic*). But they seldom if ever refute the general pictures that the theoretical formulations articulate. So, to return to Nagel's examples, no philosopher has shown that there are no subsisting abstract entities or that reality does not consist entirely of minds and their contents.

We should by no means disdain the achievements of philosophical theories. When philosophers are doing their job properly, each new formulation will be superior to the extent that it resolves the difficulties that defeated its predecessors. And, in fact, there has been considerable philosophical progress over the centuries, and particularly in the twentieth century, through increasingly better theoretical formulations. It is fair to say that we have better *theories* of knowledge than Plato or Descartes did. But these are theories that articulate the general Platonic or Cartesian *pictures* of knowledge, and we

---

22   On the picture–theory distinction, see my "Can Philosophical Beliefs Be Rationally Justified?", *American Philosophical Quarterly* 19 (1982), 328–30.

have found no way to show the decisive superiority of either of these pictures to the other.

The distinctive cultural value of philosophy lies in the dialectical interaction of its pictures and theories. The philosophical instinct has long been to insist that we need to establish just one comprehensive picture as uniquely preferable, something pragmatic liberalism suggests we are very unlikely to do. But our inability to establish the unique privilege of a general picture does not imply that we have no need to develop such pictures and maintain them through theoretical formulations. A first and crucial point is that general pictures are essential elements of human culture. We have an ineradicable urge to act out of a comprehensive understanding of our situation. Even a view, like pragmatic liberalism, that is skeptical about substantive grand narratives deploys this very skepticism as a general vision of the human predicament. Further, individuals and even entire cultures can face destruction through persistent adherence to a failing picture. The people perish not only when there is no vision but also when their vision no longer provides effective responses to the exigencies of life. When a dominant picture fails, we need others to replace it. It follows that the development of alternative pictures – a primary achievement of philosophy in the mode of creative redescription – is culturally vital.

But a picture has no value for us unless we perceive it as a live option. There are, of course, many merely affective reasons why certain pictures remain dead for us. But, at some level, intelligence is always a factor in our lives, and the viability of a general picture will always depend importantly on whether we see it as coherent and plausible. We therefore need formulations of our guiding visions that make them intellectually respectable, even if they do not vindicate them over all rivals. Only in this way can a culture satisfy its members' desire for intellectual integrity and also provide alternative pictures when the dominant ones fail. Here we find the fundamental cultural function of philosophy in all three of its modes. Creative redescription invents new pictures, while conceptual analysis and historical critique sustain the credibility of pictures by developing theories that express their content through particular deployments of concepts and arguments. In this way, while specific philosophical projects have become ever more specialized and esoteric, philosophy as a discipline remains the primary locus of the human effort to, in Sellars's famous phase, "understand how things in the broadest possible sense of the term hang together in the broadest possible sense of the term".[23] This is, of course, more a claim about general function than

---

23 Wilfrid Sellars, "Philosophy and the Scientific Image of Man", in *Science, Perception, and Reality*, New York: Humanities Press, 1963, 1.

about individual intentions. Philosophers today have many reasons for engaging in their pursuits. Some still seek or even think they have ultimate truth; others see themselves as virtual scientists or protoscientists; still others just enjoy the game of conceptual puzzle-solving or of creating new languages. But the best overall cultural sense we can make of all this activity is through the picture-theory model.

Philosophy does, then, have a distinctive subject matter (the development and explication of fundamental concepts) and a distinctive set of techniques (conceptual analysis, historical critique, and creative redescription). Given our inability to establish one account as the final truth, there is no warrant for placing philosophers at the head of our intellectual table. But our pragmatic liberal metaphilosophy shows why they have a distinctive and essential voice in the conversation.

INDEX